PENGUIN BOOKS

DAUGHTERS OF ISIS

Joyce Ann Tyldesley was born in Bolton, Lancashire. She gained a first-class honours degree in archaeology from Liverpool University in 1981 and a doctorate from Oxford University in 1986. She has extensive experience of archaeological fieldwork, including work on the British Museum excavations at Ashmunein and the Liverpool University Delta Survey; she also directed Oxford University's recent fieldwork at Tuna el-Gebel. She is now Honorary Research Fellow at the School of Archaeology, Classics and Oriental Studies at Liverpool University and a freelance writer and lecturer on Egyptian archaeology.

D0376481

DAUGHTERS OF ISIS

WOMEN OF ANCIENT EGYPT

JOYCE TYLDESLEY

PENGUIN BOOKS

PENGUIN BOOKS

Published by the Penguin Group
Penguin Books Ltd, 27 Wrights Lane, London W8 5TZ, England
Penguin Books USA Inc., 375 Hudson Street, New York, New York 10014, USA
Penguin Books Australia Ltd, Ringwood, Victoria, Australia
Penguin Books Canada Ltd, 10 Alcorn Avenue, Toronto, Ontario, Canada M4V 3B2
Penguin Books (NZ) Ltd, 182–190 Wairau Road, Auckland 10, New Zealand

Penguin Books Ltd, Registered Offices: Harmondsworth, Middlesex, England

First published by Viking 1994
Published in Penguin Books 1995
3 5 7 9 10 8 6 4 2

Copyright © J. A. Tyldesley, 1994
All rights reserved

The moral right of the author has been asserted

Printed in England by Clays Ltd, St Ives plc

For Steven and Philippa Anne Snape

Contents

Plates

Objects recovered from Professor John Garstang's Beni Hassan and Abydos excavations are here illustrated by the original excavation photographs of 1904 and 1907–9. Thanks are due to Professor Slater of Liverpool University for permission to reproduce these hitherto unpublished photographs.

1 First Intermediate Period stela showing the Ladies Hetepi and Bebi, daughters of the Steward Sennedjsui. (Bolton Museum)

2 The elaborate dress and coiffure of a New Kingdom lady. (Tomb of Ramose, Thebes)

3 Old Kingdom pair-statue of a husband and wife. (Egyptian Museum, Cairo)

4 Stela of Iteti, accompanied by his three wives and two of his daughters. (Egyptian Museum, Cairo)

5 Middle Kingdom family stela featuring the scribal assistant Iy together with his wife, his children, and his parents. The precise role of the six 'Ladies of the House' shown towards the bottom of the stela is unknown. (Bolton Museum)

6 Middle Kingdom model of a female dwarf carrying a child on her hip. (Liverpool University)

7 The dwarf god Bes. (Graeco-Roman temple of Dendera)

8 Fragment of an ivory 'magic wand' with protective deities. (Liverpool University)

9 Wooden tomb models of two servant women, each carrying a box and two ducks. (Garstang: Beni Hassan)

10 Cord fertility dolls of the Middle Kingdom. (Garstang: Beni Hassan)

Figures

Maps and Chronologies

ACKNOWLEDGEMENTS

I would like to express my gratitude to all those whose contribution has made this book possible. Paul Bahn, Eleo Gordon and Sheila Watson gave me both encouragement and practical advice whenever necessary. Angela Thomas and the staff of the Bolton Museum cheerfully provided photographic prints, while the members of the Liverpool University S.E.S. photography department, Ian Qualtrough and Suzanne Yee, were unfailingly helpful at all times. Thanks are due to Professor Elizabeth Slater of Liverpool University for permission to photograph some of the previously unpublished objects in the University archaeological collection. Above all, Steven Snape has been a remarkably patient husband, never doubting that this book, started in 1986, would eventually be finished.

Where possible, this book has included quotations from contemporary documents which give the Egyptians the opportunity to speak for themselves. Those familiar with published Egyptian literature will immediately recognize the immense debt owed to the translation work of Miriam Lichtheim, which has been used as the basis of many of the quotations given.

The line drawings included in the text have been redrawn by the author from published sources; full acknowledgement of the sources of these drawings is provided in the list of illustrations given on pages xi–xiv.

Introduction: The Geographical and Historical Background

Not only is the Egyptian climate peculiar to that country and the Nile different in behaviour to other rivers, but the Egyptians themselves, in most of their manners and customs, exactly reverse the common practices of mankind. For example, the women attend the markets and trade, while the men sit at home and weave at the loom ... The women likewise carry burdens upon their shoulders while the men carry them upon their heads ... Sons need not support their parents unless they chose, but daughters must, whether they chose to or not.

Herodotus tells of the wonders of Egypt

When the Greek historian Herodotus visited Egypt at the very end of the dynastic period, he was struck by the topsy-turvy nature of both the land and its people. There was no question about it, Egypt was a very peculiar country. The climate could only be described as unusual, the River Nile behaved like no other river in the classical world, and the relations between the sexes were simply extraordinary. Herodotus had never before encountered women who appeared to be as free as their menfolk, and he was intrigued by their behaviour. As he travelled around the country he made detailed notes of all that he observed, taking every opportunity to participate in local customs and chatting to the locals wherever possible. On his return to Greece he recorded his experiences in a combined travel-guide and history of Egypt; the first book to introduce the exotic and mysterious land of the pharaohs to European readers.[1]

Herodotus was quite correct to single out the long thin geography of Egypt as a crucial factor in the development of her people. The River Nile, flowing north through a narrow strip of cultivated land to branch into the separate streams of the Delta, dominated every aspect of Dynastic life, and it would be impossible to gain any insight into the thoughts and deeds of the ancient Egyptians without an understanding of the land in which they lived. As Herodotus himself remarked, in an often-repeated phrase, 'Egypt is the gift of the Nile.'

Egypt is an African Mediterranean country with close geographical links with Palestine and the Near East. The first cataract of the Nile, just to the south of the modern town of Aswan, marks the traditional southern boundary of Egypt, although at times of imperial expansion this border was pushed further south into Nubia. Conventionally, this southern region is known as 'Upper Egypt' while the northern area including the Nile Delta is known as 'Lower Egypt'. To the north, Egypt is bounded by the Mediterranean Sea. During the Dynastic period the narrowness of the fertile land effectively restricted expansion to the east and west of the Nile, though the deserts were exploited for natural resources as and when required. Egypt maintained fluctuating economic ties with her immediate neighbours – Nubia to the south and Syria and Palestine to the east – while contact with the more distant lands of Mesopotamia, Anatolia and Crete led to Mediterranean and Near Eastern influences being absorbed into Egyptian society. However, thanks to her abundant natural resources and her geographical near-isolation, Egypt was able to remain a basically independent and self-sufficient country throughout her long history.

The Egyptians themselves knew their country as the 'Black Land', referring to the all-important ribbon of highly fertile soil which lined the banks of the Nile. The cultivated Black Land was in turn enclosed by the 'Red Land', the barren desert and cliffs which were only suitable for the construction of burial grounds and royal tombs. The difference between the fertile Black Land and the infertile Red Land has always been both clear and extreme, and many visitors to Egypt have noted how it is literally possible to stand with one foot in the desert sand and one foot on the green cultivation. This perpetual reminder of the stark contrast between the living and the dead, the fertile and the infertile, left an indelible mark on secular and religious thought, and the constant cycle of birth, death and rebirth became an endlessly repeated theme of Egyptian life.

All hail the god Hapy who springs out of the earth to water the land!
You of the secret ways, darkness in daylight, to whom your worshippers sing.
You flood the fields which Re has made, and give drink to all who thirst.

Middle Kingdom hymn to Hapy,
god of the Nile inundation

The River Nile allowed the first Egyptians to settle successfully in an otherwise arid part of North Africa by providing a dependable source of water for drinking, cooking, washing and waste disposal. In the absence of major roads and wheeled vehicles the Nile served as the major transport route linking the towns and cities and, as the stream flowed from south to north while the prevailing wind blew from north to south, movement both up and down the country was made very easy for any boat equipped with both an oar and a sail. However, it was the annual Nile inundation or flooding which had a profound effect on the development of Egyptian culture.

Agriculture, the backbone of the Egyptian economy, was totally dependent upon the inundation. Each year, from July to October, heavy summer rains in Ethiopia caused the river level to rise dramatically, flooding all of low-lying Egypt, irrigating and cleaning the land and depositing a deep layer of fertile mud

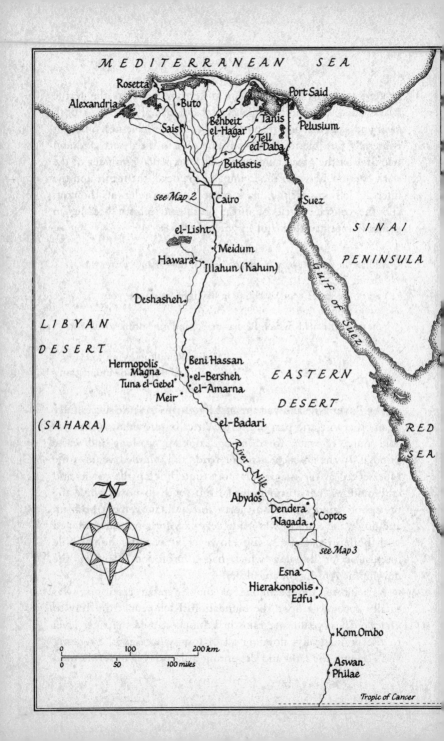

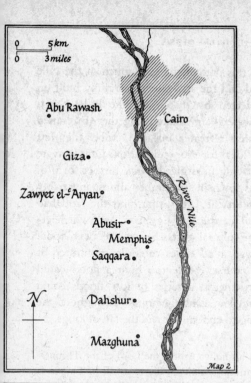

Abu Rawash

Giza

Zawyet el-ʿAryan

Abusir
Memphis
Saqqara

Dahshur

Mazghuna

River Nile

0   5 km
0   3 miles

N

Map 2

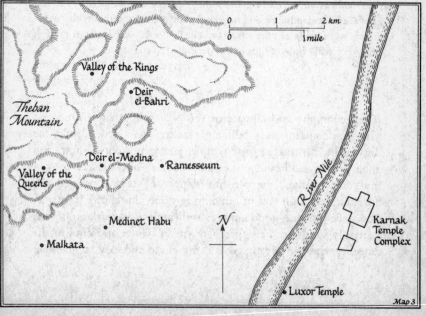

Valley of the Kings

Deir
el-Bahri

Theban
Mountain

Deir el-Medina

Ramesseum

Valley of the
Queens

Medinet Habu

Malkata

River Nile

Karnak
Temple
Complex

Luxor Temple

0   1   2 km
0   1 mile

N

Map 3

rich in minerals. During this part of the year much of the Nile valley became submerged and the settlements, carefully built on higher ground and protected by dykes, became little islands rising above the floodwaters and linked together by raised pathways. When the waters retreated in late October they left behind a thick moist soil ideal for crop cultivation. Only private gardens and the most outlying fields needed any further form of artificial irrigation. Crops sown in November almost invariably led to a splendid harvest in the late spring, and the land had plenty of time to dry under the hot Egyptian sun, which effectively killed many agricultural pests, before the next flood. The level of the Nile was at all times carefully monitored at various points along its course: while too high a flood could cause damage to the settlements, a series of low floods could become a national emergency, causing famine throughout the land and ultimately leading to civil unrest and the fall of kings.

He built as a monument to his father Amen, the Lord of the Thrones-of-the-Two-Lands, a magnificent temple on the west side of Thebes. It was built as an everlasting monument to last for all eternity. It was made of fine sandstone and worked with gold throughout; the pavements were made of pure silver and all the doors were made of gold. It was very wide and very great and decorated to endure.

> Extract from the New Kingdom
> stela of King Amenhotep III[2]

The geography and climate of the Nile valley had a profound effect on contemporary building practices. As a general rule, the Egyptians constructed their temples and tombs out of stone and their palaces and houses out of humble mud-brick. Given the hot and dry weather, the plentiful supply of Nile mud and the prohibitively high cost of building in stone, this choice of materials made practical good sense. A well-built mud-brick house was naturally insulated, being both warm in winter and cool in the summer, had the advantage of being cheap and easy to maintain and would certainly last for several generations. Unfortunately, this contrasting use of stone and mud-brick has distorted the surviving archaeological evidence. Over the passing centuries the mud-brick domestic structures have gradually crumbled, eroded and collapsed to form huge mounds of highly fertile soil which, until the relatively recent enforcement of protective legislation, were exploited by the local peasant farmers who had no understanding of their archaeological importance. Many ancient sites were simply dug up and spread on to the neighbouring fields.

In contrast, the robust rock-cut tombs, known to their owners as 'houses of eternity', and the solidly built temples, the 'mansions of millions of years', were designed to last quite literally for all eternity. While the majority of the tombs have been robbed and badly damaged, and the masonry blocks of many of the temples have been commandeered by subsequent generations, these structures have survived in a far more intact condition than the houses and palaces. They have consequently received a higher proportion of egyptological attention.[3] The unfortunate result of this bias in the archaeological evidence is an enforced reliance upon information taken from the burials of the upper echelons of society; although perfectly acceptable, this type of evidence is by no means typical of the whole population, and to base an understanding of daily life on the type of material yielded by Tutankhamen's tomb would clearly be foolish.

Fortunately, all is not gloom and doom on the archaeological front, and some extensive domestic sites have survived to be excavated. The pyramid town of Kahun and the workmen's villages of Amarna and Deir el-Medina were purpose-built housing complexes constructed to provide homes for the communities working on great royal projects.[4] These communities included not only the artisans and their overseers but also their wives, children, dependants and pets, together with those who provided services for their households such as the washermen, midwives and potters. They were by no means typical Egyptian settlements, being constructed in inhospitable and arid zones and occupied by skilled workmen rather than peasants, but they have provided us with many intimate details of ordinary, everyday activities.

The priests say that Men was the first king of Egypt, and that it was he who raised the dyke that protects Memphis from the inundations of the Nile . . . By banking up the river at the bend which it forms about one hundred furlongs south of Memphis he laid the ancient channel dry and dug a new course for the stream . . .

Herodotus telling the history of Egypt

The time-span covered by this book is vast; it stretches from the dawn of the Dynastic age in about 3000 BC until Egypt's conquest by the Greek forces of Alexander the Great in 332 BC. This is the equivalent of studying European history from a century before the founding of Rome to the present day, or American history from the War of Independence to President Clinton twelve times over. It includes thirty-one royal dynasties, the rise and fall of a vast and influential empire, and periods of chaos, anarchy and foreign invasion. No one would sensibly expect a flourishing and dynamic nation to remain culturally stagnant for well over 2,500 years and, indeed, there were always continuous and subtle changes to all aspects of Egyptian life. Nevertheless, it is startling to realize just how little the fundamental core of Egyptian society varied throughout this long period. In particular, although there were shifts in the nuances of religious thought, and changes in emphasis in various cults and mortuary practices, the underlying theology remained unaltered and basic to the Egyptians' way of life. The same stability is apparent when looking at the day-to-day life of the ordinary people; the Old Kingdom peasant wife may have worn different clothing from her New Kingdom descendant and her husband may have been labouring to build a pyramid rather than a rock-cut tomb, but their lifestyle and outlook would have been very similar. It is this continuity of thought and belief which makes the study of such a long time-span valid.

Tradition holds that Egypt was unified at the start of the Dynastic period by the warrior-king Menes, who led his fierce troops from the south to conquer the traditional enemies of the north and establish one kingdom. Menes then became the first king of the newly unified land. More realistically, it would seem that Egypt's formation must have been both more gradual and more complex, as the increasingly large agricultural communities along the Nile started to recognize the advantages of bonding together and sharing common policies. Whatever the mechanics of unification, it is clear that the resultant country was geographically too large to be ruled as a single administrative unit, and powerful local families of governors or princes were appointed to oversee the provinces which retained a certain degree of independence at all times.

Egyptian history is from the point of unification divided into dynasties, or periods of varying length defined by their different ruling families. The dynasties themselves are conventionally grouped together into three 'Kingdoms' and the so-called 'Late Period', punctuated by three 'Intermediate Periods' of varying length and character. This is not done merely to confuse the non-specialist. The Egyptians themselves never developed the equivalent of our modern calendar, preferring to date their years by reference to the length of the present king's reign. For example, wine jars labelled 'Year 9' were recovered from the New Kingdom tomb of Maya; there was no need to include the name of the king (Horemheb), as everyone at the time knew who he was. This complicated system meant that in order to understand their own history the Egyptians were forced to keep a long and very accurate chronological list of all their rulers and their reign-lengths. Fortunately, enough of these so-called king lists have survived to allow us to date long-ago events to the reign of a particular king with a fair degree of accuracy.

The Archaic period of unification and consolidation (1st and 2nd Dynasties) was succeeded by the Old Kingdom (3rd to 6th

Dynasties). This was a time of strict feudal rule, with the semi-divine king recognized as the rightful owner of all material possessions and therefore fully entitled to requisition all surplus produce. Position and power within the country were directly dependent upon royal patronage, and the heads of the political and religious establishments who controlled Old Kingdom Egypt were more often than not members of the King's immediate family. The sun-god Re soon became the principal state deity and developed an influential priesthood based at ancient Heliopolis, now a suburb of modern Cairo, while the king himself ruled his land from the nearby northern city of Memphis. The pyramids which characterize this period serve as impressive symbols of the power of the monarchy and the role of the pharaoh as god-king, indicating the extent to which the resources of the country were concentrated on specific royal monuments intended to emphasize the position of the king. No one knows what caused the Old Kingdom to collapse into a period of chaos and near anarchy, but a series of low Nile levels resulting in crop failure and famine must certainly have contributed to the growing civil unrest and the eventual breakdown of central authority.

The gradual reimposition of law and order following the disruptive First Intermediate Period (7th to 10th Dynasties) marked the start of the Middle Kingdom (11th to 13th Dynasties) and a period of peace and tranquillity throughout the land. The re-unified country was ruled by a succession of strong kings residing at Itj-Tawy, a new capital lying somewhere between the mouth of the Faiyum and the Old Kingdom capital Memphis, and the power of the hereditary local rulers was significantly reduced by a 12th Dynasty reorganization of provincial government. The 12th Dynasty survived the assassination of its founder, Amenemhat I, to become a time of great internal stability which lasted for over 200 years and allowed literature and the arts to flourish. Building works progressed and, although there were no projects on the scale of the Giza pyramids and the Sphinx, the pharaohs continued to build impressive tombs in the form of pyramids. Foreign policy became more adventurous at this time, and Egypt started to carve out an empire in the south while becoming more involved with her neighbours along the eastern borders.

Eventually, the large-scale immigration of Semitic peoples into the fertile Nile Delta became a contributory factor in the gradual de-stabilization of the Middle Kingdom. Central authority gradually collapsed and the country slowly fragmented into a small number of geographically distinct and mutually unfriendly enclaves: the 'Hyksos' Palestinian invaders and their Egyptian vassals in the north, the Nubian kingdom of Kerma in the extreme south and a small rump of independent Egyptians based, as at the beginning of the Middle Kingdom, on the southern city of Thebes. The Hyksos ruled over Egypt for approximately 100 years, bringing with them such new-fangled Asian influences as the horse, the horse-drawn chariot and the vertical loom, and retreating only when defeated in a series of vigorous military campaigns led by Ahmose, the dynamic founder of the 18th Dynasty.

The New Kingdom (18th to 20th Dynasties) quickly recovered from this brief phase of ignominious foreign occupation and soon developed into the period of greatest Egyptian wealth and prosperity, characterized by internal peace and external conquest. The high military standards set by Ahmose were continued by his descendants, and the Egyptian empire steadily expanded until, ruled from the northern capital of Memphis, it stretched from the Sudan in the south to the River Euphrates in the north-east. This policy allowed Egypt to gain control over many valuable natural resources and made it easy to open trade routes to Africa, western Asia and Greece. The new-found Egyptian wealth was reflected in the building of large-scale stone monuments such as the magnificent temples of Karnak and Luxor, and in the exquisite works of art which are typified by the spectacular golden treasures of Tutankhamen's tomb. At this time there was a large expansion of both the army and the civil service; middle-class bureaucrats were now needed to maintain the vast machinery of state.

Egypt continued to prosper during the 18th and 19th Dynasties, but by the reign of Ramesses III she was being badly affected by the movement of the 'Sea Peoples'; hordes of invaders from southern Europe who were attempting to settle in the Near East. Egypt managed to fight off these raiders but the country was greatly weakened, and during the 20th Dynasty the Asiatic empire was lost and the internal structure of the country again started to collapse.

Throughout the Third Intermediate Period (21st to 25th Dynasties) Egypt was effectively split into a number of independent units, the two most important being controlled by the High Priests of Amen who ruled over most of the south of the country, and by the 21st Dynasty of kings who ruled the immediate area around Tanis in the eastern Nile Delta. Initially relationships between these two governments were relatively amicable, and there was a degree of co-operation between the two capitals. However, the fragmentation of authority grew steadily worse, so that during the 22nd to 24th Dynasties local chieftains, often military families of Libyan descent, sprang up to simultaneously proclaim themselves pharaoh. Egypt was only brought back under central authority when a Nubian king marched north from the Sudan to reunite the country and establish the 25th Dynasty, a period of comparative stability which lasted for just over 50 years until an Assyrian invasion led by Ashurbanipal penetrated as far south as Thebes, reducing Egypt to the status of a mere province of the Assyrian Empire.

The major Egyptian collaborators who worked in conjunction with the Assyrians were an influential and wealthy family of local chiefs from the city of Sais in the western Nile Delta. These Saite rulers gradually became more and more powerful until they were able to ease out the Assyrians and again unite Egypt at the start of the Late Period (26th to 31st Dynasties). The resultant Saite phase was the final flourishing of Egyptian culture with art reverting back to the classical styles of the Old Kingdom. This strong emphasis on all things Egyptian seems to have been a calculated political move designed to emphasize the individual national character of a once-powerful country which was rapidly becoming a bit-part player on the stage of international affairs. The whole of the Near East was precariously unstable at this time and Egypt's neighbours, weakened by constant infighting, had become themselves highly vulnerable to attack. In 539 BC the Persian army, led by Cyrus II, conquered Babylon and in 525 BC Cyrus's son Cambyses entered Egypt and established the Persian 27th Dynasty.

The 28th and 29th Dynasties were periods of confusion and disunity, probably representing local resistance to Persian rule. Egypt was again, and for the last time, controlled by Egyptian rulers in the 30th Dynasty. The final king of this dynasty, Nektanebo II, had the dubious honour of being the last native Egyptian to rule over a unified country until President Nasser. He was eventually chased south into Nubia and historical obscurity by the invading Persians who established the 31st Dynasty. The subsequent brief period of Persian rule was in turn ended when Alexander the Great conquered Egypt in 332 BC, adding Egypt to his Macedonian Empire and allowing General Ptolemy to become governor, and eventually king, of the captured land. This conquest marks the end of the Dynastic Period and the start of Graeco-Roman rule. Ptolemy's Greek descendants continued to reign over Egypt until the defeat of the renowned Queen Cleopatra VII, when Egypt lost all semblance of independence, becoming a province of the Roman Empire.

Do not spare your son work when you can make him do it . . . Teach your son to write, plough, catch birds and set traps in case there is a year of low Nile, so that he will be able to reap the benefit of what he has learned.
Late Period scribal advice to parents

All through her long history Egypt retained an inflexible, pyramid-shaped society. At the very top of the social hierarchy

perched the king, or pharaoh, an acknowledged semi-divine ruler
who owned the entire land and who simultaneously acted as head
of the priesthood, the army and the bureaucracy. A long way
below him came the upper classes, a select band of privileged
families who owed their exalted position to royal patronage and
who were almost all related to the king. These fortunate few
assisted in the government of the country by functioning as high-
ranking priests, generals and senior civil servants, receiving
significant estates as payment for their hard work. Further again
down the social scale came the educated middle classes who,
being literate, were able to join the bureaucracy as scribes and
accountants, while directly beneath them were the lower middle
class semi-literate and illiterate artisans who worked as joiners,
potters, sculptors or artists. The lowest and largest layer of society
included private soldiers, servants and, above all, the peasants
who spent their lives working the land owned by either the
king, the private landlords or the religious foundations. Slaves,
who were never very numerous during the dynastic period, did
not really form an important or independent social class.

Obviously, this pyramid model gives a somewhat over-simpli-
fied view of Egyptian society, and there were many variations on
the basic pattern described above. Nevertheless, it does serve to
convey the curiously static and unchanging nature of Egyptian
dynastic life. At all times there was remarkably little movement
between the classes, and it was very difficult for anyone, male or
female, to advance from one social group to another. This was at
least partially due to the traditional Egyptian method of education
and training; fathers invariably apprenticed their sons in their
own trade or profession so that, generally speaking, a boy's
career was mapped out before his birth and whole castes of
doctors, washermen, reed-cutters or bureaucrats developed.
Young girls had even less need of career advice, as it was
automatically assumed that all daughters would marry and have
children. Denied the benefits of modern medicine girls were to a
large degree restricted by their biology, a restriction reinforced

by both cultural conditioning and the lack of modern conveniences which made the running of the household a full-time job. The vast majority of women, therefore, remained uneducated and untrained in anything other than domestic skills.

Even though the Egyptian woman enjoyed an unusual degree of freedom, it would be naive to regard her as a fully liberated prototype of the modern career woman. Indeed, all evidence suggests that men and women led very different lives. The Egyptians themselves, an instinctively conservative people who placed great value on the continuance of traditions, were happy enough to accept that everyone had his or her particular and pre-determined role to play in the maintenance of natural order and stability. This belief in a correct and unalterable way of doing things became absolutely fundamental to the Egyptian way of thought. To a people who continually sought out and emphasized the reassurance of links with the past and who at all times felt an unusually deep bond with their ancestors, the realities of an unchanging social structure were not so much stifling as immensely comforting. No one thought of questioning the uneven distribution of wealth and status throughout the community, just as no one ever questioned the inherited right of the pharaoh to rule, because these were the traditional and correct social divisions which, it was fully understood, were necessary to maintain the status quo. Egyptian daughters therefore looked forward to leading a life very similar to that led by their mother and grandmothers before them, interpreting this continuity as a sign that Egypt, and therefore the world, was functioning correctly.

1

Images of Women

[hieroglyphs]

Wherever you go, beware of approaching the women.
Old Kingdom scribal advice

The women of Dynastic Egypt created quite a stir in the ancient world. Legally free of the strict male supervision which more patriarchal societies imposed on their wives and daughters, these fortunate females appeared to their contemporaries to lead excitingly independent lives tinged with an alluring romance. In a land of exotic and unusual customs, where the king lived as a god, the gods took the form of animals and the entire population appeared obsessed with death, women were acknowledged to be one of the strangest phenomena. Their distinctive exotic beauty, coupled with fantastic rumours of lax Egyptian morals and wanton Egyptian females, simply added to their fascination and served as an inspiration to the authors and poets of Greece and Rome. It is this rather decadent image of Egyptian womanhood which has been perpetuated by more modern authors from Shakespeare onwards, so that even today the names of Nefertiti and Cleopatra conjure up a vision of the ultimate *femme fatale*.

But just how accurate is this portrait of the active, independent and sexually liberated Egyptian lady? How did the Egyptians themselves view their womenfolk? And how did the women see themselves?[1] It is not always easy for us to gain an understanding of the beliefs and cultural conditioning which lie behind the deeds of the past. Archaeological evidence, invaluable when

Fig.1   Lady carrying goods

attempting to assess material culture and used as the basis of all the subsequent chapters in this book, rarely allows an insight into ancient thought processes. For example, archaeology may tell us that Egyptian kitchens were situated at the back of the houses, furnishing us with a wealth of factual detail concerning different types of ovens and cooking utensils. It cannot, however, tell us who did the cooking. Was cooking a menial task to be despised? Or was the cook a respected member of the household, honoured for his or her skill?

Fortunately, the Egyptians have left us two contrasting means of studying their attitude towards women. An examination of contemporary arts (painting, sculpture and literature) can provide us with an idealized view of womanhood by allowing us to study the image which the Egyptians themselves wished to present to the world. At a more down-to-earth level, a consideration of the legal system and its treatment of females gives us an understanding of how, in practice, women were treated within the community. By combining these two very different types of evidence we can go at least some way towards an understanding of the woman's place in Egyptian society.

*

The idiot who looks at a woman is like a fly sucking on blood.
Papyrus Insinger, first century AD

Representational art, with its colossal stone figures, vibrant tomb paintings and delicately carved reliefs, presents us with some of our most enduring images of Dynastic women, allowing us the chance to expand our knowledge of Egyptian society by examining and contrasting the ways in which men, women and children were recorded by their fellow citizens. However, Egyptian art differed greatly in both style and function from its modern western counterpart, and it is not possible to make a literal interpretation of the abundant painted scenes and statues without some understanding of the conventions which exerted a profound influence on the work of the contemporary artists.

The ancient Egyptians did not recognize the concept of 'art for art's sake'; every single piece of their art was commissioned for a definite purpose and each image or statue had a deliberate and well-defined function. Aesthetic considerations were never the sole or even the primary concern of either the artist or his patron. This strictly utilitarian view led the Egyptians to regard all their painters and sculptors as craftsmen rather than artists and to confine their work to certain highly specific contexts, usually either the temple or the tomb. Here, standard and widely recognized formal scenes were presented not merely as a means of enhancing the décor but because they made an important contribution to the religious and/or political aspect of the building. An illustration of the king vanquishing his traditional enemies carved high on the wall of a temple, for example, both expressed the power of the monarch and reinforced the authority of the king, while a scene depicting a dead man enjoying the delights of the Afterlife added a magical strength to the deceased's endeavours to reach the Field of Reeds. Scenes painted on the interior walls of private houses were similarly impersonal. Accurate artistic 'snapshots' of Dynastic family life were extremely rare, and almost all the surviving household paintings include a fairly direct religious or magical message.

Not surprisingly, this deliberately practical emphasis stifled any impulse towards experimentation and creativity. Instead, it led to the development of strict artistic conventions and a repertoire of constantly repeated themes which satisfied the Egyptian love of tradition and continuity. Although there were many subtle changes in artistic styles throughout the Dynastic period, and although no two tomb walls are precisely identical, we find that the same conventional scenes are represented over and over again with very little variation in content.

The principal female figures depicted in formal paintings are almost invariably upper-class wives or daughters included in the scene by virtue of their relationship to a particular man. That is, they are shown in the tomb of their husband, father or son, rather than being tomb owners in their own right. It is not surprising that these women conform to a stereotyped view of the role of the Egyptian female as a passive support to her husband or father. Women take a secondary role in the proceedings; although they may be both active and prominent, they are obviously less active and less prominent than the male tomb owner. Often depicted on a much smaller scale than their spouse, they almost always stand behind their man. How far this formal representation of the relationship between men and women reflects the true situation we can now only guess, but it does seem obvious that within their tombs Egyptian husbands wished to preserve the traditional image of the man as the head of the household.

One exception to the general rule of the inert female is provided by the tombs of the queens of Egypt. Several of these women-only burials include scenes where wives act independently of their husbands; for example the 4th Dynasty tomb of Queen Meresankh ('She-Loves-Life') reveals the queen picking lotus blossoms while enjoying an informal boating expedition with her mother.[2] An even more striking contrast to the conventional depiction of passive women is provided by the representation of a besieged Asiatic town found on the wall of an Old Kingdom

*Fig. 2   Queen Meresankh boating in the marshes with her mother,
Queen Hetepheres*

tomb at Deshasha. This unique scene clearly shows the village
women fighting with knives and bare hands to defend their
homes from enemy Egyptian bowmen. Whether or not the scene
should be read as an appreciation of the bravery of the local
(non-Egyptian) women, or as a less than flattering comment on
the valour of their menfolk, is not now clear.[3]

I was an artist skilled in my art and pre-eminent in my learning . . . I
knew how to depict the movements of a man and the carriage of a
woman . . . No one succeeds in all of this apart from myself and the
eldest son of my body.

Inscription of the sculptor Irtisen

Fig. 3   Women fighting in the streets

The principal private individuals painted by the artists were almost invariably presented as perfect physical specimens dressed in gleaming white clothes, adorned with spectacular jewels and positively bursting with vigorous good health. The women, their femininity emphasized by rounded breasts and buttocks and less well-defined muscle groups, were all, without exception, beautiful. Every feature on their idealized body was shown from its best or most typical angle, and some rather contrived and contorted-looking poses developed as the artists struggled to paint their standing subjects with the head in profile, a single eye and eyebrow shown as from the front, the torso also shown from the front, the hips viewed from the side and the legs shown separately and slightly apart.

To modern eyes, accustomed to images which faithfully mirror reality and the now conventional use of foreshortening and perspective, this stylization leads to an unnatural and rather primitive-looking painting technique which makes all Egyptian two-dimensional art instantly recognizable. However, to the Egyptians, who expected to see a formalized rather than an impressionistic form, it was a necessary precaution. After all, the Egyptians reasoned with their own intensely practical brand of logic, if a part of the body couldn't be seen, it almost certainly wasn't there. It was vital that the main figures painted on tomb walls should be both seen and understood to be complete because, if by some mischance the physical body should defy the art of the embalmers and decompose after death, the spirit of the deceased might be compelled to live on in his or her painted image. Few Egyptians were willing to run the risk of surviving minus an arm or a leg in the Afterlife.[4]

The 'fairer sex', who conventionally worked indoors away from the burning Egyptian sun, were invariably painted with lighter skins than their ochre-coloured menfolk. This convention completely ignored the fact that society was racially well-mixed at all levels; as has already been noted, the Egyptians did not require their art to be an accurate representation of life. Some women were depicted with a black skin, but this did not necessarily imply a Negroid origin. Black, the colour of the fertile Egyptian soil, symbolized regeneration and was therefore used to indicate those awaiting rebirth in the Afterlife. Following this logic, a lady depicted with green skin was understood to be dead, green in this instance being the colour of life (i.e. the expectation of resurrection) rather than putrefaction. For both men and women, dead and alive, colour was used to fill in the outline of the figure without any attempt at shading, so that the image appeared complete to the pedantic Egyptian observers.

Most Dynastic men of substance chose to be preserved for posterity with stylized rolls of unhealthy-looking fat sagging around their not-insubstantial waists. This less than subtle convention was employed as a means of stressing the wealth of the subject; clearly only the richest Egyptians could afford to consume large amounts of food without needing to burn off calories during hard manual labour. Fat became firmly equated with power, a message which is made very clear in tomb scenes where skinny workmen and those of low rank are shown working beside their overweight masters. In at least a few cases the conventional upper-class paunch may have had some basis in reality. Wealthy Egyptians were inordinately fond of eating and drinking, and the mummified bodies of several New Kingdom pharaohs, including Tuthmosis II and Ramesses II, showed large folds of flabby skin over the abdominal region, indicative of a life-long weight problem.[5]

In contrast, fat Egyptian females were very rare indeed, and the assorted wives, daughters and sisters who accompanied the tomb owner always maintained an acceptably svelte appearance which was highlighted by their fashionably tight clothing. The obese and possibly steatopygic Queen of Punt and her fat daughter must have been regarded as both unnatural and unwomanly by the workmen who had the duty of recording their images on the walls of Queen Hatchepsut's temple at Deir el-Bahri. Whether this female thinness was simply an artistic convention, or whether it should be interpreted as a deliberate comment on women's less powerful relationship with men, is not clear. In any case, the fact that artists chose to depict all women as slender certainly does not mean that they actually were all slim.

The more minor female figures included in the painted scenes did not need to conform to a stereotyped image of slender feminine passiveness. As these non-central characters formed a relatively small and unimportant part of the total picture the artists felt free to take liberties with their appearance, rejecting the rather stilted formal poses appropriate to the tomb owner and his wife and adopting instead a more naturalistic and light-hearted style. Ugly, old, badly dressed and fat women all appear to enliven the backgrounds of more formal scenes, and it is these more relaxed figures shown working, resting and going about their business, who provide us with a lively and far more typical view of many aspects of everyday Dynastic life. Nubile young girls dance, play their musical instruments and perform impressive gyrations for the entertainment of their patrons, while sedate maids grind endless bushels of corn to make bread and elderly peasant women toil in the fields pulling flax and gleaning grain.

Egyptian sculpture was every bit as practical in its conception as Egyptian painting. All statues were automatically invested with magic or religious powers and could be used to represent or replace real people as necessary. Abstract or 'unnecessary' sculpture was therefore unknown in Egypt, and craftsmen confined themselves to depictions of gods, kings and wealthy individuals. All these works were ultimately intended to serve as a substitute person or god in either the temple or the tomb.

During the Old Kingdom the vast majority of private statues were carved for inclusion in the tomb. These figures provided a convenient base for the soul of the departed to receive offerings and, like the two-dimensional images, could serve as a replacement home for the spirit should the original body decay. By the Middle

Kingdom, however, most private statues were commissioned so that they could be placed in the courtyards of the great temples where they would serve as an acceptable substitute for the absent devotee and could absorb and transmit any benefits received from their proximity to the god. This tradition continued throughout the New Kingdom, to the extent that most major temples developed associated stoneworking industries. Therefore the pious pilgrim who had been unable to transport a statue from home was able to buy a custom-made figure – ranging from a few inches high to lifesize – to which his or her own name could be added. These proxy worshippers were placed in silent staring ranks facing the sanctuary; when the courtyard became too crowded they were simply removed and buried in a large pit within the sacred temple precincts.

An Egyptian had to be either rich or influential to be able to afford a substantial hard-stone statue. It is not surprising that the recovered statues provide us with a fairly accurate reflection of the more high-ranking sections of society. Most statues represent relatively wealthy men, either single men or groups of related men who have contributed to the cost of a communal statue. Husband-and-wife statues and family groups including dependent children are not uncommon, and these almost always show the wife physically supporting her husband with her arm around his shoulder in a traditional wifely pose. Whether this should be interpreted as a subservient posture, or a sign of family solidarity, is not now clear. Statues of the king and queen invariably depict the wife on a much smaller scale than her husband. This is a true reflection of the relative importance of the couple, but reveals the difference between a god and a mortal rather than that between a husband and a wife; in other family groups the couple are shown more or less to scale, and in cases where a woman of normal height was married to a dwarf the husband is clearly shown to be shorter than his wife. The woman invariably wears formal clothes which allow the artist to emphasize her sexuality by stressing the outline of her breasts. Single female statues, women-only groups

Fig. 4   Husband and wife statue

and groups where a woman plays a dominant role are very rare,
suggesting that women through either choice, economic necessity
or social opportunity did not invest in statues.

He who commits any offence against my concubine, he is against me
and I am against him. Look, she is my concubine and everyone knows
how to treat a man's concubine . . . Would any of you be patient if his
wife had been denounced to him? Then why should I be patient?

Letter from the priest Heqanakht

The letter quoted above was written by the minor Middle
Kingdom priest Heqanakht to his family.[6] It is as indicative of
domestic discord and strife as any letter written today and,
indeed, the disquieting undercurrents evident in this angry message inspired Agatha Christie to write her popular murder-
mystery *Death Comes as the End* which is set in pharaonic
Egypt.[7]

The literate Egyptians were inveterate writers, and the dry
desert conditions have ensured the preservation of monumental
inscriptions, fragile papyri and leather scrolls in which we have
been able to read not only impersonal royal pronouncements,
formal religious texts and rather dull business letters but also the
private law cases, romantic love poetry and intimate family
letters which give a human face to the sometimes rather dry
archaeological bones. Ostraca (*sing.* ostracon: limestone chips and
pottery fragments used as writing materials) were the memo-
pads of the past, and were used in their thousands as Egyptians
jotted down unimportant messages which would have wasted the
expensive papyrus. Vast numbers of these ostraca have survived,
allowing us a glimpse into the more humdrum day-to-day lives
of the ordinary people. Perhaps we should not be too surprised
to learn that personal relationships in ancient Egypt were not
very different from the relationships of today; there were many
loving and united families but, as Heqanakht's correspondence
suggests, there were also bitter inter-family quarrels over money
and status. At all times gossip and innuendo were rife while the
rumoured immoral behaviour of others was, of course, of
universal interest.

However, all this written evidence needs to be treated with a
due degree of caution. It should always be remembered that our
record is both incomplete and randomly selected – that even
though many texts have survived many more have been
destroyed, leaving whole aspects of life simply unrecorded. Those
documents which do survive present us with several problems of

interpretation. Although we are able to translate literally many of the words which the Egyptians used we do not come from the same cultural and social background and, just as a visitor from the planet Mars equipped only with a dictionary would have trouble understanding the radio commentary to a football game or the meaning of the words of a pop song, so we may be missing some of the more subtle nuances and colloquial expressions which would have been clear to the intended reader. This is particularly true of the romantic love songs and the myths and legends, where the Egyptians deliberately employed metaphors and *double entendres* to add a pleasing twist to their message. The Egyptian habit of exaggerating or even inventing the glorious deeds carved on monumental inscriptions simply adds to our confusion; the Egyptians themselves could see no reason why they should not usurp the monuments, and even the actions, of their illustrious forebears.

Above all, it should be remembered that literacy was confined to a very small percentage of the population, almost all of whom were male members of the middle and upper classes. The surviving documentary evidence therefore deals primarily with matters which concerned a restricted section of the community, and is both written from a male viewpoint and intended for a contemporary male reader. Even where a text purports to be by a woman – for example, the love poetry written from a young girl's viewpoint – it was often composed by a man and therefore gives a male interpretation of a woman's assumed feelings. Since most women could neither read nor write, many matters of purely feminine interest are simply excluded from the written record.[8]

The ship commander Ahmose, son of Abana, the justified, speaks, and says: 'I speak to all of you. I speak to let you know of the favours which have come to me. I have been rewarded with gold seven times in the sight of the whole land, with male and female slaves as well.

I have also been endowed with very many fields. The name of the brave man is preserved in his deeds; it will not perish in the land forever.'

From the New Kingdom autobiography of Ahmose, son of Abana[9]

In a tradition which started during the Old Kingdom, many Egyptian men of high rank and breeding made a permanent record of their daily activities and achievements. This lengthy and stylized 'autobiography' was preserved on the walls of their tomb. Typically, these texts detail the trials and triumphs of the deceased's life and, although invariably written in an exaggerated and, to modern eyes, rather boastful style, they can provide the student of Egyptian history with a great deal of information concerning the life of their subject. Unfortunately women, as the secondary occupants of the tomb, have rarely left us this type of information. We have no female autobiographies to compare with those of the men,[10] and the rather muted epithets which are traditionally used to praise a dead woman 'Whom the People Praised' or 'Guardian of the Orphan's Heart' are both vague and rather meaningless.

Prescription for safeguarding a woman whose vagina is sore during movement: You shall ask her 'What do you smell?' If she tells you 'I smell roasting', then you shall know that it is *nemsu* symptoms from her vagina. You should act for her by fumigating her with whatever she smells as roasting.

Extract from the *Kahun Medical Papyrus*

Only one particular type of document offers us the opportunity to see the real Egyptian woman stripped of her modest veil of privacy. The so-called Medical Papyri[11] – handbooks listing all the known symptoms and suggested cures for a variety of common ailments and accidents – combine with the details recorded from the surviving human burials and mummified remains to provide us with a fascinating insight into the daily life of the Egyptian doctor and his patients. This scientific evidence indicates that the average indigenous Egyptian woman was relatively short in stature with dark hair, dark eyes and a light brown skin. She had an average life expectancy of approximately forty years, assuming that she was able to survive her childhood and her frequent pregnancies.

The idyllic scenes which decorate many tomb walls give the impression that the Egyptians were a fit and healthy race untroubled by sickness. This impression is flatly contradicted by the medical evidence which indicates a population at the mercy of a wide variety of debilitating and life-threatening diseases ranging from leprosy and smallpox to spina bifida and polio. Even less serious-sounding afflictions such as diarrhoea, coughs and cuts could prove fatal without modern medicines, while the majority of the population suffered intermittently from painful rheumatoid joints and badly abscessed teeth. The 18th Dynasty *Edwin Smith Papyrus* paints a vivid picture of the dangers which could be encountered in a society where major building projects were conducted with only the most minimal of safety precautions and where warfare was relatively common. This papyrus, a specialized work dealing with the treatment of horrific industrial wounds, includes typical case histories: 'Instructions concerning a gaping wound in his head smashing his skull' or, more seriously, 'Instructions concerning a gaping wound in his head penetrating to the bone, smashing his skull and rendering open the brain'. Not surprisingly, this latter was classed among the ailments 'not to be treated'.

The reverse of the *Edwin Smith Papyrus* presents us with information more relevant to a study of women. At some time in the past an Egyptian scribe or doctor has used the back to jot down a curious assortment of magical texts and prescriptions for a variety of complaints. These include a 'recipe for female troubles', two prescriptions 'for the complexion' and one recipe 'for some ailment of the anus and vicinity'. In their apparently random mixture of practical advice, scientific knowledge and superstitious ritual these prescriptions clearly indicate the thin line that always existed between ancient medicine and magic. Indeed, the Egyptian physicians did not attempt to differentiate between the effectiveness of rational scientific treatment and amuletic or supernatural cures, just as they did not distinguish between medical complaints and problems such as persistent dandruff and facial wrinkles which we would now regard as cases for a beautician rather than a doctor. Instead, they took the view that all people were born healthy, and that disease and infirmity, if not the direct result of an accident, were caused either by a parasitic worm or by an evil spirit entering the body. It therefore made sense to take practical measures to alleviate uncomfortable physical symptoms while relying on magical spells to banish the evil spirit and thereby cure or remove the illness.

The *Ebers Medical Papyrus*, also dating to the 18th Dynasty, is perhaps the most scientifically advanced of the Egyptian medical documents. It is less specific in its content than the *Edwin Smith Papyrus*, but shows the same mixture of sympathetic magic and good advice when dealing with more common Egyptian ailments, internal diseases and general afflictions such as baldness and bad breath. The section dealing with specific male problems is very short, detailing four particular illnesses (itching, priapism, impotence and gonorrhoea). The much longer section on women's matters deals primarily with reproduction and associated problems such as contraception, breastfeeding and child welfare. Surprisingly, for a country whose funerary rites encouraged the dissection of the deceased, knowledge of the internal workings of the female body was fairly limited. Gynaecology was not a specialist subject, and there were some strange misunderstandings with regard to the function of the female organs. For example, although the position of the cervix was known, no mention is recorded of the ovaries, and the uterus itself was believed to be fully mobile and capable of floating freely within the female body. As a wandering womb was thought to cause the patient great harm, various means were developed to tempt the itinerant organ back to the pelvis, the most widely used being the fumigation of the unfortunate patient with dried human excrement.

Prescription to cause a woman's uterus to go to its correct place: tar that is on the wood of a ship is mixed with the dregs of excellent beer, and the patient drinks this.

Extract from the *Ebers Medical Papyrus*

There was also a mistaken assumption that a healthy woman had a free passageway connecting her womb to the rest of her body, an assumption which became absorbed into later Greek medical wisdom. Many fertility tests were designed to locate any obstruction in this corridor which would prevent conception. The *Kahun Medical Papyrus* therefore advised that the patient should be seated on a mixture of date flour and beer; a fertile woman would vomit after this treatment and the number of retches would give a sure indication of the number of potential pregnancies. A similar prescription is recommended by the *Berlin Medical Papyrus*. Alternatively, in a test later used by Hippocrates, a garlic or onion pessary could be inserted in the vagina and left overnight; if by morning garlic could be detected on the patient's breath she was thought able to conceive. Occasionally, physicians were able to pinpoint the exact cause of female sterility: when the king of the Hittites contacted his ally Ramesses II requesting the services of an Egyptian doctor who could help to cure his sister's childless marriage the king wrote back pointing out, with more truth than tact, that as the lady in question was about sixty years old, hopes of a cure were slim.

Then the peasant said to his wife, 'Look, I am going down to Egypt to bring food from there for my children. Go and measure out for me the remains of last year's barley which is in the barn.' His wife measured out twenty-six gallons of barley for him. The peasant then said to his wife, 'Look, you keep twenty gallons of barley as food for you and your children. Now make these six gallons of barley into bread and beer for me to eat on the days which I am travelling.'

From the Middle Kingdom *Story of the Eloquent Peasant*

Egyptian fiction was a relatively late development, gradually growing in subtlety from the straightforward action-packed heroic tales popular during the Old Kingdom to the more complex and challenging allegories of the Middle and New Kingdoms. Throughout the Dynastic age, however, women were included in the stories only as subsidiary figures peripheral to the main plot. Wives and daughters may have provided food and clothing for their intrepid menfolk but they never accompanied them on their adventures, appearing content to stay behind and run the home. Indeed, the extreme male-oriented content of the stories and their undoubtedly masculine appeal make it difficult to dismiss the impression that surviving Egyptian fiction represents only those tales which were told by men to men. It may well be that the corresponding stories popular among groups of women were never written down; this would certainly explain the dearth of romantic fiction and the complete absence of domestic details which would presumably not be of interest to men. The consistent portrayal of loyal but passive and rather insignificant wives and daughters in the surviving fiction confirms the impression presented by the contemporary paintings and sculpture, that Egyptian men and women led essentially separate lives with different but complementary duties.

Towards the end of the Dynastic period, when Egypt was experiencing increasing foreign influence, the tradition of writing about good but rather negligible women was suddenly halted as scribes started to depict more realistic females with both a good and a bad side to their character.[12] Indeed, soon the women included in the stories were more bad than good. This abrupt change of attitude is apparent in both the fictional tales and the scribal instructions which were used as set texts in all Egyptian schools; by the Late Period scribe Anhsheshonq was writing about wives in a way that suggests that he himself did not enjoy an entirely happy home life:

Let your wife see your wealth but do not trust her with it . . . Do not open your heart to your wife, as what you say to her in private will be repeated in the street . . . If a wife does not desire her husband's property, she is in love with another man.

Ankhsheshonq held a very ambivalent attitude towards women, for in the same work he also expresses his admiration for the good woman of noble character, who 'is like food which arrives in times of famine'. Did he feel that a good woman was a rare thing? Or were his comments on untrustworthy wives simply the ancient equivalent of the disparaging 'mother-in-law' jokes still popular with some male comedians today?

Several fictional females were presented in a distinctly unfavourable light. The 19th Dynasty *Story of Two Brothers*, for example, tells of the rift which developed between the brothers Anubis and Bata when Anubis's scheming spouse first attempted to seduce her brother-in-law and then, her amorous advances rejected, accused him of attempted rape:

Now the wife of his elder brother grew afraid so she took fat and grease and made herself appear as if she had been beaten, in order to tell her husband, 'It was your younger brother who beat me.' Her husband returned home in the evening according to his daily routine. He reached his house and found his wife lying down and seeming to be ill. She did not pour water for his hands in the usual manner, and she had not lit a fire for him. His house was in darkness and she lay vomiting . . .

Anubis, foolishly trusting his false wife, instantly prepared to kill his brother who, magically forewarned by his favourite speaking cow, was forced to run away from home to face a life

of danger, drama and adventure. Unfortunately Bata also proved
to be a bad judge of the female character, and he too was
eventually betrayed by a faithless wife.

A similarly unpleasant woman was featured in the New
Kingdom *Tale of Truth and Falsehood* where the rather naive
Truth, already betrayed and blinded by the lies of his more
devious brother Falsehood, was seduced by a glamorous but
selfish lady. Although the woman bore Truth's son she treated
her former lover very badly, making him serve as the humble
doorkeeper of her house. It was only when the son was old
enough to question his paternity that Truth was finally accorded
his correct position in the family.

> When I see you my eyes shine and I press close to look at you, most
> beloved of men who rules my heart. Oh, the happiness of this hour,
> may it go on for ever! Since I have slept with you, you have raised up
> my heart. Never leave me!
>
> New Kingdom love song

Lyrical love songs and romantic poems were popular throughout
the Dynastic age. These semi-erotic verses, with their explicit
references to sexual intercourse mingled with a series of more
veiled allusions to love-making, allowed young Egyptian girls a
chance to express their own sexuality by making it quite clear
that a woman can desire a man just as a man desires a woman.
There is always a danger that the verses represent wishful thinking
on the part of male poets wistfully conjuring up enchanting
images of a non-existent world full of sexually receptive females.
They do, however, indicate that Egyptian society was unusually
relaxed in its attitude towards the relationships between two
unattached and consenting parties, and was apparently untroubled
by women expressing feelings of love and sexual arousal.

> Keep your wife from power, restrain her . . . In this way you will
> make her stay in your house.
>
> Old Kingdom scribal advice directed at young men

The role of the woman in Dynastic art and literature is very much the image of a stereotyped female seen through the eyes of the man. In paintings and in sculpture she represents the dutiful wife, daughter and mother, while in literature she provides a loyal support for her more adventurous spouse. She is invariably passive and submissive; her private life and thoughts are very much a blank. Although this type of evidence does give us some understanding of Egyptian family hierarchy – we can see, for example, that the husband clearly considered himself to be the head of the household, and can guess that men had little understanding of the woman's daily routine – the real woman still remains tantalizingly hidden behind a mass of convention and tradition. This idealized image of the Egyptian woman and the Egyptian marriage can, to a certain extent, be balanced by a consideration of how women were actually treated within the community.

Unfortunately, no Egyptian book of laws has survived. However, there is enough evidence in the form of court documents and legal correspondence to show that, in theory at least, the men and women within each social class stood as equals in the eyes of the law. This equality gave the Dynastic Egyptian woman, married or single, the right to inherit, purchase and sell property and slaves as she wished. She was able to make a valid legal contract, borrow or lend goods and even initiate a court case. Perhaps most importantly of all, she was allowed to live alone without the protection of a male guardian. This was a startling innovation at a time when the female members of all other major civilizations were to a greater or lesser extent relegated to a subordinate status and ranked with dependent children and the mentally disturbed as being naturally inferior to males. The contemporary written laws of Mesopotamia and the later laws of Greece and Rome all enshrined the principle of male superiority, so that the regulation of female behaviour by males was seen as a normal and natural part of daily life throughout most of the ancient world.[13]

In Mesopotamia the *Code of Hammurabi,* which consolidated Babylonian law in approximately 1750 BC, included many regulations relating to the control of female behaviour and the proper conduct of a marriage. In particular, it emphasized the complete authority of the male within the home, with wives and children treated as the disposable property of the husband. Although women were allowed certain very important legal and economic rights, including the right to own property and the right to a protective and binding marriage agreement, these rights were strictly limited. For example, it was very difficult for a wife to divorce an unsatisfactory husband, and a woman had no control over the disposal of her dowry which legally passed to her sons at her death.[14]

The laws and customs of Greece were if anything more repressive in their treatment of women, condemning all wives and daughters to a perpetual and suffocating protection.[15] Respectable Greek women, effectively excluded from all public life, had few legal rights unless they acted with the full consent of their *kurieia* or male legal guardian. As a result, many upper-class women led unsatisfactory half-lives, closely confined within their own quarters where they spent long days working at the loom and supervising the household. Only in Sparta were young girls permitted to enjoy healthy exercise and positively encouraged not to spend too long at their weaving; this liberal behaviour was considered to be shockingly lax in ultra-conservative Athens. Under strict Athenian law women were effectively owned either by their father or by the husband who had been selected for them. Their dowries were at all times under the control of their husbands and they were neither allowed to inherit nor to make valid legal contracts. Their children became the property of the father and his family.

The Roman woman was also expected to behave with a becoming modesty, although she was permitted to enjoy a wider range of social activities than her Greek sister. It was quite acceptable for a Roman matron to dine with male guests, visit shops and temples and even play a restricted role in furthering her husband's career, and indeed male Greek visitors to Rome were thrown into embarrassed confusion when first attending banquets at which the ladies of the household were also present. Despite this additional freedom, however, the Roman woman remained under her father's legal control until she married, when her father had the option of transferring his guardianship to the new husband, thereby allowing the bride exactly the same legal rights as any daughter of the groom. If the father did not exercise this option he remained financially responsible for his daughter who was legally still a member of his household. Again the woman required the consent of her guardian in all formal legal matters, and again she was unable to act as the guardian of her children.

How did the unusually liberated women of Egypt develop and retain their equal legal status? This is an intriguing question which, as yet, has no entirely satisfactory answer. Early egyptologists, unduly influenced by the pioneering work of Frazer,[16] felt that the legal freedom of the Egyptian women provided direct proof that the Egyptian system of government had evolved from a pure matriarchal system.[17] This theory is now known to be totally false, and it seems likely that the answer must be sought in a consideration of the more unusual aspects of Egyptian culture. The legal subjugation of women in other societies seems to have been designed to ensure that women were denied the sexual freedom allowed to men, and thereby prevented from indiscriminate breeding. If this was a direct result of the need to provide a pure ruling élite and to restrict the dispersal of family assets, the unique position of the god-king and the absence of a strictly defined 'citizen' class made similar considerations irrelevant in Egypt. The rigid nature of the Egyptian class system and the traditional pattern of matchmaking meant that those assets which were held privately were unlikely to be dissipated on marriage, while the remarkable fertility of the Nile valley reduced the competition for access to resources

*Fig. 5   Stela of the child Mery-Sekhmet shown in the
arms of his unnamed mother*

experienced in less fortunate societies. The recognition that
descent could pass through both the female and the male lines,
a characteristic of several African cultures, must also have
been instrumental in protecting the rights of women. The
Egyptians consistently regarded the female line as an important
one, and mothers were frequently honoured in the tombs of their
sons.

Their equal status allowed women full access to the legal
system. Women were able to bring actions against fellow citizens
and give valid evidence in court, and they were liable to be
publicly tried for their crimes. Egyptian justice was based on a

court or arbitration system. Both rich and poor were entitled to lodge formal complaints, and each legal case was considered purely on its own merits by a local magistrate. More important cases were heard before a specially convened tribunal or jury of fellow citizens while the vizier, who was in practice the head of the Egyptian judiciary, judged the most grave and complex issues himself. Although bribery of the officials was a recurrent problem, and those from powerful families often held undue influence over the courts, justice was theoretically available to all Egyptians regardless of sex or class. Ostraca recovered from Deir el-Medina indicate that women were, however, generally less likely to be involved in legal action than their menfolk, reflecting the fact that women played a less prominent role in public life. Those women who were forced to make a court appearance were more likely to be defendants than plaintiffs, and we have legal documents dealing with cases where women were tried for non-payment of debts, theft and even the neglect of a sick relative.

The case of Mose, a bitter legal wrangle involving a complex tangle of forged documents and lying witnesses, clearly demonstrates the woman's right to inherit property, to act as a trustee and to bring a complaint before the law courts. Mose, a bureaucrat employed in the treasury of Ptah at Memphis, proudly recorded the entire dispute on the wall of his Sakkara tomb.[18] He tells us how his ancestor, a certain captain Neshi, received a small estate as a reward for his loyal services to the king. This estate remained intact within the Neshi family for over two hundred years, passing down from generation to generation and always administered by a trustee appointed to act on behalf of the legal heirs. During the reign of King Horemheb a man named Khay was appointed trustee of the estate, but his appointment was challenged by the Lady Wernero, Mose's grandmother, and the court eventually confirmed Wernero's position as trustee for her five brothers and sisters. Unfortunately Takharu, one of Wernero's sisters, made an official objection to this new trusteeship, and so it was decided that the land should be divided into six equal portions and shared out between all the legal heirs. Mose's father, Huy, and his grandmother, Wernero, both appealed against this judgement, but before the issue could be resolved Huy died and Mose's mother Nubnofret was evicted by Khay from her one-sixth share of the land. Although Nubnofret immediately lodged a formal complaint before the court she was unable to prove her right to the land as Khay had submitted forged documents in evidence, and therefore Khay retained possession of Mose's inheritance. It was only when Mose grew old enough to plead his own case, presenting several sworn testimonies to the Grand Court of the vizier, that the dispute was finally settled in Mose's favour.

I am a free woman of Egypt. I have raised eight children, and have provided them with everything suitable to their station in life. But now I have grown old and behold, my children don't look after me any more. I will therefore give my goods to the ones who have taken care of me. I will not give anything to the ones who have neglected me.

Last will and testament of the Lady Naunakhte

The right to own property was a very important legal concession, providing a degree of security for all unmarried, widowed and abandoned women and their dependent children. The 20th Dynasty last will and testament of the Lady Naunakhte illustrates the extent to which women were able to dispose of their own goods as they wished. Naunakhte, the mother of eight children, had acquired considerable wealth from her family and from her first husband but had grown old and increasingly dependent upon her offspring. She swore her will before a court tribunal, specifying that she wished her property to be split only between the five children who were continuing to care for her in her old age, and specifically disinheriting those children who had ignored her plight. However, recognizing that she could not prevent her husband's share of the joint property plus his personal possessions from being divided according to his wishes, she conceded that 'as regards these eight children of mine, they shall come into the division of the possessions of their father to a proportionate part'. Clearly, the families of 3,000 years ago could be as unreliable as those of today.

The deed of transfer made by the Priest Wah:

I make this deed of transfer for my wife, Sopdu's daughter Sheftu, known as Teti, of everything that my brother left to me. She herself shall pass it on to any of the children that she shall bear me, as she wishes. I am giving her the three Asiatics which my brother gave to me, and she may give them to any of her children, as she wishes. As for my tomb, I shall be buried in it and my wife also, without any interference from anyone. Furthermore, my wife shall live in our home which my brother built for me, without being evicted by any person . . .

Middle Kingdom last will and testament

Property acquired by a couple during a marriage was legally regarded as a communal asset, and so in addition to her own possessions a wife was entitled a share of any such joint property.[19] This share passed to her children at her death, or to the woman herself if she was divorced, while the remaining two-thirds were divided firstly between the husband's children and then between his brothers and sisters. In addition, a widow automatically inherited a percentage of her husband's private property and, indeed, some husbands used their knowledge of the legal system to ensure that their partner would receive the bulk of the joint estate by legally transferring property to their wife before death, somewhat as present-day inheritance tax is avoided by those who resign themselves to giving away their goods during their lifetime.

A more devious means of preventing brothers or sisters from laying claim to matrimonial property involved the husband adopting his wife as his child; a fascinating Middle Kingdom

legal document gives details of the adoption of the woman
Nenufer by her husband Nebnufer: 'My husband made a writing
for me and made me his child, having no son or daughter apart
from myself.'[20] This declaration, made in front of witnesses, was
legally binding and Nenufer was able to inherit all Nebnufer's
property as she was both his wife and his daughter. Seventeen
years later Nenufer, now a widow, made an important addition
to the legal deed, telling how she and her husband had purchased
a slave girl to act as a surrogate mother, presumably to Nebnufer's
children. This slave had borne two girls and one boy who had
been freed and in turn adopted by Nenufer, and then as Nenufer's
brother had expressed a wish to marry one of the girls, he had
also been adopted by his sister so that he might receive his share
of the family property. Nenufer's legal right to inherit property,
make a legally binding will, adopt a child and free a slave are all
made explicit in this text.

Unfortunately, during the Graeco-Roman period when the
Greek laws, customs and language started to have a profound
influence on the Egyptian way of life, the woman's right to equal
status was slowly but surely eroded away. At this time many
Greek families settled in Egypt and closely cloistered Greek
women protected by the legal guardianship of their *kurieia* started
to live side by side with the free-born Egyptian women. Many
Egyptians, seeing the exotic Greek lifestyle as preferable to their
own, rushed to embrace the new modes of behaviour; indeed,
we have documents confirming that several non-Greek women
who had no legal need for a guardian actually applied to have
one appointed, perhaps in the hope that others might mistake
them for sophisticated Greeks rather than provincial Egyptians.
By the Roman period, when Roman traditions were added to
the Greek and Egyptian cultural mix, women had lost many of
their former rights and privileges, so that although continuing
local customs allowed them to remain less suppressed than the
women living in Rome, they were nowhere near as emancipated
as their Dynastic forebears had been.

2

Married Bliss

> Found your household and love your wife at home as
> is fitting. Fill her stomach with food and provide
> clothes for her back ... Make her heart glad, as long
> as you live.
>
> Old Kingdom *Wisdom Text*

Those of an unromantic or cynical disposition may take the view
that marriage is little more than a simple economic contract
drawn up between a man and a woman, intended to create an
efficient working unit and strengthen alliances while protecting
interests in property and legitimizing children. Love may, or
may not, be an additional bond which unites the participants; it is
certainly not fundamental to a successful marriage. For women in
particular the wedding ceremony, marking the important change
in status from daughter to wife, also represents the recognized
transition from child to adult and the start of a new role in
society. Very unfairly, married women are almost universally
regarded with more respect than their unmarried sisters; indeed,
the view that an unmarried woman is a woman who has failed in
her main role in life is one which is expressed with monotonous
repetition by both men and women of different cultural
backgrounds and different historical periods.

All these generalizations are true of marriage in ancient Egypt,
where the formation of a strong and unified family provided
much-welcomed protection against the harsh outside world. And
yet the Egyptians, far more than any other past civilization, have
passed on to us, through their paintings, their statues and, above

all, their lyric love songs, their satisfied contentment with the romance of marriage. To marry a wife and beget many children may have been the duty of every right-thinking Egyptian male, but it was a duty which was very much welcomed: the Egyptians were a very uxorious race.

Tradition and biology combined to ensure that marriage followed by motherhood would be the inevitable career-path for almost all Egyptian women, and mothers trained their young daughters in domestic skills accordingly. Once a girl had reached adolescence she had no real social role, being neither child nor wife, and so she remained in a kind of protective limbo, living in her father's house until a suitable match could be found. The best marriages were widely agreed to be those arranged between members of the same family, or between neighbours of the same social standing and professional class, and scribe Ankhsheshonq advised parents 'don't let your son marry a bride from another town, in case he is taken away from you'. Just as modern Egyptian peasants acknowledge the right of a paternal male cousin to claim the hand of his father's brother's daughter, so their ancient forebears gave preference to marriage between first cousins or uncles and nieces which would prevent the splitting of family property and the inherited right to work land, an important consideration in an agricultural community. The genetic implications of inbreeding do not seem to have worried the Egyptians unduly, although several examples of congenitally deformed skeletons recovered from local cemeteries suggest that occasional problems did occur.

The state itself was remarkably relaxed in its attitude to marriage and, unlike almost all other ancient civilizations, the Egyptians placed no official restriction on unions with foreigners. There was no perceived need to preserve the purity of the Egyptian race, so exotic beauties were frequently included in the New Kingdom royal harem, while a stela found at Amarna shows an Egyptian woman and her foreign husband, easily identified by his unusual hairstyle and dress, sitting peacefully

Fig. 6   Foreign women and their children

together sipping beer through straws. In marked contrast, both the Greeks and the Romans placed a very high value on the inherited right of citizenship which was legally confined to the upper echelons of society, and it was at least in part due to their desire to protect the purity of the bloodline that the tradition of segregating women from men developed. The Egyptian tolerance of mixed marriages extended to unrestricted slave-marriages, both between two slaves or between a free person and a slave:

Year 27 of the reign of Tuthmosis III. The royal barber Sabestet appeared before the tribunal of the royal house testifying: my slave, my property, his name is Imenjui. I fetched him with my own strength when I accompanied the sovereign. I have given to him the daughter of my sister Nebta as a wife, her name is Takamenet.

New Kingdom legal document

This approach is in sharp contrast to the complex inheritance rules which were enforced in Egypt during the period of
Roman control, when it was clearly regarded as desirable that
people should be pressured to marry only within their own
caste:

Children born to a townswoman by an Egyptian husband have the
status of Egyptians and inherit from both parents. If a Roman of either
sex marries anyone of the status of a townsman or of an Egyptian
without being aware of their status, their children take the status of the
inferior parent. If a Roman or a townsman marries an Egyptian wife
in ignorance of her status, the children may take the status of the father
after *erroris probatio*. If a townswoman marries an Egyptian husband
in the mistaken belief that he is a townsman she is not to blame, and if
the declaration of birth of children is made by both the status of citizen
is granted to the offspring . . .[1]

The most unusual aspect of the state's lenient attitude towards
marriage was the complete lack of any taboo against the marriage
of close relations. Most societies feel that the union of children
with parents, or brothers with sisters, is undesirable and take steps
to ensure that it does not occur. Egypt was a notable exception
to this rule. However, incest was certainly not as rife as popular
fiction would suggest. With the exception of the royal family
who intermarried to safeguard the dynastic succession and to
emphasize their divine status, there is no real evidence for
widespread brother–sister marriages until the Roman period,
while parent–child incest is virtually unrecorded. The brother–
sister marriages which are recorded are more likely to be between
half-brothers and half-sisters than full siblings. Unfortunately for
modern observers, the Egyptians employed a relatively restricted
kinship terminology, and only the basic nuclear family were
classified by precise kinship terms (father, mother, brother, sister,
son and daughter). All others had to be identified in a more
laborious manner, such as 'mother of the mother' (maternal
grandmother) or 'sister of the mother' (maternal aunt). To make

matters even more confusing the precise family names could also be applied to non-family members, so that 'father' could be correctly used to indicate a grandfather, stepfather, ancestor or patron, while 'mother' could describe either a grandmother or even a great-grandmother. The use of the affectionate term 'sister' to encompass a wide group of loved women, including wife, mistress, cousin, niece and aunt, taken in conjunction with a theology which condones the brother–sister marriage of principal deities such as Isis and Osiris, has contributed to our misunderstanding of the prevalence of brother–sister incest, and there has been a general reluctance to lose the image of the intriguingly decadent Egyptian lifestyle conveyed by these errors in interpretation.

A similar misconception has grown up around the subject of Egyptian polygamy. Although there were no laws to specifically prohibit polygamous marriages, and in spite of the fact that Herodotus firmly believed that only the Egyptian priests were expected to remain monogamous – thereby implying that all other Egyptians chose to be polygamous – multiple marriages were not as common as has often been supposed. Polygamy, when not actually illegal, has always been a rich man's hobby, and things were no different in ancient Egypt where only the more wealthy members of society could afford to indulge in the luxury of more than one wife. Confusion has arisen in this matter because of the Egyptian habit of depicting one or more dead first wives together with their living successor on their joint husband's tombstone. The most often-quoted evidence used to support the theory of polygamous Egyptian marriages consists of a papyrus written by the Lady Mutemheb in which she clearly states that she is the fourth wife of her husband Ramose, adding that two of his other wives are dead while one is still living. Although the precise circumstances of this marriage are not spelt out to us, there is nothing further to suggest a polygamous alliance, and it would seem far more logical to assume that

Ramose had divorced his third wife before marrying his fourth. Serial polygamy, or re-marriage following bereavement or divorce, was comparatively common, and again scribe Ankhsheshonq had an opinion to offer: 'Do not take to yourself a woman whose husband is still alive, in case he should become your enemy.'

He is a neighbour who lives near my mother's house, but I cannot go to him. Mother is right to tell him 'stop seeing her'. It pains my heart to think of him, and I am possessed by my love of him. Truly, he is foolish, but I am just the same. He does not know how much I long to embrace him, or he would send word to my mother.

New Kingdom love poem

The matchmaking involved a series of negotiations conducted between the father of the bride and either the groom or, less commonly, his father. Yet again Ankhsheshonq had an opinion on the selection of a suitable partner, recommending that his son should 'choose a prudent husband, not necessarily a rich one, for your daughter'. A widow was able to negotiate on behalf of her fatherless girls, but it was not until the very end of the Dynastic period that matrimonial tradition was relaxed enough to allow the bride and groom to negotiate their own marriage. Although surviving texts make it clear that the bride was 'given' in marriage by her father to the groom we have no idea whether this was purely a conventional turn of phrase, directly comparable with the tradition of fathers symbolically 'giving away' their legally independent daughters which still survives in western marriage ceremonies, or whether the daughter had little or no say in the choice of her husband. The idea of the caring Egyptian father of many family portraits deliberately contracting his daughter to marry against her will, or refusing to permit a love match without good reason, is certainly difficult for us to accept, and we have no textual evidence to suggest that women were ever forced into marriage.

There were no legal age restrictions on marriage, although it has generally been assumed that a girl would not be considered eligible before the onset of puberty and menstruation, which would have occurred at about the age of fourteen. A 26th Dynasty document recording a father's refusal to agree to his daughter's wedding because she was too young and 'her time has not yet come' supports this view. However, evidence from Rome, where female puberty was legally fixed at the age of twelve regardless of the physical development of the girl concerned, indicates that ten- or eleven-year-old brides were not uncommon, and we have no reason to doubt that such young girls were also married in Egypt. Indeed, it is only within the past fifty years that in modern rural Egypt marriage with girls as young as eleven or twelve has been prohibited by law. There is certainly textual evidence from the Graeco-Roman period for Egyptian girls marrying as young as eight or nine, and we have a mummy label, written in demotic, which was made out to identify the body of an eleven-year-old wife.

The bridegroom, particularly in an uncle–niece marriage, was likely to have been considerably older and more experienced than his immature child-bride; Ankhsheshonq recommended that men should marry when they reached the age of twenty, while scribe Ptahotep considered that a youth should not marry until he had become a respectable man. To assume that the young brides were not sexually active before the onset of their periods would be very naive and, despite the availability of a range of contraceptives, the problem of fertile but physically immature children themselves becoming mothers must have contributed to the high levels of infant and maternal mortality during pregnancy and childbirth.[2] Strabo gives some indication of the widespread acceptance of pre-pubertal sex by describing at some length the religious dedication of a young and beautiful high-born girl to the service of Amen or Zeus: 'She becomes a prostitute and has intercourse with whoever she likes until the purification of her body takes place.' By the purification of the body Strabo meant the onset of her menstrual periods. Although it is possible that Strabo may have misunderstood the situation, or may have been misled by helpful locals inventing lurid stories to interest the foreigner, it is clear that this story is regarded as one of general interest, and not one of revulsion.

I see my sister coming. My heart exults and my arms open to embrace her. My heart pounds in its place just as the red fish leaps in its pond. Oh night, be mine forever, now that my lover has come.

New Kingdom lover's song

In western societies marriages have become unions with strong legal implications which are matters of concern to the state bureaucracy. They may in addition be regarded as religious unions requiring the approval of a priest. This outside involvement creates an established wedding protocol, with a requirement to take certain legal vows, register with various authorities and in some countries even undergo simple blood tests. As a result, it becomes relatively easy for anyone to determine whether or not a couple are actually married, and the moment of the actual wedding is usually clearly defined. The ancient Egyptians took a very different approach to marriage, regarding it as a purely personal matter between two individuals and their families which was of little or no concern to the state and which required no associated religious or legal ceremony. There was therefore no compulsory registration of the marriage, and although a form of marriage contract could be drafted either at the time of the wedding or, more usually, later, this was not a legal necessity and certainly did not constitute a marriage agreement. Consequently, although the Egyptians themselves were very clear about who was and who was not married to whom, the intricacies of their family life are now not always apparent to us.

The most obvious difference between our modern and the ancient Egyptian marriage is the complete lack of any prescribed wedding ceremony. There was no Egyptian word meaning wedding, no special bridal clothes to be worn, no symbolic rings to be exchanged and no change of name to indicate the bride's new status. There may have been the consumption of a special wedding meal, perhaps involving the eating of salt, but this is only a tentative suggestion based on the interpretation of one broken line of text.[3] In the absence of all other visible evidence for wedding ceremonies, we must assume that the cohabitation of the happy couple served as the only outward sign that the marriage negotiations had been successfully concluded, and so it was by physically leaving the protection of her father's house and entering her husband's home that a girl transferred her allegiance from her father to her husband, becoming universally acknowledged as a wife. She took with her all her worldly possessions, the 'goods of a woman', which are usually specified as including a bed, clothing, ornaments, mirrors, a musical instrument and an expensive shawl which may well have been the equivalent of our bridal veil. The nuptial procession, where the young bride in all her finery was escorted through the streets by a happy crowd of friends and relations, must have been an occasion for great family rejoicing; the ancient Egyptians were inveterate party-givers who seized every opportunity for throwing a lavish banquet, and we may assume that the wedding celebrations went on well into the night.

We do not know how much importance or ritual, if any, was attached to the consummation of the marriage. Until comparatively recently the defloration ceremony formed a definitive part in the celebration of an Egyptian wedding, being witnessed by a variety of married female relatives who could vouch for the honour of the new bride and her family. Indeed, the deflowering most often occurred with the young bride firmly restrained while either the groom or a female relation used a finger covered in clean gauze to break the hymen and draw the blood necessary to prove her purity. In ancient Egypt, where the chastity of unmarried females was not considered to be of overwhelming importance to society, the consummation of the marriage may well have been a more private and less harrowing ceremony. It does seem likely that consummation was necessary to make a marriage legally valid and binding, as is the case in many societies today. Certainly in contemporary Mesopotamia, where the bride was expected to prove herself fertile, the marriage was not a true marriage until conception had occurred, and it was only after the birth of a child that the dowry became payable.

The groom was not required to pay his new father-in-law a bride-price, although in a tradition arising during the New Kingdom he was expected to hand over a token gift of money and sometimes corn to his wife. The actual financial value of this payment varied, ranging from negligible to the purchase price of a slave, and it seems to have represented a consideration which made the marriage agreement binding on both parties, perhaps somewhat as a new husband is today expected to provide his wife with a wedding band during the marriage ceremony. Whether this tradition is the survival of an earlier custom of actually making a payment to the father, either as compensation for removing the bride and her services from her birth-family, as consideration to mark the transfer of the right of ownership of the bride, or even a straightforward purchase price paid for the bride, is unclear.

In his turn, the father of the bride contributed to the well-being of the happy couple by donating wedding presents of domestic goods and food, often continuing to supply substantial quantities of grain for up to seven years, until the union became generally recognized as well-established, therefore a true marriage rather than a simple 'living together'. Towards the end of the Dynastic period it became fashionable to record these 'dowries' in a legal contract which could be used to prevent dispute and protect the economic rights of the woman and her children in the unhappy event of a divorce. These marriage contracts were not a part of the marriage itself, and were often drawn up after the couple had produced several children.[4] The example quoted below represents a Graeco-Roman contract, with the Egyptian-born Horemheb agreeing that his wife Tais will be adequately compensated should the marriage fail:

If I divorce you as my wife, and hate you, preferring to take another woman as my wife, I will give you two pieces of silver beside the two pieces of silver which I have given you as your woman's portion . . . And I will give you one third of everything which will be owned by you and myself furthermore.

It is very difficult for us, looking back from a different culture and through thousands of years, to really understand the accepted day-to-day rights and duties of Egyptian married life. We may know that the husband was almost invariably the breadwinner while the wife worked in the home, but we cannot fully appreci-ate the subtleties of the situation, particularly as women have left no record of their daily existence, thus, we have no idea of how the wife expected to be treated by her husband, or how each regarded the function of the other. Did husbands view their wives as equal partners in the marriage, or were they considered to be inferior in every way? Were women deferred to within the home, or were they verbally abused? Was wife-beating unheard of, or accepted by both as an absolutely normal aspect of family life scarcely worthy of comment? Inscriptions from the tomb-chapels of the Old Kingdom suggest that the perfect wife was both submissive and compliant, 'she did not utter any statement which repelled my heart', although this ideal did not necessarily reflect real life, and Ankhsheshonq's comment 'may the heart of a wife be the heart of her husband', hints that marital disagree-ments may have been more common than men liked to admit. Scribal instructions, written for the guidance of young unmarried men, generally suggest that in an ideal world the husband would treat his wife with respect while retaining control of his household and its members. Perhaps the best indication of how the husband himself perceived his moral duty towards his wife can be gleaned from reading a detailed letter written during the 19th Dynasty by a man wishing to ingratiate himself with the dead wife whom he believed to be haunting him:

I took you as my wife when I was a young man and you were still my wife when I filled all kinds of offices. I did not divorce you and I did not injure your heart ... Everything I acquired was at your feet, did I not receive it on your behalf? I did not hide anything from you during your life. I did not make you suffer pain in anything I did with you as your husband. You did not find me deceiving you like a peasant and making love with another woman. I gave you dresses and clothes and I had many garments made for you.

The legal situation is somewhat easier for us to follow. The new husband assumed the father's former role of protecting and caring for the bride, although he in no way became her legal guardian. The wife was allowed to retain her independence without becoming legally subservient to her spouse, and was able to continue administering her own property. Although the husband usually controlled the joint property acquired during the marriage, it was acknowledged that a share of this belonged to the wife; she was able to collect her portion when the marriage ended. One Ptolemaic text gives us a very clear picture of the legal equality of women when it records the business deal of an astute wife who lent her spendthrift husband three *deben* of silver, to be paid back within three years at a hefty annual interest rate of 30 per cent.

I shall not leave him even if they beat me and I have to spend the day in the swamp. Not even if they chase me to Syria with clubs, or to Nubia with palm ribs, or even into the desert with sticks or to the coast with reeds. I will not listen to their plans for me to give up the man I love.

New Kingdom love song

The marriage was ended, as is the case today, either by the death of one of the partners or by divorce. The death of a spouse

loomed as an ever-present threat to happiness as life expectancy
was not high and reminders of mortality were everywhere. Very
few couples survived into middle age without losing most
members of their immediate family, and the death of several
children would have been accepted with resignation. Young girls
married to much older men must frequently have been widowed
before they left their teens, while the very real dangers associated
with pregnancy and childbirth contributed to the many mother-
less families. Fortunately, the woman's right to inherit one-third
of her husband's property meant that a widow was not forced
either to rely on the charity of her children or to return to her
father's house, although convention decreed that the bereaved
should be cared for by their family whenever necessary. Vulnerable women without the protection of a male were clearly to be
pitied, and were regarded as being in need of protection. As the
Eloquent Peasant flattered his judge in the New Kingdom fable
'for you are the father of the orphan, the husband of the widow
and the brother of the divorced woman . . .' Tomb scenes
indicate that loving couples torn apart by death confidently
expected to be re-united in the Afterlife. In the meantime re-
marriage after widowhood was very common, and funerary
stelae indicate that some individuals married three, or even four,
times. We do not know whether there was a prescribed period of
mourning for widows, although most societies impose a waiting
period of approximately six months following bereavement
which allows proper respect to be paid to the dead husband
while ensuring that there is no doubt over the paternity of
posthumous children.

Let Nekhemut swear an oath to the lord that he will not desert my
daughter . . . As Amen lives and as the Ruler lives. If ever in the future
I desert the daughter of Telmont I will be liable to hundreds of lashes
and will lose all that I have acquired with her.

Although many marriages were both stable and happy, some

ended in divorce. This was without doubt a serious matter for those involved but, just as the marriage itself was not seen as a matter of legal formality, so the divorce could be brought about by mutual agreement without the costly help of lawyers and courts. Those who had had the foresight to draw up a marriage contract were bound to honour its terms, while those who were involved in acrimonious disputes over the division of joint property could invest in a legal deed to resolve their differences. These legal cases were, however, unusual, and the majority of marriages ended by the couple simply splitting up, with the wife leaving the matrimonial home and returning to her family house, taking her own possessions together with her share of the joint property and occasionally, in cases where she could in no way be regarded as a guilty party, a fine paid by the husband as a form of compensation. In a few rare cases it was the wife who owned the house, and consequently the husband who was expected to leave. This parting, and the returning of all the woman's property, ended the husband's obligation to maintain his wife and set both parties free to marry again. We do not know who had custody of the children and who had the duty to pay for their upbringing and education, although it is generally assumed that they were left in the care of their mother. If so this is a further indication of the liberal Egyptian attitude towards women's rights, which was in marked contrast to accepted practice in Greece or Rome where the male head of the household was the sole guardian of the dependent children and a divorced wife lost all legal rights to her offspring. In patriarchal Rome, a pregnant widow was obliged by law to offer her newborn baby to her dead husband's family; only if they had no use for the child was she given the chance to raise her baby herself.

The right of a man to end an unhappy alliance by 'repudiating' an unsatisfactory wife is known from the 12th Dynasty onwards and almost certainly existed earlier in Egyptian history. The corresponding right of a wife to initiate a divorce is only documented from the New Kingdom onwards but, given that

Egyptian law consistently treated married women as independent individuals, it would appear that it simply went unrecorded in earlier times. There are certainly very few recorded case histories dealing with a woman repudiating her husband; whether this indicates that women were less fickle or had lower expectations of their partners is not clear. It may be that, in a society which placed great emphasis on fertility, and consequently on youth, an elderly wife would think twice about rejecting her husband as she might well be unable to find a replacement willing to maintain her. As there were no legally defined grounds for divorce almost any excuse could be cited as a reason to end the alliance and in effect the marriage could be terminated at will. In practice, financial considerations and perhaps pressures from the two families concerned, who may well have been related, must have provided some restraint. There is no indication that divorce was regarded as a social stigma for a man, although the repudiated wife, particularly one rejected in favour of a younger and more attractive or more fertile bride, may well have felt publicly shamed.

Do not divorce a woman of your household if she does not conceive and does not give birth.

> Late Period scribal advice

A diverse variety of reasons have been recorded for the ending of marriages, many of which would be familiar to the divorce lawyers of today. Marriages often failed because of mutual incompatibility, because the husband wished to devote himself to his work, or because one party had fallen in love with another. The rejection of an infertile wife was a common enough tragedy, although not one that society approved of. A 21st Dynasty letter which has survived from the workmen's village of Deir el-Medina quotes the unusual and almost certainly apocryphal story of a man and wife who had been married for over twenty years. When the husband fell in love with another woman he looked for a reason to end his marriage, and decided on 'I repudiate you because you have no sight in one eye.' Not surprisingly his wife, who had been partially blind throughout the entire marriage, was not particularly impressed by her husband's feeble excuse and roundly mocked him for taking twenty years to notice her deformity.

For a long time egyptologists believed that concubines, the official mistresses of both married and unmarried men, were accepted throughout Egyptian society although they were not generally accorded either the respect or the legal rights reserved for married women. It now appears that the number of official concubines may have been seriously overestimated as there has been an unfortunate tendency to classify all otherwise unidentified single women as concubines. A growing understanding of the textual evidence is starting to indicate that many of the unmarried ladies attached to households actually served as administrators, musicians or maids. Even in the letters of Heqanakht, where the Lady Iutemheb is described as *hbsw.t*, a term which has not been found in any other text but which has been traditionally taken to mean concubine, it is by no means certain that the lady in question was not an official second wife.[5]

Do not fornicate with a married woman. He who fornicates with a married woman on her bed, his wife will be copulated with on the ground.

                                          Late Period advice to young men

Married women were certainly not allowed any degree of sexual licence and adultery – 'the great sin which is found in women' – was the most serious marital crime which a wife could commit, and one which would almost certainly lead to ignominious divorce and the total loss of all legal rights. Men in turn were expected to respect another man's sole right of access to his wife, and indulging in sexual relations with a married woman was frowned upon, not for moral reasons, but because it was a sure and certain way of enraging a cuckolded husband. Even a relationship between a willing unmarried woman and a married man could be fraught with danger, and one letter which has survived from Deir el-Medina tells how a group of villagers ganged together to confront a woman known to be conducting a clandestine affair with the husband of a neighbour.[6] The mob could only be prevented from seriously assaulting both the woman and her family by the timely intervention of the local police. The wronged wife had attracted the sympathy of her community, and the adulterous husband was ordered to regularize his affairs and obtain a divorce at once, as the people could not be restrained from acting for a second time. As in many cases of adultery the woman was clearly seen as a temptress corrupting a weak but essentially innocent man, and Egyptian myths and wisdom texts, all written by males, are full of dire warnings to stay clear of other men's wives who would use all their feminine wiles to snare them into sexual relationships.

Then she spoke to him, saying 'You are very strong. I see your vigour every day.' And she desired to know him as a man. She got up, took hold of him, and said 'Come, let us spend an hour lying in bed together. It will be good for you, and afterwards I will make you some fine new clothes.'

New Kingdom *Tale of Two Brothers*

A wife caught in adultery was open to the harshest of physical punishments from her husband. In theory she could be put to death; the New Kingdom *Westcar Papyrus*, a collection of stories about the fabulous Old Kingdom court of King Cheops, tells how an unfaithful wife was burned and her ashes scattered on the River Nile, while in the *Tale of Two Brothers* Anubis eventually kills his guilty wife and throws her body to the dogs, thereby denying her an honourable burial. Diodorus Siculus reports that the adulterous Egyptian wife was liable to have her nose cut off, while her partner in crime would be savagely beaten. In practice divorce and social disgrace seem to have been the accepted penalty, and the wife repudiated on the grounds of adultery was roundly condemned by everyone.

Prescription to make a woman cease to become pregnant for one, two or three years; grind together finely a measure of acacia and dates with some honey. Moisten seed-wool with the mixture, and insert it in the vagina.

Ebers Medical Papyrus

Illegitimate children appear to have suffered no specific hardships or discrimination in Dynastic Egypt, although in the New Kingdom *Tale of Truth and Falsehood* a young fatherless boy was cruelly taunted by his schoolmates: ' "Whose son are you? You don't have a father." And they reviled him and mocked him.' Several contraceptives and even abortion-procuring prescriptions were available for those couples who wished to avoid a pregnancy; these were generally concocted from a diverse range of curiously unpleasant ingredients and frequently included a measure of crocodile dung. The use of animal excrement as a contraceptive appears to be a peculiarly widespread phenomenon: in southern Africa elephant droppings have often been used as a prophylactic, while the English *Boke of Saxon Leechdoms* of AD 900 cheerfully suggested that those wishing to avoid children should 'take a fresh horse turd and place it on hot coals. Make it reek strongly between the thighs up under the raiment.'[7] The efficacy of these methods is unknown, although it is tempting to assume that the application of a judicious amount of any type of dung to the private parts may well have cooled the ardour and made the use of any further precautions unnecessary. Perhaps not surprisingly, no evidence for 'male' contraceptives such as condoms or recipes for potions to be applied to the male genitalia have been recovered; methods such as coitus interruptus (withdrawal of the penis before ejaculation) or coitus obstructus (full intercourse with the ejaculate entering the man's bladder due to pressure on the base of the urethra) would naturally leave no trace in the archaeological record.

Man is more anxious to copulate than a donkey. What restrains him is his purse.

> Observation of Scribe Ankhsheshonq

The more intimate aspects of married life were very important to the Egyptians, who held the continuing cycle of birth, death and rebirth as a central and often repeated theme in their theology. Intercourse naturally formed an integral part of this cycle, and the Egyptians displayed no false prudery when dealing with the subject of sex. Unlike most modern views of heaven, which tend to concentrate on spiritual rather than physical gratification, potency and fertility were regarded as necessary attributes for a full enjoyment of the Afterlife, and consequently false penises were thoughtfully moulded on to the mummified bodies of dead men, while their wives were equipped with artificial nipples which would become fully functional in the Afterlife. Female fertility dolls with wide hips and deliberately emphasized genitalia were often included among the grave goods of men, women and children to help the deceased regain all lost powers. Although clearly sexual symbols, these figurines are often carrying tiny baby dolls, emphasizing the fact that sex was regarded as just one of the more pleasing aspects of the wider subject of fertility. There was no artificial distinction drawn between the enjoyment of sex and the wish to produce children, and a woman's fertility consequently contributed to her sexual attractiveness. The clear and artificial division which most westernized societies make between sex and reproduction can be seen when trying to picture a provocatively pouting *Playboy* centrefold posing with her newborn infant.

The Egyptians were certainly not coy about sexual matters. However, as most of the evidence which they have left us comes from religious or funerary contexts where explicit references to

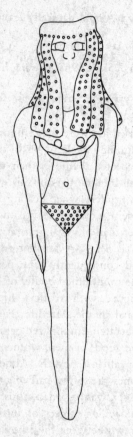

Fig. 7   Pottery fertility figurine

intimate subjects would have been considered inappropriate, we do not have much opportunity for archaeological voyeurism. Love songs, myths and stories all make rather vague and veiled references to intercourse, while crude graffiti, dirty jokes and explicit drawings scribbled on potsherds are far more basic. One of the world's earliest examples of pornography, the so-called *Turin Erotic Papyrus*, contains a series of cartoons depicting several athletic couples cavorting rather self-consciously in a wide variety of imaginative and rather uncomfortable-looking poses. Unfortunately, we do not know whether the papyrus was supposed to be a true record of events observed in a brothel or, as seems far more likely, simply represented the draughtsman's more extravagant fantasies. Certainly, basing our understanding of conjugal relations on the *Turin Papyrus* would be similar to believing all that is suggested by blue movies to be typical of modern western life. More down-to-earth evidence compiled from texts and ostraca confirms that the more conservative 'face-to-face' positions and intercourse from behind were the preferred sexual postures for most couples.

Then Seth said to Horus: 'Come, let us have a feast day at my house.' And Horus said to him: 'I will, I will.' Now when evening had come, a bed was prepared for them, and they lay down together. At night, Seth let his member become stiff, and he inserted it between the thighs of Horus. And Horus placed his hand between his thighs and caught the semen of Seth.

New Kingdom *Story of Horus and Seth*

We must assume that, as in any sophisticated society, more unusual sexual tastes did exist, but the Egyptians themselves maintained a discreet silence in these matters. Homosexual activity, which was by no means frowned upon in many parts of the ancient world, seems to have played little part in Egyptian daily life; the *Book of the Dead*, that indispensable guide to the Afterlife, lists abstinence from homosexual acts among the virtues but gives us no indication of how common such acts might have been. The homosexual episode in the *Story of Horus and Seth*, quoted above, has been variously interpreted as either a symbol of Seth's general unfitness to rule or as a sign of Seth's physical dominance over his nephew. The Middle Kingdom version of this tale credits Seth with the immortal line 'How lovely your backside is.' Horus then reports this unexpected advance to his mother, Isis, who advises her

Fig. 8 A prostitute enjoying sex with a client

son to catch Seth's semen, thereby avoiding the humiliation of impregnation by his enemy.

As in many societies where men write the histories, lesbianism seems to have passed completely unrecorded. Rumours of more fantastic sexual behaviour were recorded by Herodotus, who seems to have been particularly fascinated by the seamier side of Egyptian life: 'In my lifetime a monstrous thing happened in this province, a woman having open intercourse with a he-goat.' Even if this was true, it was clearly not a common occurrence. Necrophilia involving the abuse of freshly dead female bodies in the embalming houses, also hinted at by Herodotus, is again totally unrecorded by the Egyptians themselves.

Take to yourselves a wife while you are young, so that she may give you a son. You should begat him for yourself when you are still young, and should live to see him become a man.

New Kingdom scribal advice

In the days following her wedding the young bride would have eagerly looked for the telltale signs which would indicate that a baby was on the way. It would be very difficult for us to over-emphasize the importance of her fertility to the Egyptian woman. A fertile woman was a successful woman. She was regarded by men as sexually attractive, was the envy of her less fortunate sisters and, as the mother of many children, she gained the approval of both society and her husband. Every man needed to prove his masculinity and potency by fathering as many children as possible, and to do this he had to have the co-operation of a fruitful wife. The wife, for her part, needed many children to please her husband, ensure her security within the marriage and enhance her status in the community. Mothers had an important and respected role within the family, and were frequently represented in positions of honour in the tombs of both their husband and sons. Children were not, however, simply status symbols. Both husband and wife appear to have loved their

Fig. 9   A prostitute painting her lips

offspring dearly, and Egyptian men had no misplaced macho feelings that made them embarrassed or ashamed of showing affection towards their progeny. To produce a large and healthy brood of children was every Egyptian's dream, and babies were regarded as one of life's richest blessings and a cause for legitimate, if occasionally exaggerated, boasting: we must either assume that the 11th Dynasty army captain claiming to have fathered 'seventy children, the issue of one wife' was over-counting to emphasize his virility, or else feel deeply sorry for his wife.

The Egyptians were by no means unusual in their desire to father many offspring. Peasant societies traditionally show a great respect for fertility, and nowhere is this more true than in modern rural Egypt where a great man can easily be identified by his many sons and the unfortunate woman who shows no signs of pregnancy becomes the subject of endless speculation and gossip less than a year into her marriage. To remain childless is a tragedy in a country where parents stress their parenthood by themselves taking the name of their eldest son, using the prefix *abu* (father of) or *om* (mother of), and where women without children are politely referred to as *om el-ghayib*, 'mother of the absent one'. In these circumstances the concept of waiting to start a family, or perhaps restricting the number of planned children, becomes incomprehensible, and sterile men have been known to kill themselves rather than admit that they are incapable of fathering a child. The ancient Egyptians would have felt at one with their modern counterparts in this matter.

Do not prefer one of your children above the others; after all, you never know which one of them will be kind to you.

Late Period advice to parents

There are very few societies where female babies are actively preferred to males, and Egypt was no exception to this general rule. Although girls were clearly loved by their parents, as witnessed by several family portraits which include daughters in formal but affectionate poses, boy children undeniably conveyed greater status. This preference for boys may be hard for us to condone but is perhaps easy to understand. In any society with no efficient welfare or pension system children represent a financial investment for the future. Boys, who traditionally work outside the home, have a high-earning potential while girls, whose work within the home is unwaged, will marry and devote their work to the good of their husband's family. In ancient Egypt the eldest son also had an important part to play in his parents' funeral ritual; a role which could not be adequately performed by a daughter.

The preference for boy children was never as extreme as it was in other ancient societies, and the Egyptians never developed the tradition of overt female infanticide – the abandoning of girl babies at birth – which became accepted practice in both Greece and Rome. This legalized form of murder was to its practitioners simply a late form of abortion, and as such remained valid Roman law until AD 374. It allowed the father the sole right to refuse to rear any child, just as the father had the sole right to authorize his wife to have an abortion. The mother had absolutely no say in the matter, and an unwanted infant was simply exposed on the local rubbish dump soon after birth.

Double the food which your mother gave you and support her as she supported you. You were a heavy burden to her but she did not abandon you. When you were born after your months she was still tied to you as her breast was in your mouth for three years. As you grew and your excrement was disgusting she was not disgusted.

New Kingdom scribal instruction[8]

Although the detailed mechanism of menstruation was not fully understood the significance of missing periods was clear, and most Egyptian women were able to diagnose their own pregnancies and even forecast the expected delivery date without any medical interference. Those who were in doubt could consult a doctor who, for a fee, would conduct a detailed examination of the woman's skin, eyes and breasts, all of which are known to undergo marked changes in the first few weeks following conception. As an additional test, a urine sample was collected from the hopeful mother-to-be and poured over sprouting vegetables or cereals, with subsequent strong growth confirming pregnancy. The changes in the levels of hormones present in the urine, monitored in our modern pregnancy-testing kits, had a stimulating effect on the vegetation. Following a positive test it was even possible to anticipate the sex of the unborn child by a further study of the growing power of the mother's urine; if it was sprinkled on both wheat and barley a rapid growth of barley would indicate a boy, wheat a girl. The physicians also developed a number of tests which could be used to determine whether a childless woman was ever likely to become pregnant. A physical inspection of the lady could prove particularly informative in this respect as, 'if you find one of her eyes similar to that of an Asiatic, and the other like that of a southerner, she will not conceive'. An expert examination of the breasts could be used to indicate a fertile woman, a newly pregnant woman and even the sex of an unborn child.

Certain vegetables were strongly equated with fertility, and so vast quantities of lettuce were consumed by those wishing to conceive. The Egyptian lettuce grew tall and straight, rather like a modern cos lettuce, and when pressed it emitted a milky-white liquid. It is therefore not entirely surprising that this vegetable became associated with the ithyphallic god of vegetation and procreation, Min, and was firmly recommended by the medical papyri as a sure cure for male impotence. The experts, however, differed over the precise effects of lettuce. Discorides and Pliny believed that it should be taken to repress erotic dreams and impulses, while Hippocrates felt that it was actually an anti-aphrodisiac. Pliny recommended leeks rather than lettuce to stimulate the sexual appetite.

Sadly, although the skill and wisdom of the Egyptian doctors was famed throughout the ancient world, even the most experienced of physicians could offer no real hope to those faced with the tragedy of a childless marriage. The Egyptians well understood what had to be done to make a woman pregnant but they were less certain of the actual mechanics of conception, and without this knowledge backed up by sophisticated laboratory techniques infertility was almost invariably blamed on the wife.

Consequently, barren marriages were often 'cured' by divorce, with the husband simply taking a different and hopefully more fertile partner; whether in these circumstances anyone realized that the man himself might have been the infertile partner is not clear. A second practical means of ending sterility was adoption. The short life expectancy and high birth rate meant that there was a readily available supply of orphaned children, and infertile couples frequently adopted the child of a poorer relation.

He who is ashamed to sleep with his wife will not have children.

Scribe Ankhsheshonq

The lack of even the most basic medical help, and the air of mystery and ignorance which surrounded the creation of a new life, meant that those who longed for pregnancy were far more likely to turn to religion and magic than to professional doctors. In all societies and at all times conception and childbirth have attracted numerous superstitions and old wives' tales, and we can assume that Egyptian girls were no different in trying out the unofficial remedies passed down by word of mouth from one generation of women to the next. Unfortunately, it is precisely this sort of information which is lacking from our record of women's lives. The type and extent of information which is lacking is suggested by Winifred Blackman's 1927 survey of the peasant communities of modern Egypt which included a whole chapter devoted to fertility rites and rituals, all of which were very important to the hopeful mothers-to-be, but none of which would yield material evidence for the archaeologists of the future. For example, she noted that:

It is a popular belief in Egypt that if a dead child is tightly bound in its shroud the mother cannot conceive again. Therefore the shroud and the cords binding it are always loosened just before burial, dust also being put into the child's lap. The dust is put there, so I was told, in order to keep the body lying on its back. The woman who gave me this information said that sometimes a body twists round when decomposition sets in, and if this happens the mother cannot have another child. If, in spite of precautions, the woman as time goes on seems to have no prospect of again becoming a mother she will go to the tomb of her dead child, taking a friend with her, and request the man whose business it is to do so to open the tomb. The disconsolate mother then goes down inside the tomb where the body lies, and steps over it backward and forward seven times, in the belief that the dead child's spirit will re-enter her body and be born.

More alarmingly, Miss Blackman observed that 'sometimes if a woman has no children her friends will take her to the railway and make her lie down between the lines in order that the train may pass over her'. This frightening rite gives some indication of the despair felt by women who are prepared to risk their lives for the chance to conceive a child. The ancient Egyptians have left us no evidence for similar fertility rituals, although we do know that a variety of amulets, worn next to the skin for increased efficiency, was available. The hippopotamus goddess Taweret, the bringer of babies to childless women, was a very popular charm, as was the dwarf god Bes.

Who makes seed grow in women and creates people from sperm. Who feeds the son in his mother's womb and soothes him to still his tears. Nurse in the womb. Giver of breath. To nourish all that he made.

The Great Hymn to the Aten

Childbirth itself was not generally considered to be a matter for either medical or male interference, and the medical papyri offered little practical advice to the midwives who customarily assisted at the delivery. Indeed, the whole process of birth developed into a female-controlled rite far beyond the experience of most men, and consequently we have no contemporary description of childbirth. This means that our understanding of the single most important event in the Egyptian woman's life has

to be pieced together from fragments of surviving stories and
myths combined with the illustrations of divine births carved
on the walls of temple *mammisi*.[9] Not surprisingly, this
type of evidence is very strong
on ritual and symbolic content
but rather weak on practical
details. The *Westcar Papyrus*
gives us our most detailed
account of childbirth when telling the story of the miraculous
birth of triplets to the Lady
Reddjedet. We are told that
for her delivery Reddjedet used
a portable birthing stool, and
that she was assisted by four
goddesses who arrived at her
house disguised as itinerant midwives. Isis stood in front of the
mother-to-be and delivered the
babies, Nephthys stood behind

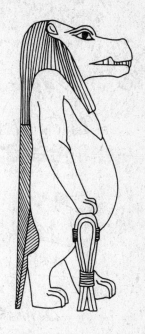

Fig. 10   The goddess Taweret

her, and Hekat used an unspecified technique to 'hasten' the
births. Meskhenet then fulfilled her divine role by telling the
fortunes of the new-born babies while the god Khnum gave life
to their bodies. All three infants were washed in turn, the
umbilical cords were cut, and they were placed on a cushion on
bricks. Reddjedet then presented the midwives with a payment
of corn, and 'cleansed herself in a purification of fourteen days'.

Although ostraca recovered from Deir el-Medina suggest that
women in labour may have entered a specially constructed 'birth
bower', a tent-like structure with walls hung with garlands (*see*
Chapter 8), these representations probably have more symbolic
than literal meaning with most births occurring within the

Fig. 11   The goddess Hekat

family home. For her delivery the naked mother-to-be either knelt or squatted on two low piles of bricks or sat on a birthing-stool, a seat with a hole large enough for the baby to pass through. Gravity was used to assist the birth, and the midwife who squatted on the floor was able to help the mother by easing the baby out. Most women were left to give birth unaided, although for more difficult cases there were several approved procedures intended to 'cause a woman to be delivered'; these included bandaging the lower part of the abdomen and the use of vaginal suppositories. The only surgical implement used by the midwife was the obsidian knife which was used to cut the umbilical cord after the delivery of the afterbirth; this knife had an unknown ritual significance. We do not know what happened to the afterbirth, but it seems likely that it would have been disposed of carefully. Traditionally, in Egypt, the fate of the placenta is believed to be directly linked to the life of the baby, and it is often safely buried at the threshold of the house or thrown into the Nile to ensure the survival of the infant. It may even be that the afterbirth, rich in iron, was partially eaten by the new mother. A piece was occasionally offered to the newborn child, and if it was refused, or if the baby turned its head downwards, groaned, or cried 'no' rather than 'yes', this was taken to be a very bad omen, indicating that the infant would soon die. The umbilical cord was also regarded as important; in the *Myth of Horus*, Horus recovered the umbilical cord of his murdered father and buried it safely at Herakleopolis Magna.

The *Westcar Papyrus* provides us with one of the few Egyptian references to multiple births. Twins do not seem to have been particularly welcomed: '. . . we shall fill her womb with male and female children, and save her from giving birth to twins', an attitude which perhaps reflects the additional dangers involved in a multiple birth. Although we do know of examples of Egyptian twins these are few and far between, which has led to suggestions that either one or both of a set of twins may not have been allowed to live. This is a theory, however, which is very difficult to prove, and one which does not immediately agree with the often-repeated belief in the Egyptian love of children.[10]

Unfortunately, tragedies associated with childbirth were all too common. Female pelvic abnormalities sufficient to have made childbirth difficult, if not impossible, have been recognized in several mummies and serve to stress this point; one of the worst examples is the 12th Dynasty mummy of the Lady Henhenet which shows a dreadful tear running from the bladder to the vagina, almost certainly caused during childbirth when a large baby was dragged through the mother's abnormally narrow pelvis. The royal family was not exempt from these tragedies, and the body of Mutnodjmet, wife of King Horemheb, was recovered with the body of a foetus or new-born child, suggesting that the queen had died attempting to provide an heir to the throne. Surprisingly few mummified or buried babies have been recovered, and it is likely that in many cases an infant who was stillborn or who died soon after birth was not regarded as a full member of society and consequently not accorded full burial rites; the recovery of infants buried under village houses implies that the dead baby itself may have had some religious or superstitious value. This suggestion is reinforced by the discovery of two miniature coffins of gilded wood which had been carefully placed in the tomb of Tutankhamen. Each contained an inner coffin and a tiny mummified foetus. These could be the remains of two premature children born to the young king and his queen, Ankhesenamen, but the inclusion of the small bodies within the tomb may have had a more complex symbolic meaning as yet unexplained.

The new mother was expected to 'purify' herself for fourteen days following the delivery. The term 'purification' was also used to describe menstruation, indicating an understandable confusion between menstrual bleeding and the lochia or discharge from the womb which follows childbirth. Whether the use of this apparently emotive term, with its connotations of impure or dirty, should be taken to indicate some religious or ritual avoidance of 'unclean' bleeding women, or whether it was simply a colloquial expression with no deeper significance than 'the curse', is unclear. It does indicate, however, that the new mother was allowed a period of rest after the birth, with her female relations taking over her household duties and allowing her to concentrate on recovery and caring for the new arrival.

I made live the names of my fathers which I found obliterated on the doorways . . . Behold, he is a good son who perpetuates the names of his ancestors.

Middle Kingdom tomb inscription

The mother named her new baby immediately after the birth, presumably following an advance briefing by the father, thereby ensuring that her child had a name even if she or he then died. Names were very important to the Egyptians, who felt that knowledge of a name in some way conferred power over the named person or object. One of their greatest fears was that a personal name might be forgotten after death, and rich men spent a great deal of money building commemorative monuments to ensure that this would not occur. Dying a 'second death' in the Afterlife – the complete obliteration of all earthly memory of the deceased including the name – was almost too awful to contemplate, and specific spells 'for not perishing in the land of the dead' were included in the texts routinely painted on the wooden coffins.

Most non-royal Egyptians were given one personal name but could also be distinguished by his or her relationship to others, for example, as in the case of Ahmose, son of Abana, the subject of a famous New Kingdom war biography. We know of many examples of personal names being favoured repeatedly within one family; a good example is the family of the New Kingdom Third Prophet of Amen, where the sons were named in alternate generations Pediamennebnesttawy (literally 'Gift of Amen who is Lord of the Thrones of the Two Lands') and Hor (literally 'Horus'). Family names were also given to girls, and it was not considered confusing that both a mother and one or more of her daughters should share the same personal name. Presumably these women were distinguished from each other by their nicknames. The Egyptians certainly did not baulk at giving their children very long names; Hekamaatreemperkhons, son of Hekhemmut, would not have felt particularly hard done by, although again it is perhaps not surprising that nicknames were both common and widely used. In the absence of a favourite family name it was considered a good idea to include the name of a local god or goddess within a child's name, and some children like the above-mentioned Pediamennebnesttawy were named in a way that suggests that they were considered to be the specific gift of a particular deity. Some names emphasized the relationship between the child and her mother or family, such as Aneksi, 'She belongs to me' or Senetenpu, 'She is our sister'. Naming children in honour of members of the royal family was also popular, and attractive animals or flowers made nice names; Susan, 'a lily', was a favourite Egyptian girl's name.

My son, O King, take thee to my breast and suck it . . . He has come to these his two mothers, they of the long hair and pendulous breasts . . . They draw their breasts to his mouth and evermore do they wean him.

Old Kingdom *Pyramid Texts*

It was customary to breast-feed infants for up to three years, much longer than is common in western societies and way beyond the point where the child would be happily eating solid foods. Not only did breast milk provide the most nutritious, most convenient and most sterile form of food and drink available for babies, it also had a certain contraceptive effect, reducing the chances of the new mother becoming pregnant too soon after she had given birth. There was no false prudery over breast-feeding, and the image of a woman squatting or sitting on a low stool to suckle a child at her left breast became symbolic of successfully fertile womanhood, frequently depicted in both secular and religious Egyptian art. The medical papyri suggested that the quality of the milk should be tested before feeding the infant; good milk should smell like dried manna but 'to recognize milk which is bad, you shall perceive that its smell is like the stench of fish'. To ensure a copious supply of milk the same texts advise rubbing the mother's back with a special mixture, or feeding her with sour barley bread. Mother's milk, particularly the milk of a woman who had borne a male child, was regarded as a valuable medical commodity, useful not only for feeding babies but also for increasing fertility and even healing burns. It was often collected and stored in small anthropomorphic pots shaped like a woman holding a baby.

Mothers of high birth and those who were unable to breast-feed left the feeding of their baby to a wet-nurse. Wet-nursing was one of the few well-paid jobs which was open to women of all classes, and the unfortunately high rate of female mortality during childbirth meant that it was a profession always in demand. It was usual for the parents to draw up a legal contract with the chosen nurse, who would undertake to feed a child for a fixed period of time at a fixed salary. Late-Period contracts usually included a clause stating that the nurse should not indulge in sexual intercourse for the duration of the employment, as this may have resulted in pregnancy and possibly ended the lactation. There was no shame attached to working as a wet-nurse and

Above: First Intermediate Period stela showing the Ladies Hetepi and Bebi, daughters of the Steward Sennedjsui.

Left: The elaborate dress and coiffure of a New Kingdom lady.

Left: Old Kingdom pair-statue of a husband and wife.

Below: Stela of Iteti, accompanied by his three wives and two of his daughters.

Right: Middle Kingdom family stela featuring the scribal assistant Iy together with his wife, his children and his parents. The precise role of the six 'Ladies of the House' shown towards the bottom of the stela is unknown.

Top left: Middle Kingdom model of a female dwarf carrying a child on her hip.

Top right: The dwarf god Bes.

Above: Fragment of an ivory 'magic wand' with protective deities.

Right: Wooden tomb models of two servant women, each carrying a box and two ducks.

Top: Cord fertility dolls of the Middle Kingdom.

Above: Reed brush and basket, typical household implements of the New Kingdom.

Top right: Large basket...

Bottom right: ... containing a foldaway stool.

Above: New Kingdom ladies listening to a musician.

Left: Wooden model of a *djeryt*.

indeed, during the Dynastic period, the position of royal wet-nurse was eagerly sought after as it was one of the most important and influential positions that a non-royal woman could hope to hold. Royal wet-nurses were therefore often married to, or were mothers of, high-ranking court officials. During the Roman period the position of wet-nurse became less valued. We have a number of contracts from this time which make it clear that nurses were being paid to rear totally unrelated foundlings who were presumably the abandoned babies rescued from the local dump. These children were later sold by their owners, a practice which made sound economic sense at a time of high slave-prices.

When death comes he steals the infant from the arms of the mother just as he takes him who has reached old age.

New Kingdom scribal instruction

The high levels of infant mortality meant that childhood illnesses were always worrying times for the mother. Very few parents could afford to take their sick children to consult doctors, and anyway the lack of some of the most basic of medical skills meant that little effective treatment was available. If, for example, a child had teething trouble the standard cure was to offer the infant a fried mouse to eat; this must certainly have presented a challenge to a baby without molars. Illnesses such as measles which we today regard as trivial were, without proper treatment, fatal. Not surprisingly, mothers turned again to folk wisdom and magic to protect their darlings, placing their trust in a variety of charms, amulets and spells:

Perish, you who come in from the dark. You who creep in with your nose reversed and your face turned back, and who forgets what he came for. Did you come to kiss this child? I will not allow you to kiss him.

New Kingdom medical advice

The evil spirit described in this incantation cunningly wore his nose reversed so that he would not be recognized sneaking into the house. These spells were known to be so effective that they were frequently written on a small scrap of papyrus packed into a specially carved wooden or gold bead and carefully suspended around the neck of the beloved child to ensure maximum protection. Two thousand years later, little had changed in the Egyptian village and as Miss Blackman observed: 'To prevent or cure disease in their children the women will go to one magician after another and purchase from them amulets and written charms, not grudging for a moment the expenditure of what may be to them considerable sums of money. Numbers of these prophylactics may be seen hanging from the necks of the hapless infants.'

There is no question that the care of babies and children, not only her own but also her younger brothers and sisters, her grandchildren and the children of friends and relations, would have played a major part in any Egyptian woman's life. Royal children are occasionally depicted with male child-minders or tutors but, as a general rule, it was women who cared for children. Unfortunately, this type of work is not easily detected in the archaeological record, and in consequence we are left with very little knowledge of Egyptian child-care practices.[11] The most important aspect of child-care, however, is clear; all surviving evidence indicates that most parents were loving and conscientious guardians who made every effort to ensure a happy and carefree childhood for their offspring.

Parents bought or made a wide range of toys for their darlings, and boys and girls were able to enjoy carved wooden animals, miniature boats, wooden balls and spinning tops which would still delight any modern child. For those who could not afford such luxuries there were the open fields to play in and the river and canals to swim in, while thick Nile mud was always in plentiful supply for use as modelling clay; several primitive clay dolls and animals, presumably made by children themselves, have been recovered from workmen's villages. However, as might be expected in a hard-working society where teenage marriages were common and formal education a luxury, childhood was a relatively short-lived experience in ancient Egypt. As the children grew older they were gradually introduced to the work which they would be doing for the rest of their lives. Young children were expected to supervise their tiny brothers and sisters or to take care of the animals, girls helped their mothers around the house while older boys were sent to school, worked in the fields or started to learn their trade. 'Teenagers' as a distinct class of young adults simply did not exist. At the age of thirteen or fourteen a daughter would be eagerly anticipating her own marriage, while her mother, probably herself less than thirty years old, could look forward to the pleasant prospect of acquiring a new son-in-law and becoming a respected grandmother.

3

Mistress of the House

Do not control your wife in her house when you
know she is efficient. Do not say to her 'Where is it?
Get it' when she has put something in its correct place.
Let your eye observe in silence; then you will recognize
her skill, and it will be a joy when your hand is with
her. There are many men who don't realize this, but if
a man desists from strife at home he will not find it
starting. Every man who establishes a household should
hold back his hasty heart.

New Kingdom scribal advice

In the ancient Egyptian mind housework was very firmly equated
with women's work. Domesticated house-husbands were quite
simply unknown, and the married woman's most coveted title of
Mistress of the House was a constant reminder of her principal
wifely duty: to ensure the smooth day-to-day running of her
husband's home. It seems very unlikely that either sex would
ever have dreamed of questioning the inevitability of this division
of labour. Males and females were understood by all to be
different types of people destined to live very different lives, and
any upsetting of this natural order would clearly have been
wrong. In every household, therefore, the wife was nominally
responsible for all domestic tasks. Naturally, the amount of
housework which any individual was personally required to
undertake was dependent upon her social status. A queen had no
need to disrupt her social life to cook, clean or change nappies,
while a wealthy society lady could rely upon the help of a large
number of servants including maids, cooks, nurses and brewers,

but was expected to supervise and order their activities. A poor woman would need to perform all the domestic tasks herself, helped only by her unmarried daughters and her other close female relations. Given the absence of modern luxuries such as running water, electricity, gas, supermarkets and motorized transport, the care of the home was a full-time occupation involving a great deal of hard physical work.

We have surprisingly little information about the size or composition of the typical Egyptian household, although archaeological evidence suggests that, as in present-day rural Egypt, the western-style nuclear family was unusual and the extended family was the general rule, with family groups of six or more adult members being common. Such extended family units were economically highly efficient, particularly in rural areas where all the members of one family worked the same plot of land. Perhaps more importantly, they represented security for their members, providing welcome physical and financial support in a society with no formalized welfare programme and a rather crude legal system. From the woman's point of view, domestic chores must have been very much eased by sharing with the other females in the household, and childcare would not have been the problem which it is for many mothers today. However, to modern eyes at least, there was a price to pay for this security: the almost complete lack of privacy in the average Egyptian home. Society had absolutely no regard for the individual's need for solitude, and the western concept of parents and even children requiring their own personal space would have seemed incomprehensible to people who regarded sharing their sleeping quarters with four or five other family members as reassuring rather than invasive.

Although some young boys left home to enlist in the army, daughters almost invariably remained with their parents until marriage. They then left their family to live with their husband, either joining him in establishing a new home or moving in with their new in-laws and all their dependent children. Consequently, the population within each house varied from year to year, dwindling as the older members died or married out only to swell again with new births and the introduction of new brides. Contemporary census information indicates that the immediate household of a soldier named Hori, a resident on the Middle Kingdom housing estate of Kahun, was fairly typical. The dimensions of his house measured 12 × 15 metres, and into this rather cramped space he packed his wife, his baby son Snefru, his mother and five assorted female relations who may well have been his dependent unmarried sisters. When, many years later, Hori died and Snefru became head of the household he continued to provide a home for his mother, his widowed grandmother and at least three of his maiden aunts.[1] A similar picture of apparent overcrowding is obtained from the more wealthy household of the priest Heqanakht which included his mother Ipi, his concubine Iutemheb, his five sons and an unspecified number of assorted daughters, daughter-in-laws and servants.

Almost all Egyptian houses, rich or poor, whether built as homes for the living, the dead (tombs) or the gods (temples), followed the same basic pattern, with an open public area or courtyard leading through semi-private reception rooms into a private area. In the houses this private area was firmly restricted to women, children and immediate male family members. This pattern is still followed in most Egyptian villages today, where convention dictates that many domestic activities may occur in front of the house and that guests may be entertained in the main reception area, but male visitors will never expect to set foot in the private women's quarters at the back of the house. Whether there were areas of the ancient Egyptian house specifically reserved for men is less clear, although illustrations preserved in tombs suggest that women were in no way confined to their quarters or prevented from mixing socially with the men of the household. To be ordered back to the women's quarters was considered a dire

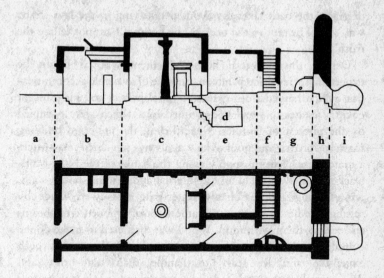

KEY

a   Street
b   Room with boxed bed or birth bower
c   Main room
d   Cellar
e   Storeroom or bedroom
f   Stairs to roof
g   Kitchen with oven
h   Village hall
i   Cellar

Fig. 12   Cross-section and plan of a typical Deir el-Medina house

disgrace: the oath taken by women testifying in the law courts was 'may I be sent to the back of the house if I am not telling the truth'.

Despite this universal houseplan there was, as might be expected, a wide discrepancy in the scale of available accommodation which ranged from extensive royal palaces and magnificent country estates to small one-roomed huts which were occupied by the poorest of families. Nevertheless, the preferred building material for rich and poor alike was always sun-dried mud-brick, a material in plentiful supply along the banks of the Nile. Mud-brick was used to build all the internal and external house walls, while strong and reasonably watertight roofs were made by resting bundles of reeds on a framework of wooden cross-beams and sealing them with mud. Wood was then used to make doors, columns and window frames as required. Stone was both expensive and less easy to handle than mud-brick and consequently only used in domestic architecture when there was no alternative – for example, at Deir el-Medina, there was no convenient source of either water or mud to make the cheaper and lighter bricks. Wealthy householders did occasionally employ stone for high-visibility status symbol features such as thresholds, door-frames and the bases of wooden pillars, and these expensive stone components were often salvaged and re-used by subsequent generations when the less durable mud-brick surrounds had collapsed. In the grandest of households these stone fitments bore carved inscriptions and were painted in bright colours.

The use of mud-brick imposed certain limitations on the Egyptian architects. Their first priority was always to avoid the damp soil which would cause the house walls to decay and collapse, and consequently all villages and towns were sited as far away from the highest level of the inundation as was practical. This would have been a sensible precaution even if building in stone. The mud-brick also had a direct effect on the internal structure of the houses, as the walls had to be relatively thick in order to support the load-bearing roof while the roof itself had to be relatively narrow due to the shortage of timber to span the gap between the walls. Any increase in house size therefore required a corresponding increase in internal divisions to support the roof, and only those wealthy enough to incorporate free-standing pillars in their plans were able to construct imposing and spacious halls. However, there were definite advantages to using mud-brick. The houses were cheap and easy to build and, as mud-brick is an efficient insulating material, remained both cool in the summer and warm in the winter. As an added bonus it was easy to extend or divide up the properties, and throughout their useful lives most mud-brick buildings underwent a series of DIY alterations designed to adjust the available living space to suit the ever-changing needs of the occupants.

Your heart rejoices as you plough your plot in the Field of Reeds. You are rewarded with what you have grown. You gather a harvest rich in grain.

> Inscription from the New Kingdom tomb of Paheri

Throughout the Dynastic period Egypt was ruled from a succession of different capital cities, with Memphis, Thebes, Amarna and Pa-Ramesses each serving at different times as the principal seat of government and home to the royal court. Local administration was delegated to the forty or so regional capitals which acted as the centres for all provincial bureaucracy, while other towns such as Abydos grew in size and importance due to their links with major cult temples. These flourishing urban centres were always the exception rather than the rule, and the vast majority of the population lived the lives of rural peasants, inhabiting small and politically insignificant villages and farming the surrounding land. The importance of agriculture to the economy and to the general well-being of Egypt was never underestimated by her people. Rural living, in a rather glamorized and sanitized form, was widely perceived to be the ideal way of life for all right-thinking upper-class Egyptians, and wealthy individuals spent many a happy hour relaxing in the countryside while watching the local peasants toiling in the fields. Their idea of the ultimate heaven, or the Afterlife, was to supervise the performance of basic agricultural tasks in the ever-fertile 'Field of Reeds'.

It is not surprising that the most widely coveted residence, often depicted in tomb scenes of the Afterlife, was a spacious ranch-style country bungalow or even a two-storey villa set in its own extensive grounds and further sheltered from the hurly-burly of life by a protective mud-brick wall. In an ideal world this perfect home would have an impressive columned portico, elegant and well-proportioned central reception rooms and extensive family quarters, servants' rooms and of course a well-fitted kitchen. Outbuildings would provide further accommodation and storage areas, and the flat roof, reached by a narrow external staircase, would have a multitude of uses. The formal landscaped leisure garden, artificially irrigated and lovingly tended by hard-working gardeners, would include a shallow artificial pool with ornamental fish, many colourful and exotic flowers and shrubs, and leafy trees to provide welcome protection from the harsh glare of the midday sun. There may even be a private shrine or chapel situated within the garden wall. The estate would naturally have a private well and perhaps even its own little farm to supply fresh produce for the household. To enjoy this bucolic existence, untroubled by the stresses of city life and, naturally, with enough labourers to perform the necessary agricultural and domestic tasks, was every rich Egyptian's dream.

The gardener carries a yoke which makes his shoulders bend with age; it causes a nasty swelling on his neck, which festers. He spends his morning watering his leeks and his evening tending to his herbs, having already toiled in the orchard at noon. He works himself into an early grave far more than do the other professionals.

From the Middle Kingdom *Satire of the Trades*

The Egyptian rural idyll came closest to reality at the city of Akhetaten, King Akhenaten's custom-designed capital set in the desert sands of Middle Egypt. In this arid and unpromising place luxurious villas were constructed for the wealthiest court officials and bureaucrats. Some of the more spacious homes had twenty or more internal rooms including a large master bedroom with *en suite* bathroom facilities, and were surrounded by delightful pleasure gardens enclosed by thick mud-brick walls. The servants' quarters and storage areas were set a little apart from the main house in order to ensure maximum peace and quiet for the residents. Sadly, Akhenaten's city proved to be indeed a dream, and the new capital was abandoned after less than twenty years' occupation.

The more typical Egyptian village must have appeared very much like its modern counterpart, with closely-packed thick-walled houses of varying size arranged higgledy-piggledy along narrow passageways and courtyards, and new buildings or extensions springing up as and when required with absolutely no formal planning procedure. The average villager probably lived in a modest four- or five-roomed house which would have been home to the extended family, the family dependants, the family pets, the foodstores and perhaps a few birds and a sheep or two being raised for food. It is perhaps fortunate for family sanity that due to the good weather most tasks could be performed out of doors, either in front of the house, in the yard or on the useful flat roof, and the overcrowded homes were frequently little more than bases used for eating and sleeping.

The houses, especially the better built ones, admirably suit the Egyptian climate. There is only one thing lacking to make them really pleasant places to live, and that is greater cleanliness within the houses themselves and within the streets. The salvation of the people lies in the fact that they lead essentially an outdoor life, the houses being regarded almost solely as places to sleep and cook in; otherwise the mortality would be considerably higher than it is.

Miss Blackman's comments on modern Egyptian village housing

Town and city houses were generally smaller than their village counterparts and, as land within the walled town was at a premium, they were often built in terraced rows without the luxury of a garden or yard. To compensate for their enforced narrowness the houses grew upwards, and homes two, or even three, storeys high were designed. Actual depictions of urban life are rare, but it is clear that the towns were very densely occupied and in certain more central quarters rather squalid, with the tall buildings crammed together around the important public buildings and excluding the light from the narrow streets. Purpose-built housing complexes such as Deir el-Medina or Amarna, with their organized ranks of neat buildings arranged along straight streets and right-angled road junctions, give a false impression of the efficiency of Egyptian urban planning; these towns were atypical in being conceived for one purpose and built relatively quickly by the state. In contrast, the long-established centres of trade and commerce evolved slowly and randomly. The lack of any official sanitation or waste-disposal system, the overcrowded conditions and the ubiquitous presence of the animals needed for food must have made town life at times unappealing, if not downright unhygienic, particularly during the long hot summer days; the attractions of country life must have been widely felt.

Preserved on the wall of the Theban tomb of Djehutynefer, a New Kingdom Royal Scribe and Overseer of the Treasury, is a complete sectional plan of his comparatively spacious town house, built in one of the more salubrious areas of uptown Thebes. It appears to have been at least three storeys high, although given the conventions of Egyptian art these layers may actually represent various parts of the house lying one behind the other. The lowest floor, or basement, was apparently the servants' quarters, where the mundane domestic activities such as breadmaking, brewing and weaving could proceed out of sight of the owner and his family. The elegantly tall public reception rooms on the first floor had high windows designed to maximize coolness and must have been suitably impressive for distinguished visitors, while the top level included the private and less formal family and women's rooms. Five conical grain-silos were placed on the flat roof, which was also apparently used for some cooking and food processing, although the logic behind placing the grain storage on the roof is not immediately apparent; perhaps it reduced the number of vermin infesting the grain? Such luxurious town houses were very much a privilege of the wealthy, and artisans lived in far less splendid accommodation, rarely having access to more than three or four narrow rooms plus the flat roof which could be sheltered from the sun by simple screens and used as an outdoor room.

Fig. 13 *Woman carrying domestic provisions*

The homes built for the Theban necropolis workers at Deir el-Medina were all identically long and narrow, measuring about 15 x 5 metres. They included a square reception area leading into a larger inner room, a storage room or small bedroom, and a small courtyard which served as a kitchen and which often included an underground storage area. External stairs led up to the roof where the entire family probably slept during the heat of the summer. At Amarna, a less prosperous town, the most menial labourers were housed in very cramped accommodation, with each of the seventy-two housing units measuring only 5 x 10 metres. These houses were divided into a main living area, a bedroom or storage area and a kitchen, while the porch was used to shelter animals and the roof served as an additional room. Dotted among these rather squalid houses were the larger homes built for the artisans; square-shaped dwellings with a large, columned reception room, several bedrooms and storage rooms and an outside cooking area.

To expel fleas in a house: sprinkle it throughout with natron water until they pass away.

To prevent mice from approaching: fat of cat is placed on all things.

To prevent a serpent from coming out of its hole . . . a bulb of onion is placed in the opening of the hole and it will not come out.

Housekeeping hints from the *Ebers Medical Papyrus*

Given the heat, the overcrowded conditions, the lack of basic sanitation and the presence of both foodstores and animals within the home, it is not surprising that domestic pests became a constant nuisance almost impossible to control. Many harassed housewives resorted to perfuming every room in the house with a sweet-smelling incense blended from myrrh, frankincense and spices; this had the dual benefit of masking any unpleasant odours while efficiently fumigating both the house and its contents. Flies must have been an ever-present menace and, although the smoke from the cooking fire may have deterred some of the less determined insects, proven repellents such as 'oriole fat' were much in demand. The lack of an efficient waste-disposal system unfortunately meant that all types of domestic refuse, including decaying food and human-waste products, had either to be carried to the local dump or tipped in the nearby river or canal; many householders could see no reason to go to all this trouble and simply threw their trash out into the street, causing the level of the ground to rise almost imperceptibly from year to year. Fortunately, the hot climate ensured that the domestic refuse decomposed relatively quickly if rather malodorously. The unsavoury heaps of decaying refuse between the houses were obviously highly attractive to vermin, and many of the homes which have been excavated give evidence of large-scale infestation by mice and rats. Pets may have helped to reduce the numbers of rodents and perhaps have deterred snakes, but those faced with more persistent problems had to use mechanical trapping devices or simply resorted to blocking the holes with stones or cloth plugs.

The washerman launders at the riverbank in the vicinity of the crocodile . . . His food is mixed with filth, and there is no part of him which is clean. He washes the clothes of a menstruating woman. He weeps when he spends all day with a beating stick and a stone there . . .

Extract from the Middle Kingdom *Satire of the Trades*

Despite the lack of concern over hygienic waste disposal, great importance was attached to personal and household cleanliness. The Egyptians were famed throughout the ancient world for their sparkling white clothes, and Herodotus remarked approvingly that their garments were 'constantly fresh washed and they pay particular attention to this'. Those who were wealthy enough to take advantage of a commercial laundry service enjoyed the luxury of having their dirty linen collected at the door and returned when clean, dry and ironed or re-pleated. In spite of the rather deprecatory quotation given above the professional washerman was not necessarily a despised or lowly individual, and the chief washerman of the royal household was often a young man of noble birth who was universally recognized as occupying a position of some privilege and who was ranked only slightly lower than the king's sandal-bearer. It is very unlikely that such an exalted and well-bred officer would ever have stooped to a degrading manual task, and he would instead have confined his duties to supervising the work of others less privileged than himself.

Unfortunately, the professional washermen were mainly employed to undertake the extensive laundry of the large temples and the more wealthy households, and laundries were an undreamed-of luxury for most women. The family washing therefore became an important, time-consuming and physically demanding chore which had to be performed on a very regular basis. On washday, the dirty garments were piled into baskets and carried to the bank of the river or a nearby canal where they were rolled into a ball and wetted. Natron-soap was then applied, and the laundry was either pounded vigorously with a wooden paddle or rubbed repeatedly over smooth stones before rinsing thoroughly in running water. The clean linen was then shaken, wrung out and left to dry and bleach in the sun. When dry the cloth was ironed or smoothed, carefully folded, and taken back to the house where it was replaced in its basket or storage chest. The few laundry scenes which have been preserved in tombs show that washing was a developing science; during the Middle Kingdom the professional washermen used the same simple methods as the housewives but by the end of the New Kingdom the washermen were heating large jars of water at the riverbank. This innovation allowed the washermen to give the clothes a hot wash and presumably remove far more dirt.[2]

The house itself was cleaned with the aid of a short-handled broom made from stiff vegetable fibres, and several contemporary illustrations show crafty servants first sprinkling drops of water to encourage the dust to settle and then using remarkably modern-looking brushes to sweep the floor clean. Linen rags, the useful remnants of household sheeting and clothing too small to be saved for funeral bandages, were recycled and served as dusters. The houseproud housewife was helped in her dusting by the scarcity of furniture, carpeting and curtains to trap dust particles; even the most luxurious homes were somewhat bare by modern western standards, and most of the furniture which has been recovered has come from the excavation of tombs rather than from houses. Although the internal mud-brick walls were often plastered and painted with bright and elaborate scenes, furniture was to a large extent considered both unnecessary and a waste of space, and the concept of decorative but non-functional ornaments and knick-knacks was unknown.

It was both customary and comfortable to sit or squat on the floor and, although roughly made stools, some as low as 16 cm high, were used by all the people, formal chairs with backs and arms were relatively expensive status symbols used only by the upper classes. Short footstools were highly popular with the chair-using élite. Small individual tables or eating-stands were manufactured to co-ordinate with the chairs, but again these were by no means considered essential domestic equipment and, as in modern rural Egypt, food was usually served on woven mats spread on the floor. The diners sat or squatted round the mats and helped themselves to whichever dish they fancied. Although spoons and knives were used in the preparation of food, eating with the fingers was considered perfectly polite at all levels of society. We even have a delightfully informal depiction of King Akhenaten enjoying a large joint of beef while Queen Nefertiti holds a whole roast bird in her right hand.

How great is the lord of his city. He is a cool room that allows a man to sleep until the dawn.

Middle Kingdom *Hymn to King Senwosret III*

The bedrooms were similarly stark. Indeed, specific bedrooms were a luxury enjoyed only by the more wealthy who could afford to be extravagant with their space; most families had fairly informal sleeping arrangements, needing only a mat or a folded linen sheet and a curiously hard curved stone or wooden headrest to be sure of a good night's dreams. This portable sleeping paraphernalia could easily be packed away at dawn when the room needed to resume its daytime function. Those rooms which were specifically intended to be bedrooms often had a low brick platform built along one wall to serve as the base for a mattress of thickly folded linen sheets which prevented cold, damp and perhaps insects reaching the sleeper. The wooden beds which were available were both costly and space-wasting, an important consideration in the overcrowded houses, and were consequently used only by the very wealthy who greatly prized them as status symbols; Scribe Ipuwer repeatedly lamented that during the anarchical First Intermediate Period 'He who did not sleep on a box owns a bed', and 'Those who owned beds are on the ground, while he who lay in the dirt spreads a rug.' His sense of outrage at this impropriety and reversal of the natural hierarchy was only calmed with the coming of law and order, when he was able to report:

It is good when beds are made ready and the masters' headrests safely secured. When everyone's need is filled by a mat in the shade, and a door shut on him who sleeps in the bushes.

The best of the beds were fitted with integral 'springs' made from rushes and interlaced cord. Curiously, some of the earliest beds had such a pronounced slope towards the foot that it was apparently necessary to employ a footboard to prevent the unconscious sleeper from slowly sliding downwards. This design defect was corrected during the New Kingdom when beds became far flatter and presumably more comfortable for the restless sleeper. The remaining bedroom furniture was minimal. There may have been a low stool to sit on while dressing the hair and applying makeup, and elaborate cosmetic and jewel boxes would have been prominent in the boudoirs of the wealthy. Perhaps because of the shortage of good Egyptian wood, fitted bedrooms were unknown and wardrobes, cupboards and chests of drawers were rarely used. Instead, a wide range of chests, boxes and woven baskets with tie-fasteners was used to store folded clothing, linen and personal possessions.

One item which could be found in all the rooms of the house was the lamp. The sun sets both quickly and early during the

Egyptian winter, and there was a need for some form of artificial lighting if family life was to continue after the evening meal. Lamps ranged in design from very simple oil-burning bowls with floating cloth wicks to sophisticated and surprisingly modern-looking standard lamps; long carved wooden pillars designed to support a large pottery oil-burning lamp. Fires, torches and portable braziers were all used to increase this rather dim light while providing welcome warmth during the colder winter evenings. Nevertheless, the Egyptian house must have been a rather gloomy place after dark, and the majority of the population rose at daybreak and retired to bed at dusk.

The kitchen was extremely simple by modern standards, typically including a cooking fire, one or more small circular ovens, grinding equipment, pottery vessels and storage space for all the food and utensils necessary for the preparation of the household meals. As wood was both expensive and in short supply the fuel used in cooking was almost invariably dried dung which had the advantage of burning with a long-lasting, odourless and clean heat and was free to those who had access to animals. Sheep dung in particular burns for a very long time, and ready-prepared cakes of sheep droppings mixed with straw have been recovered from some of the Amarna kitchens. The manure had to be collected on a daily basis and moulded into suitable firebricks by mixing with water and straw before drying in the sun, a rather time-consuming and unglamorous duty which, just as in modern Egypt, was presumably delegated to the more junior females and the children. Once laid, the fire could easily be lit by means of a simple bow drill or the spark from a struck flint.

The oven was a squat, beehive-shaped clay mound about three feet tall, fitted with internal shelving and with a hole at the base designed to allow the removal of ash. It was principally used to bake bread, although food could also be cooked in a saucepan placed on the flat oven-top, and the cook sat or squatted in front of the mouth of the oven while preparing her food. Those who preferred to cook on an open fire used a tripod-like contraption

Fig. 14   Woman baking

while boiling and roasting, and were able to bake directly in the
embers of the fire. Contemporary illustrations suggest that the
oven was occasionally situated on the roof of the house although,
bearing in mind the ever-present risk of fire, this seems unnecessar-
ily dangerous; it may be that the artists intended to depict the
ovens outside the houses but that differences in artistic approach
and perspective have led to misinterpretations by modern eyes.
Archaeological evidence certainly confirms that ovens and cooking fires were often situated away from the home, presumably to
reduce discomfort from the heat and smoke of cooking as well as
the associated risk of fire. For example, at Amarna the kitchens
were built on the eastern side of the houses and were connected
to the living quarters by means of a covered passageway. Where
the oven or fire was inside the house it was generally positioned
well away from the door, and the kitchen roofing was provided

with airholes to allow some of the heat, smoke and smells to escape upwards. Even so, the atmosphere in the enclosed kitchen must at times have seemed unbearably hot.

They live on bread made of spelt which they form into loaves . . . they eat many kinds of fish raw, either salted or dried in the sun. Quails also, and ducks, and small birds, they eat uncooked, merely first salting them. All other birds, with the exception of those which are set apart as sacred, are eaten roasted or boiled.

Herodotus' comments on the Egyptian diet

The provision of a good and plentiful supply of food and drink for the family and its guests was one of the most important duties of the housewife and one which, if performed efficiently, could bring both pleasure and honour to the whole household.[3] Almost all peoples enjoy eating a well-cooked and tasty meal with congenial companions, but the Egyptians seem to have been inordinately fond of feasting, drinking and entertaining their friends at home. If the numerous dire warnings against gluttony recorded in the scribal instructions are considered in conjunction with the scenes of epicurean banquets preserved on tomb walls, it would appear certain that the most direct route to the Egyptian man's heart was via his somewhat bulging stomach. The blatant overeating of the sedentary upper classes was clearly a cause of concern to the more abstemious members of the population:

When you sit down to eat in company shun the foods you love. Restraint only needs a moment's effort, whereas gluttony is base and is reproved. A cup of water will quench your thirst and a mouthful of herbs will strengthen your heart . . . Vile is he whose belly still hungers when the meal time has passed.

Old Kingdom scribal advice

This enviable ability to overeat was a direct result of Egypt's efficient administration of her much-admired natural resources.

Egypt, rightly described by Herodotus as the 'gift of the Nile', was an extraordinarily fertile country teeming with edible wild plants and animals and home to a flourishing agricultural economy which year after year yielded vast supplies of grain and meat. Famine among the lower classes, a direct result of the failure of the inundation, was certainly not unknown during the Dynastic period but it was a relatively rare disaster, and the mountains of grain hoarded during the good years were generally sufficient insurance against the future lean. Even the largest of the Egyptian towns and cities was closely linked with the countryside, so that all the population were able to enjoy year-round access to a healthy variety of seasonal fresh foodstuffs.

The availability of high-quality food had a direct effect upon the evolution of Egyptian culinary techniques, with the top chefs consistently favouring very simple recipes, relying on the quality and freshness of their ingredients to produce appetizing dishes and showing no urge to experiment with adventurous sauces or elaborate combinations of tastes and textures. This fortunate situation may be contrasted with the problems faced by the ancient Roman chefs who, isolated from fresh food by a combination of distance, bad transport links and lack of refrigeration, were forced to devise spicy and highly flavoured dressings and sauces to disguise the repetitive nature of a diet monotonously high in preserved and often slightly rancid foods. The Egyptians had no need to mask the natural flavours of their ingredients and, with the possible exception of stews or soups, the food remained plain and unadorned; it was the variety of different dishes served together which tempted the Egyptian tastebuds. There was therefore little culinary experimentation; contemporary illustrations and the works of later classical authors show that boiling was regarded as the traditional and most fuel-efficient method of cooking meat and vegetables while baking was used for bread and honey- or date-sweetened cakes. Fowl were usually roasted on a skewer and both meat and fish were occasionally grilled.

One very real problem shared by both the Roman and the

Fig. 15   Two New Kingdom ladies attended by a servant at a banquet

Egyptian cooks was the hot weather; without refrigeration no food could be kept for any length of time and, although grain and some fruit and vegetables could be stockpiled for future use, meat and fish had to be dried or pickled before they could be stored, while milk and dairy products needed to be kept as cool as possible in damp earthenware pots. The problem of valuable meat going bad before it could be eaten was to a certain extent solved by the practice of slaughtering animals immediately before cooking, while the gregarious Egyptian habit of redistributing food by means of a dinner party also ensured that there was little leftover meat to go to waste. As polite guests would naturally extend reciprocal invitations to their hosts this system ensured that the net consumption of prestige foods by each individual remained constant. In contrast, there was no effective means of keeping bread fresh and, though its low fat-content meant that the bread could be kept for a day or so, it would almost certainly have been necessary to do a minimal amount of baking every two or three days. This cooking probably took place in the morning as the main meal of the day was a long and leisurely occasion enjoyed indoors while the fierce heat of the noon sun made outside work unattractive. The only other meals which had to be prepared were a light breakfast taken early in the morning and perhaps a small supper or snack to be eaten before retiring to bed.

Unfortunately, we have no ancient Egyptian recipe books to allow us to re-create the dishes served to the pharaohs. However, we do have a surprising collection of ready-cooked foods. The Egyptians, with their uniquely practical approach to death, tried to ensure that the deceased would not pass hungry into the Afterlife by providing food, wherever possible, to be enjoyed within the tomb. Indeed, during the Old Kingdom whole meals were often interred with the body; the best-preserved example of this is the 2nd Dynasty tomb of an elderly woman buried at Sakkara which included a full dinner carefully set out on the floor.[4] The menu was as follows:

> Loaf of bread
> Barley porridge
> Roast fish
> Pigeon stew
> Roast quail
> Cooked kidneys
> Leg and ribs of beef
> Stewed figs
> Fresh berries
> Honey cakes
> Cheese
> Grape wine

The excavator of this tomb, Professor Emery, noted with interest that the deceased lady, whose body was substantially less well-preserved than her picnic, had suffered from an unfortunate jaw disability and, while alive, would certainly have been unable to eat such a demanding meal since she would only have been able to chew on one side of her mouth. Her menu is strikingly similar to the banquet served to mourners at the interment of King Tutankhamen over one thousand years later, when the eight guests were presented with nine ducks, four geese, sundry cuts of beef and mutton, bread, a selection of fruit and vegetables and wine. These dishes were all served together and, as in modern Egypt, the guests helped themselves to the foods which they preferred. There was no particular emphasis placed on eating food hot from the kitchen as there is in many colder western cultures.

Make a great offering of bread and beer, large and small cattle, fowl, wine, fruit, incense and all kinds of good herbs on the day of founding Akhetaten . . .

Extract from the Amarna Boundary Stela

The exact quantity, quality and variety of food available to the individual chef naturally differed from household to household. The primary source of food for most was the daily ration earned by those members of the family who were literally 'bread-winners'. In the absence of an official currency all workers were paid in kind in the form of rations; the composition of the ration varied from period to period but it invariably included either grain or beer and bread. The minimum daily ration seems to have been ten standard-sized loaves, and a Middle Kingdom story confirms this by telling us that the daily ration allotted by the Eloquent Peasant to feed his wife and family were ten loaves of bread and two jugs of beer. Those with more prestigious employment naturally received far more than this basic allowance, with daily payments of hundreds of loaves being made to the senior bureaucrats who then subdivided their portion between their household and their estate workers. The most generous

rations of all were those sacrificed to the gods; offerings of one
thousand loaves or a whole oxen were not unusual and, since
these were then redistributed among the priests and temple
workers, the Egyptian clergy became some of the best-fed people
in the land. As Herodotus noted with more than a twinge of envy:

They consume none of their own property and are at no expense for
anything. Every day bread is baked for them of the sacred corn and a
plentiful supply of beef and goose flesh is assigned to each.

In addition to the basic bread or grain ration most families
were able to increase their food supplies by hunting, trapping
and fishing, while even those living in the crowded towns and
cities were able to rear a few fowl, sheep or a goat to eat up
scraps of waste food and produce a daily supply of eggs, milk
and cheese. The larger estates of the wealthy were practically
self-supporting, maintaining their own granaries, bakeries and
farms and staffed by their own servants. Those thrifty householders who were able to accumulate an excess of one product,
perhaps by growing their own vegetables or by making extra
bread, were able to barter their surplus at the market and buy in
an even greater variety of food. Thus, while the menus of the
poor and less enterprising usually involved a fairly dull and
rather flatulent rotation of bread, onions, lettuce, radish and
pulses, the more successful were able to tuck into mouthwatering
mounds of succulent meat, poultry and fish, served with a
selection of fresh fruits and vegetables and accompanied by bread
and cakes.

Do not eat bread while another stands by, without offering your
portion to him. Food is always here. It is man who does not last.
                                        Advice offered by Scribe Any

Bread was by far and away the most important food prepared
by the Egyptian housewife. In the absence of other high-

carbohydrate foods such as potatoes, pasta, rice and bananas, bread was the staple component of the diet, doubly important as the major ingredient in the popular home-brewed beer. Bread was consumed in vast quantities, enjoyed by rich and poor alike, and frequently presented as a desirable offering to both the gods and the dead. To the Egyptians bread stood as a symbol representing all foods, and to be without bread either in this life or the next was simply unthinkable. It is not surprising that baking was a motif featured time and time again in tombs, either in the form of painted scenes or small model bakeries, while the importance of having enough bread to eat was constantly stressed in folk tales and proverbs.

Without the convenience of shop-bought milled flour daily breadmaking was a relatively hard grind. It was necessary to process all the household flour by hand on a stone saddle quern; in a household of five or six adults with the healthy appetites of manual workers this must have been a daunting task. Once ground and passed through a sieve, the rather gritty flour was mixed with water and salt to make an unleavened chapati or pitta-type bread which could be quickly cooked on a flat stone placed either within the oven or on an open fire. Leavened loaves were made by kneading the flour with yeast and water to form a stiff dough. Spices, salt or flavourings could be added before baking to improve the taste, while the addition of fat, eggs and sweet dates made the basic loaf into a tasty cake. The bread was either shaped by hand or pressed into a mould and then allowed to rise before baking within the oven. Not surprisingly, many different varieties and shapes of loaf were produced. There were over fifteen words used to differentiate between the different types of bread baked during the Old Kingdom, and over forty New Kingdom words for bread and cakes. The most popular breads were semi-circular loaves shaped by hand and tall pointed loaves which were baked in distinctive conical moulds, but more elaborate breads baked into the shape of animals or even female figures were eaten on special occasions.

Better is bread with a happy heart than wealth with vexation.

New Kingdom proverb

In contrast to bread, meat, especially beef, was a very highly prized food but one which was not enjoyed by the majority of the population with any degree of frequency. It was theoretically possible for anyone to purchase the cuts of beef which represented the distribution of surplus meat from the temples, but meat was always a luxury commodity eaten only by the rich. Considering the lack of refrigeration and the prevalence of flies and dirt the beef would probably not have appeared particularly tempting to modern eyes; indeed, no one from the western plastic-wrapped and hygiene-obsessed supermarket culture who has seen a modern open-air Egyptian butcher's shop is likely to forget the sight in a hurry. Some prosperous individuals did own one or more cows but it was only the most wealthy or the larger temple estates who could afford to maintain a herd of non-working cattle as a food source. These food-cattle were fattened up by force-feeding on balls of bread, and were slaughtered only when they were almost too obese to walk, yielding a tender and fatty meat. Less wealthy cattle owners made the best use that they could of their investments by exploiting their cows primarily for their milk and dung and even using them in ploughing and threshing. Only at the end of its working life was a privately owned cow slaughtered, and the resulting meat must have been flavoursome but rather stringy and tough. Once a cow had been killed no part of the animal was ever wasted; brains, entrails, ears, tongue and feet were all consumed with relish and even the blood was saved to make a tasty black pudding. The fat had a multitude of uses, and 'ox grease' was a commonly used ingredient in patent medicines. The upper classes, less concerned about waste, are depicted eating only the prime cuts of beef.

'Small cattle' – that is, sheep, goats and to a lesser extent pigs – were fairly widely kept and consequently far more easily available to ordinary families. Hearty and nourishing meals of boiled mutton or goat stew were particularly enjoyed by the prosperous middle classes, although there is some indication that sheep may have been avoided by the conspicuously devout members of the upper classes in cities such as Thebes where the ram was venerated as a god. Sheep and goats were particularly important as a source of fresh milk, a great delicacy which was enjoyed as a hot drink and frequently used in cooking and which was, of course, vital for the production of cheese and clarified butter. Just as in many parts of the world today, pork was the subject of a more widespread religious taboo and was theoretically not acceptable as a food. However, archaeological evidence suggests that this ritual avoidance was not strictly observed. Herds of swine were clearly depicted on tomb walls, and the rubbish dumps of both Amarna and Deir el-Medina included quantities of pig bones suggestive of widespread pork consumption. Pigs are certainly very efficient animals as they eat up and re-cycle the waste food which would otherwise spoil in the hot climate, and they have the additional fringe benefit of providing a free street- and house-cleaning service.[5]

The Nile contains every variety of fish and in numbers beyond belief; for it supplies all the natives not only with abundant subsistence from the fish freshly caught but it also yields an unfailing multitude of fish for salting.

Diodorus Siculus

Fish, a highly nutritious and tasty food full of protein and minerals, was enjoyed by all levels of society, and undoubtedly made a very important contribution to the diet of the very poor who might otherwise have experienced protein deficiency. Although harpoon-fishing was a favourite hobby of upper-class men, and the professional fishermen employed an impressive variety of lines, nets and traps to earn their livelihood, it was not actually necessary to own any tackle to go fishing in Egypt, and many enterprising food gatherers simply waited until the swollen waters of the inundation dropped and then picked up the dead and dying fish left stranded high and relatively dry in the muddy fields. Once caught the fish could either be grilled and eaten fresh or preserved by wind-drying, smoking, salting or pickling in oil before storing.

Birds were another important and easily accessible source of food for the less wealthy. Although chickens were unknown until the very end of the New Kingdom, ducks and geese were widely available and could easily be raised within even the smallest home, while domesticated doves and pigeons were bred in purpose-built cotes. The ever-present waterfowl could be either trapped or netted as desired; hunting scenes do show wildfowlers earnestly stalking relatively small birds with large and aggressive-looking spears and throwing sticks, but these rather over-the-top methods were probably regarded as enjoyable sport rather than serious hunting techniques. Once caught the birds were housed in wooden cages and fattened up on grain before consumption. This system had the great advantage of providing a source of fresh meat without any need to worry about pickling or drying. The bird was simply kept alive until needed and then killed – by having its neck broken – just before cooking, as is still the custom in Egypt today, where it is common for almost all kitchens to be home to one or two live birds. The eggs produced by the captives made a useful addition to the household diet and could be supplemented by the eggs of wild birds.

Fresh fruit and beans, pulses and vegetables also played a major nutritional role in the daily diet. The Egyptians were famous throughout the ancient world for their excessive consumption of raw vegetables, particularly onions, garlic and leeks, while melons and cucumbers enjoyed such widespread popularity that even the Children of Israel, freed at last from vile bondage in Egypt, could only lament:

Will no one give us meat? Think of it. In Egypt we had fish for the asking, cucumbers and watermelons, leeks and onions and garlic. Now our throats are parched; there is nothing wherever we look except this manna.

Manna, the so-called 'bread of heaven', was probably the secretion of the small insects which live on tamarisk twigs; this delicacy is still collected and eaten by the present-day Bedouin, who regard it as a tasty treat. The Egyptian onions, which were small and round, probably tasted far sweeter than the larger European onion which is eaten today. They were enjoyed at almost every meal, and even had a degree of religious symbolism – the Sokar festival held at Memphis to celebrate the winter solstice required priests to don a wreath of onions and to sniff bunches of onions while walking in the sacred procession. Egyptian garlic was also smaller than its modern counterpart, and may not have been as strongly flavoured.

Beans, which are highly nutritious, were consumed in vast quantities by the poor. Chickpeas, broad beans, brown beans (*ful medames*) and lentils were all grown from the Predynastic period onwards and must have made appetizing and filling dishes when boiled, mashed with garlic and oil and stuffed inside a flap of unleavened bread. More adventurous bean recipes could have included chopped onion, egg, and even fried balls of bean mixture similar to the *filafil* still served in Egypt today.

The tradition of generous hospitality which prompts modern Egyptians to share their meals with the strangers of a few minutes' acquaintance has its roots in the gregarious customs of Dynastic Egypt. Semi-formal banquets were an important aspect of Egyptian social life and, as there were no restaurants or cafés, these were always held at home. In the absence of theatres, cinemas and night clubs, these dinner parties formed the main entertainment for the upper classes, and were hugely enjoyed by all. It is perhaps fortunate that those who were rich enough to throw such lavish parties were also rich enough to employ servants to cook the food and clean up the resultant mess.

Unfortunately we have no written description of the progress of a banquet, and our information is therefore derived from the painted feasts recorded on tomb walls. These scenes suggest that, although there was every likelihood that a formal banquet would eventually dissolve into a drunken orgy of overeating, it always started with an ostentatious display of good manners and prim behaviour. As correct etiquette was universally regarded as a mark of good breeding the Old Kingdom sage Ptahotep provided a useful guideline for the socially inept:

If you are one of the guests at the table of one who is greater than you, take what is given as it is set before you. Look at who is sitting before you, and don't shoot many glances at him as molesting him offends the Ka. Don't speak to him until he speaks to you – you don't know what may displease him. Speak only when he has addressed you, then your words will please his heart.

On arrival the party guests were greeted by scantily dressed young serving-women who presented them with a fragment garland of exotic flowers and a heavily perfumed wax cone to be worn on the head. There was no formal segregation of married men and women, and the servants led the most important couples to the places of honour: low chairs or stools placed next to individual tables groaning under heaps of delicious food. Those of lesser importance were happy to sit or squat on mats spread on the floor, and helped themselves to the same food as their social superiors. Throughout the meal extra food and wine were circulated by the servants, and the feasters were entertained by a spectacular succession of nubile girl dancers, acrobats and musicians singing rather mournful songs intended to encourage a proper appreciation of life. The injection of a potentially rather depressing note into the proceedings in no way deterred the cheerful feasters, and Herodotus tells us that all banquets routinely ended with a rather abrupt reminder of death; a small model mummy being exhibited to the revellers by a gloomy servant who warned the revellers to 'drink and be merry, for when you die you will be just like this'. This anecdote possibly tells us more about Herodotus' gullibility than Egyptian dining customs.

Although the tomb-wall party guests are served a tempting buffet, they are never actually depicted eating. They do, however, drink, and their cups are repeatedly replenished by the ever-willing maids. This slight inconsistency has prompted some linguists, influenced by the fact that the Egyptian word *sti*, 'to pour', also means to impregnate, to suggest that the scenes may be interpreted as a form of visual pun intended to emphasize the fertility of the deceased. Certainly more overt sexual references would have been considered out of place on a tomb wall.[6]

Yesterday's drunkenness will not quench today's thirst.
Late Period advice to young men

No accomplished host would have dreamed of inviting his guests to a meal without providing an unlimited supply of the finest wines for their enjoyment.[7] Wine was drunk by men and women alike, and there seems to have been no prohibition on serving women alcohol. In-deed, occasional scenes of indis-creetly drunken ladies being horribly and publicly sick show that intemperance at banquets was regarded as a rather amus-ing joke for all, particularly when the sufferer was a woman: one lady depicted in the tomb of Paheri even orders the servant somewhat rashly to 'Give me eighteen cups of wine, I want to drink to drunk-enness; my throat is as dry as

Fig. 16   Lady vomiting at a banquet

straw.' The most universally popular party tipple was red wine made from grapes, a drink widely enjoyed from the beginning of the Old Kingdom onwards. The mass production of white wine probably didn't start until the Middle Kingdom, although by the classical periods Egyptian whites were well respected by the bon viveurs of the classical world: the Greek–Egyptian Athenaeus admiringly described the wine of the Mareotic region as 'excellent, white, pleasant, fragrant, easily assimilated, thin, not likely to go to the head, and diuretic', the Taeniotic wine as 'better than Mareotic, somewhat pale, has an oily quality, pleasant, aromatic, mildly astringent' and the wine of Antylla province 'surpassing all others'.

Do not indulge in drinking beer lest you utter evil speech and don't know what you are saying.

Instructions of Scribe Any

Wine was very much the expensive pleasure of the upper classes. Poorer and less sophisticated drinkers drowned their sorrows in vast amounts of home-brewed beer, the favourite 'soft' drink of ancient Egypt which was sweetish, non-fizzy and thick, and unfortunately so full of floating impurities that it frequently had to be drunk through a special filtering straw. This beer was certainly nothing like the bottled 'Stella' sold in Egypt today, and was probably far more nutritious than alcoholic. However much an acquired taste, the beer was both cheap and easily available, and was apparently enjoyed by all who drank it, even winning praise from the discerning Diodorus Siculus as 'in smell and sweetness of taste not much inferior to wine'. Beer was the usual drink offered to the gods and to the deceased, and it was a valued ingredient in medicine.

Brewing was a very important offshoot of baking, and as such was traditionally regarded as a female activity. The process was relatively simple. Ground flour was mixed with water, kneaded into a stiff dough with added yeast and given a light baking in the oven. The loaf was then crumbled and placed in a fermenting jar with extra damp flour and more beer added. When brewed, the beer was strained through a sieve into a jar and stoppered to prevent further fermentation which would make the drink too acidic to be enjoyable. A similar brewing technique is still used today in the manufacture of the home-made Nubian beer known as 'booza'.

4

Work and Play

𓈖𓏏𓐍𓏤𓏏𓂋𓏏𓏥

I'll make you love the scribe's job more than you love
your own mother. I'll make its beauties obvious to
you, for it is the greatest of all professions, and there is
none like it in all the land . . . See, there is no worker
without an overseer except for the scribe, who is
always his own boss. Therefore, if you can learn to
write, it will be far better for you than all the other
careers which I have listed before you, each one of
which is more wretched than the last.

Middle Kingdom scribal propaganda

Education and literacy were the keys to professional advancement
in Dynastic society. Writing developed in Egypt at about 3000
BC, and from this point onwards only those who could combine
an ability to read and write with a basic grasp of arithmetic were
eligible to compete for prestigious posts as administrators and
accountants in the three major white-collar employment sectors:
the civil service, the army and the priesthood. The rather vague
title of 'scribe', which could be applied to anyone who was
literate regardless of occupation, quickly became one of the most
prestigious of Egyptian accolades, and many wealthy and
influential men chose to stress their high status by being sculpted
in the typical scribe's pose: seated cross-legged with a reed brush
poised to write on a roll of papyrus stretched across the knees. In
addition to enhanced employment prospects, the literate received
an enviable range of fringe benefits. Most importantly, the educated were exempt from the indignities of hard manual labour,
always something to be avoided in ancient Egypt. Instead, they

were able to reinforce their more elevated status by mingling with the equally refined upper classes rather than the uncouth peasants. In stark contrast, the illiterate and uneducated laboured under a severe social handicap, constantly banging their heads against an unpassable and unavoidable barrier to promotion. Quite simply, anyone who was anyone in ancient Egypt could read and write.

The basics of reading and writing were acquired either at home or at school before the trainee scribe, following the long-established custom of teaching via apprenticeship, progressed to working under the direct supervision of an older and more experienced professional. Often this supervisor was a close male relation such as a father or an uncle. During the Old Kingdom wealthy families employed tutors to equip their children with a primary education, and this tradition of private coaching for the upper classes continued well into the New Kingdom. However, during the prosperous Middle Kingdom, formal day-schools known as the 'Houses of Instruction' were established in association with the royal palaces and temples. Here, select bands of young boys received a good basic education designed to provide the ever-expanding state with a much needed supply of well-trained bureaucrats. These schools were not, unfortunately, noted for their imaginative or stimulating lessons, and the pupils studied very little beside reading, writing and, to a lesser extent, arithmetic. Every day the students, some as young as five years of age, attended alfresco morning classes where they passed their time endlessly chanting, copying and re-copying a series of classical texts which increased in complexity and dullness as the pupil advanced in proficiency.

When your mother sent you to school, where you were taught to read and write, she cared for you each day with bread and beer at home. When you yourself become a man and take a bride, and become settled in your house, pay attention to your own son, and bring him up carefully as your mother raised you.

New Kingdom scribal instruction

There were no specialized or simple reading books designed to encourage the development of tender young Egyptian minds. Instead, the first book to be studied, a lengthy text known as the *Kemit*, was a standard compilation of polite Middle Egyptian phrases, model letters and guidance to young scribes, written in an old-fashioned vertical script which must have been as dauntingly unfamiliar to the young students of the New Kingdom as Chaucer's Middle English would be to the primary school children of today. Once this formidable academic hurdle had been overcome, students were faced with a succession of more advanced traditional works, with modern literature being considered only after three or four years when the pupil had become reasonably fluent in both his reading and writing. The so-called *Wisdom Texts* formed an integral part of this scribal training. These texts, which have furnished many of the quotations given in this book, developed during the Old Kingdom and remained very popular throughout the Dynastic period. They always followed the same format, and were written as lists of rather long-winded and idiosyncratic advice dictated by a revered master to his son or favourite pupil. The opinions on offer ranged from the general to the highly specific, and much of the advice still holds good in the modern world:

If a man's son accepts his father's words, then no plan of his will go wrong.

Old Kingdom *Wisdom Text*

Do not tell lies against your mother; the magistrates abhor this.

Middle Kingdom *Wisdom Text*

Lend a hand to an elder drunk on beer; respect him as his children should.

New Kingdom *Wisdom Text*

He who spits in the sky will have spittle fall on his head.

Late Period *Wisdom Text*

The schoolboy's studies were made particularly tedious by the unique Egyptian tradition of employing three different types of writing at the same time, each style being considered appropriate to a specific type of document. The most popular and frequently used type of writing was a curly-looking script running from right to left. Specially developed to be written quickly with a fine paintbrush, this so-called cursive hieratic was the writing of everyday life and, consequently, the most widely studied and read. In contrast, hieroglyphic was a highly specialized, intricate and rather time-consuming form of writing reserved for monumental inscriptions of everlasting importance which could be carved or painted slowly and with great care. Cursive hieroglyphic, written from left to right, fell between these two extremes, being the writing of the semi-formal religious, magical and scientific texts. Towards the end of the Dynastic period changes in the Egyptian language led to the development of demotic, a fourth type of script which was used mainly for business purposes. Egyptian pupils, struggling to cope with different styles of writing, would have envied their modern counterparts faced only with the need to distinguish between the highly similar 'joined-up' lower case writing, sloping italic writing and printed capital letters.

Don't waste your day in idleness, or you will be flogged. A boy's ear is on his back. He listens when he is beaten.

Traditional scribal advice

The Egyptian schoolmasters were invariably very strict with their young charges, regarding frequent beatings as an integral and essential part of the learning process. As one Egyptian adult ruefully reminisced with his former mentor, 'You smote my back, and so your teaching entered my ear.' Leaving aside the question of corporal punishment, the approved teaching method differed markedly from current western educational practice. In particular, reading was taught by the constant memorizing, reciting and then writing of whole phrases which were regarded as one entity; there was no attempt to teach the pupils how to analyse a sentence by considering each word, or how to build up the spelling of a particular word by identifying and pronouncing the individual component signs and letters. Nor were the pupils encouraged to develop independent thoughts or to express themselves in imaginative prose. Instead, each conventional phrase was learned parrot-fashion so that it could be reproduced as a whole. This system of block learning goes a long way towards explaining why many Egyptian documents, even private letters, are so full of identical phrases that they manage to give the impression of being written by the same scribe. Some Egyptian letters consist entirely of these conventional phrases, and represent little more than a generalized greeting without any personal content, somewhat as a modern pre-printed birthday or Christmas card or even a brief postcard can serve as a rather impersonal gesture of contact today.

Instructing a woman is like holding a sack of sand whose sides have split open.

Late Period opinion of Scribe Ankhsheshonq

There is no direct evidence to show that girls ever accompanied their brothers to school. Indeed, as primary education was merely the first step towards a vocational training, and as few girls if any were expected to progress to high-status professions, most parents would have baulked at the unnecessary expense required to educate their daughters. After all, formal education was a privilege reserved for very few boys and the majority of the population remained both illiterate and uneducated. Nevertheless, and in spite of Scribe Ankhsheshonq's rather bigoted opinion, society did not object in principle to the education of females. Although the only Egyptian woman to be depicted actually putting pen to paper was Seshat, the goddess of writing, several ladies were illustrated in close association with the traditional scribe's writing kit of palette and brushes.[1] It is certainly beyond doubt that at least some of the daughters of the king were educated, and the position of private tutor to a royal princess could be one of the highest honour. The very influential New Kingdom official Senenmut, Steward of Amen during the reign of Queen Hatchepsut, clearly regarded his position as tutor to Princess Neferure, daughter of Hatchepsut and heiress to the Egyptian throne, as the high point of his unusually successful career.

More surprising is the evidence provided by ostraca recovered from Deir el-Medina which suggest that at least some ordinary housewives were able to read and write. These texts, which seem to be informal notes jotted down to jog the writer's memory, deal with fairly trivial female concerns such as laundry lists, underwear and dressmaking advice, and as such are certainly not the type of document which a woman would employ a scribe to write

Fig. 17   The goddess Seshat

on her behalf. It would, however, be wrong to extrapolate from this evidence and deduce that the majority of housewives were educated. Presumably the standard of literacy in a town like Deir

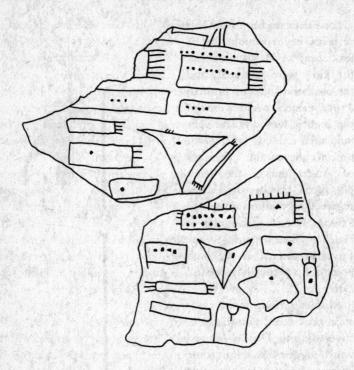

Fig. 18   Primitive hieroglyphs from Deir el-Medina

el-Medina, which included a high percentage of educated draughtsmen, masons and artists together with their families, was far higher than in a purely agricultural community where few peasant men and women would ever need reading and writing skills. It is interesting that Deir el-Medina has also yielded a number of non-hieroglyphic symbols which were obviously used by the illiterate or partially literate as a means of identifying their personal property. These signs, which vary from simple geometric shapes to more intricate hieroglyph-like figures, have been found on house and tomb walls, but are most commonly used to identify laundry which was sent to the washerman.

There's nothing better than a book; it's like a boat sailing on the water.

Middle Kingdom *Satire of the Trades*

Very few of the privileged women who received a primary education were able to progress via formal apprenticeships into professional careers. This is not necessarily because there was an official ban on women occupying influential posts and, indeed, no such veto has ever been recorded. Instead, it reflects the fact that a girl would be embarking on her nuptial and domestic responsibilities at precisely that age when her brother might expect to commence his training. Without all the conveniences of modern life, including efficient contraception, the mistress of the house had more than enough work to fill her day, and she would certainly have been unable to take on the commitment of a full-time career. After all, the upper-class wife derived her status from her husband's position in the community and she had no need to work to increase either her social standing or her personal wealth.

A wife was, however, expected to support her husband in his chosen career, to the extent that she might even be called upon to act from time to time as his official representative. The clearest surviving example of a wife deputizing for her absent husband is recorded in a New Kingdom letter written to the Scribe of the necropolis, Esamenope, by his wife Henuttawi.[2] Henuttawi tells how, at her husband's request, she supervised the reception of two ships of grain intended to pay the monthly rations of the Theban workmen. Unfortunately, when the ships were unloaded there was an obvious shortfall in the number of grain sacks, and Henuttawi, without herself directly challenging the sailors, proposed that the matter should be investigated further as someone had obviously tampered with the cargo during the voyage. Although it would have been more usual for a son to take over Esamenope's role, no one questioned Henuttawi's right to act officially on her husband's behalf, and her ability to carry out her role effectively seems to have been accepted by all.

Those wealthy ladies who were lucky enough to find themselves with time on their hands turned to the temple in an attempt to occupy their spare hours profitably while enhancing their social status. Religion, the one eminently respectable 'career' always open to royal and upper-class Egyptian women, was an approved interest for non-working females just as our modern society actively approves of those public-spirited women who have no need to take paid employment but who undertake a certain amount of voluntary work for charity. Egyptian public life was very much dominated by men, and in all the big provincial centres of Egypt the male élite held important and high-profile positions such as mayor, magistrate or senior civil servant. Their wives were free to take an equally prominent corresponding interest in the local temple where they often served as priestesses, particularly when the cult was that of a female deity. The duties of these upper-class priestesses were somewhat nebulous. Whether or not they were expected to be regular celebrants at the temple is open to question, and it seems very likely that these were purely honorary positions conferred automatically on all large-scale temple benefactors. It would certainly be wrong to class these priestesses as mere temple employees, and it seems likely that they were expected to make donations to the temple coffers rather than receive payment for their services.

Good speech is more scarce than greenstone, and yet it may be found amongst the talk of maids at the grindstone.

Old Kingdom *Wisdom Text*

The traditional Egyptian division of labour decreed that the man should work outside the home while the woman worked within it. This view was reinforced by the contemporary literature which constantly depicted active men supported by passive wives, and was subtly emphasized by the artistic convention of depicting light-skinned 'indoor' women married to sun-bronzed 'outdoor' men; in this context, 'outdoor' may be taken as a symbol for employment outside the home. Tomb paintings conform totally to the conventional view of daily life, so that we have very few scenes showing women working in anything other than purely domestic contexts, and no scenes showing a woman performing any work of great importance. But, it must be remembered that these tomb walls were painted to depict a way of life which was deliberately both idealized and stereotyped: just as upper-class Victorian and Edwardian morality maintained that a woman's place was in the home, conveniently ignoring the thousands of women who were forced to work for a living, so the Egyptian scenes emphasize that paid work was, quite properly, the prerogative of men. The scarcity of tomb scenes showing women supervising cooking perhaps gives us some indication of the lack of realism in these conventional images.

As might be expected, the true situation seems to have been less straightforward, and it would be a grave mistake to underestimate the economic importance of the Egyptian woman, just as it would be a mistake to ignore the contribution made by her children who, in the absence of any form of protective legislation, were able to take full-time jobs from a very early age. Many women did, in fact, need to work outside the home in order to supplement the family income. The work available to these women may be divided into three broad categories: those who were both well connected and well educated were able to take professional posts, usually as domestic administrators or supervisors; those with the appropriate skills and talents entered the female-dominated music, weaving and mourning industries; while those with little or no formal training entered domestic service.

Several female job titles have been preserved on tomb walls and funerary stelae.[3] However, these titles cover a relatively restricted range of duties, and it would appear that the professions open to women were limited both by tradition and educational opportunity. Once the purely honorary accolades (Sole Royal Ornament, King's Acquaintance, etc.) and the more lowly

servant's tasks (Hairdresser, Grinding Girl, etc.) are excluded
from the list, it becomes clear that the majority of the better-
educated women worked either as domestic administrators or as
supervisors of mainly female activities.[4] Their work was almost
invariably indoor work and often, but not always, they were
employed by other high-ranking ladies who maintained their
own retinues of mainly female attendants. This sexual division of
labour is underlined by the many depictions of private life which
show female servants attending to their mistresses while their
husbands are served by men, and it extended into religious life
where, as a general rule, Egyptian male gods were served by
male priests and female gods by female priestesses.[5] Even young
children demonstrate a degree of segregation in their play, so that
illustrations invariably show the boys devising their own games
apart from the girls.

The female supervisors and managers predominantly exerted
their control over female workers engaged in what were
perceived to be female activities. Thus, from the Old Kingdom
onwards we know of women working as 'Supervisor of Cloth',
'Supervisor of the Wig Workshop', 'Supervisor of the Dancers of
the King' and even 'Supervisor of the Harem of the King' – all
typically female-linked occupations. These titles were not
uniquely confined to women – there were certainly some male
overseers of wig-making, dancing and music – but the female
managers were, as a general rule, responsible for the women
dancers and singers and the production of women's wigs. However, although men occasionally supervised the female workers in
these trades, we have no direct evidence for women ever managing male workers. The work of the female administrators was
confined to private or royal households, and it is striking that,
although there were literally thousands of scribes employed in
the civil service, we know of no woman occupying an influential
bureaucratic post. Similarly, but perhaps less surprisingly, we
know of no women employed in any high-ranking capacity in
the army or in agricultural administration.

The highest-ranking administrative title ever held by a woman belonged to the Old Kingdom Lady Nebet, wife of Huy, 'Sole Royal Ornament' and 'Hereditary Princess, Daughter of Geb, Countess, Daughter of Merhu, She of the Curtain, Judge and Vizier, Daughter of Thoth, Companion of the King of Lower Egypt, Daughter of Horus'. The vizier held the most powerful and prestigious position in ancient Egypt; a position which was, in theory at least, non-hereditary. As the king's right-hand man he was frequently a member of the king's immediate family and, second only in importance to his monarch, he acted as both senior civil servant and chief judge. It would certainly have been very unexpected for a woman to hold such an important position of authority and circumstantial evidence indicates that, although Nebet was clearly accorded the title of vizier, the actual duties of the office were undertaken by her husband, Huy.[6] No other woman was accorded the honour of this title until the 26th Dynasty.

The female administrators seem to have held their most influential posts during the Old Kingdom; evidence from the Middle and New Kingdoms indicates that women retained their salaried domestic work but were now no longer classed as supervisor or overseer, and were not included in even minor positions of authority in the royal palaces. We certainly know of several women 'stewards' and some 'treasurers' active in the private sector during the Middle Kingdom. One such professional administrator was the 'Treasurer, Keeper of the Property of her Lord, Tchat', whose name and titles are mentioned several times on the walls of the 12th Dynasty private tombs at Beni Hassan.[7] The Lady Tchat worked as an official in the household of the influential local governor Khnumhotep where she was obviously held in the highest regard; reliefs in Khnumhotep's own tomb, where Tchat is several times depicted standing close to the Mistress of the House, Khety, indicate that she played a prominent role in family life. Tchat combined her role of treasurer to the household with that of concubine to its master. Eventually, following Khety's death, she gave up her official duties to marry Khnumhotep, thereby making her two surviving sons legitimate heirs to their natural father.

The sky and the stars make their music for you while the sun and the moon praise you. The gods exalt you, and the goddesses sing their song to you.

Verse from the Temple of Hathor, Dendera

Music was a particularly lucrative career which was open to both men and women and which could be pursued either on a freelance basis or as a servant permanently attached to an estate or temple.[8] Good performers were always in demand and a skilful musician and composer could gain high status in the community; for example, the female performing duo of Hekenu and Iti were two Old Kingdom musicians whose work was so celebrated that it was even commemorated in the tomb of the accountant Nikaure, a very unusual honour as few Egyptians were willing to feature unrelated persons in their private tombs. The sound of music was everywhere in Egypt, and it would be difficult to overestimate its importance in daily Dynastic life. The labourers in the fields sang popular folk songs as they worked, the sailors on the Nile matched their strokes to the rhythm of a traditional shanty, and the army marched to the sound of the drum and the trumpet. Leisure hours were filled with singing and dancing, nubile all-female song and dance troupes were a standard after-dinner entertainment, and even the heavy coffins were dragged to the burial grounds to the accompaniment of a rhythmic clapping. It is therefore deeply disappointing that, despite the survival of several instruments and many artistic representations of musical activities, we have very little idea of how this music actually sounded. In the absence of a recognizable music theory and notation, attempts to replicate the sounds enjoyed by the pharaohs are bound to be little more than interesting conjecture.

Fig. 19   All-female dinner band

The typical Egyptian secular orchestra included a large percussion section with rattles, clappers and drums helping to define the beat of the music, and strong wind and string sections with a combination of clarinets, double oboes and flutes and at least one harp. The players were supervised during the Old Kingdom by a conductor who stood in front of the performers, indicating the rhythm and pitch of the music by a complicated series of hand gestures. This conductor appears to have become superfluous to requirements at some stage during the Middle Kingdom, and was no longer depicted by the New Kingdom artist. At this time lyres and lutes were first introduced into Egypt from Asia; these very quickly became very popular additions to the standard postprandial ensemble.

All the Egyptian gods and goddesses were understood to enjoy a good tune, and so the temples employed bands of musicians and choirs of singers and dancers to enhance communication

Fig. 20   Female percussion group

with the deities. These temple musicians, both men and women, were employed on a regular basis and given frequent coaching sessions by official instructors who worked hard to ensure that the clapping and singing were as perfect as possible. More high ranking were the official songstresses of the deity; many upper-class women described themselves as religious songstresses, even including their title on their funerary monuments; it would appear that this should again be classed as an honorary temple position rather than a paid job. These ladies were certainly held in highest regard, and at Abydos there was even a special cemetery reserved for the songstresses of a number of gods and their stillborn babies.

Holy music for Hathor, music a million times, because you love music, million times music, to your soul, wherever you are. I am he who makes the singer waken music for Hathor every day at any hour she wishes.

Middle Kingdom song to Hathor

Very few of the gods actually played any instrument; the only one to be regularly depicted performing for his own evident pleasure was Bes, the ugly dwarf god who was associated with women and childbirth. Goddesses were generally more strongly identified with music than their male counterparts and, while the goddess Merit was recognized as the personification of music, it was Hathor, goddess of love, 'Mistress of Music' and attendant at royal births, who was most closely linked with music, in particular with one musical instrument: the sistrum which was played only by women. It was a rather large loop-shaped rattle with a long handle, often featuring the head of Hathor, which had initially represented the papyrus reeds of the Nile Delta where, mythology decreed, Hathor had been forced to hide with her young son. Eventually the sistrum lost all trace of its original meaning and instead started to serve as a religious symbol for life itself. It consequently became absorbed by other deities, and was particularly identified with the cult of Isis at the end of the Dynastic period. The playing of the sistrum was often accompanied by the rattling of the heavy *menit* bead necklaces which the female musicians carried in their spare hand. To a lesser extent, the round tambourine was also associated with both women and religion; New Kingdom illustrations suggest a link between this tambourine and the cults of both Hathor and Isis, while we know from the surviving temple birth houses that the beating of round tambourines was the appropriate way to mark the divine birth of a king.

Music was occasionally associated with women for more prosaic reasons. The *Turin Erotic Papyrus*, for example, includes one scene where a prostitute has hastily dropped her lyre to copulate with an over-eager client, while a crude sketch on a piece of wood recovered from a New Kingdom Theban tomb shows a woman who is actually engaged in full intercourse with a man but who still clings on to her lute. The clear inference is that prostitutes used their musical skills to entice their clients, and a link between music, femininity, sex and even childbirth is again suggested by the Bes tattoos on the musical prostitute's thighs. Less tastefully, to modern eyes, figurines which show male harpists with their instruments resting on disproportionately erect penises again emphasize the link between music and sexuality.

The weaver in the workshop is in a worse position than the woman in labour. With his knees pushed up against his chest he is unable to breathe the air. If he misses just one day of weaving he is given fifty lashes. He has to bribe the doorkeeper with food to let him see the light of day.

Middle Kingdom *Satire of the Trades*

Throughout the ancient world cloth production was primarily associated with women. In near-contemporary Greece and Rome this specialization of duties was taken to extremes, and the mistress of the house was held responsible for the provision of all the cloth (invariably wool) which would be needed by her family. This included all the clothing, sheeting, towels and shrouds, and was a daunting undertaking for any woman. Fabric manufacture became a very highly rated domestic task, to the extent that wool-work, spinning and weaving, rather than knitting, eventually became synonymous with woman's work and was expected of females of all ranks and ages. A virtuous wife could easily be identified by her skills at the loom, and even the most noble of Greek ladies was expected to spend a large part of her day weaving in order to provide the clothing for the household and its dependants.[9] As the large and heavy loom could not easily be transported, this effectively condemned her to spending many hours working alone at home.

The situation in Egypt was far more flexible. Commercial

weaving was still a female-dominated industry, particularly during the Old Kingdom when the hieroglyphic sign representing 'weaver' was a seated woman holding what appears to be a long, thin shuttle, but not all women needed to learn how to weave. Cloth could easily be obtained by barter, and any surplus of home-produced linen could be exchanged for other household items at the market. Lower-class Egyptian men were not embarrassed to be seen working at the loom, and several labourers at Deir el-Medina happily excused their absence from work by explaining that they had needed to stay at home and weave. Larger-scale commercial weaving occurred in the workshops attached to temples and large estates where both women and, to a lesser extent, men were employed, and also in the royal harem where the finest of the royal linen was produced. Although the ladies of the harem may themselves have done some of the more intricate threadwork their real function was to supervise and train the female workers in the weaving sheds; weaving formed just one of the valuable economic sidelines of the royal women.

Linen was by far the most important cloth produced in Egypt. Flax, the plant from which linen is derived, was not native to Egypt but was introduced in Predynastic times when it quickly became an important crop, essential for the production of both linen and linseed oil. Flax remained an economically valuable commodity throughout the historical period. When it is considered that the wrapping of one mummified body could use over 375 square metres of material, the importance of flax farming can be fully appreciated. Even though it was customary to recycle used household cloth and bandages in mummification, there must have been a constant demand for new linen.

The actual manufacturing process was fairly simple if time consuming. The flax was harvested by pulling the whole plant out of the ground in order to preserve the stalk; the younger the crop, the finer would be the finished thread. After an initial preparation of the fibres the flax was spun on a small hand-held spindle to produce a ball of thread, the twist of the thread being to the left as flax naturally tends in this direction when drying. The spun thread was then woven into cloth on a loom. Horizontal hand-operated ground looms made of wood were used by both men and women in commercial workshops until the Hyksos invaders of the Second Intermediate Period introduced the more mechanically efficient vertical loom. This new-style loom was operated exclusively by men. The finished material was carefully marked in one corner by either the weaver or the owner, and was stored either as bolts or large sheets (up to 2 metres wide and occasionally over 25 metres long) in special woven baskets or wooden chests. A variety of grades of cloth was produced, with the finest and most delicate linens being rightly prized all over the ancient world.

Death is before me today like a man's longing to see his home when he has been many years in captivity.

Middle Kingdom text

Some women were able to gain employment as professional mourners, an exclusively female occupation. These specialists were hired to enhance the status of the deceased by openly grieving at his or her funeral. They were not, therefore, an essential part of the funeral ritual, although they did add to its impact. As far as we can tell from contemporary tomb illustrations, the job involved donning a traditional mourning dress of white or blue-grey linen and following the funeral cortège while making an ostentatious display of grief which included loud wailing, beating exposed breasts, smearing the body with dirt and tearing at dishevelled hair; all signs of uncontrolled behaviour, the 'disorder of sorrow', which presented a marked contrast to the sedate, spick-and-span image which Egyptian women normally admired. Occasionally, very young girls accompanied their mourning mothers to work, and the New Kingdom tomb of Ramose at Thebes shows a group of professional grieving women which includes a tiny girl whose youth is made apparent

Fig. 21   Mourning women from the tomb of Neferhotep

by both her small stature and her nakedness. A more important role in the funeral ritual was played by the two women chosen to impersonate the two *djeryt*, Isis and Nephthys, the sisters of Osiris who assumed the shape of birds while searching the world for their dead brother. These two women wore an archaic form of sheath dress and a short neat wig. They walked next to the sledge which was used to drag the body towards the tomb, and had an entirely passive role in the ceremony.

A few women also acted as official mortuary priests and, just like the often-quoted Hekanakhte, they received payment for ensuring that the tomb of the deceased was correctly maintained, with all the ritual offerings duly made. These roles were generally hereditary, with the care of the tomb being passed from father to son or daughter until the funding of the endowment expired.

The servant who is not beaten is full of curses in his heart.

Late Period employment advice

An Egyptian woman of good character could always find employment as a servant; the lack of modern conveniences, such as electricity and plumbed water, meant that there was a constant demand for unskilled domestic labour. A servant's wages were relatively cheap, and most middle- and upper-class homes had at least one maid who could be trained in domestic skills while helping out with the more arduous household chores. Girls entered domestic service at a relatively young age, and anxious mothers relied upon responsible householders to protect their inexperienced daughters while providing them with a good basic training. This concern for the welfare of the younger servants is well illustrated by a private letter written during the New Kingdom. The Scribe Ahmose had become worried about the fate of a servant girl who had been specifically entrusted to his protection but who had unaccountably disappeared, apparently on the orders of his superior, the treasurer Ty:

What is the reason for taking away the servant girl who had been given to me but who has now been given to someone else? . . . As far as I am concerned I am not worried about the loss of her value, as she is very young and does not yet know her work . . . But her mother sent a message to me, saying 'You have allowed my child to be taken away when she was entrusted to you . . .'[10]

Domestic servants appear to have been closely tied to their master's services, but they could lose their position if their behaviour was not considered appropriate to their situation:

Now, as soon as you receive this letter from Sahathor, have the housemaid Senen thrown out of my house. See, if she spends just one more night in my home, watch out! I will hold you responsible for any evil which she may do to my concubine.

Middle Kingdom letter written by Hekanakhte

Servants should not be confused with slaves who, although in many cases required to perform the same range of tasks, remained at all times the legal property of their masters and mistresses.[11] Owners had many rights over their slaves who could be sold, transferred, emancipated or rented out at will, but they acknowledged a corresponding duty to feed, clothe and care for their property, just as they cared for the well-being of their free servants. Despite the popular movie scenes which show Cecil B. de millions of slaves toiling, suffering and dying under the hot Egyptian sun, slavery was relatively rare in Egypt. Such slaves as there were were either born into slavery or else represented the unfortunate victims of war:

I have brought those whom my sword spared as numerous captives, pinioned like birds before my horses, also their wives and children in their thousands and their cattle . . .

> Inscription of Ramesses III

Some slaves were also imported into Egypt by foreign slave-dealers. It would be wrong, however, to suggest that all the foreign workers in Egypt were slaves; the comparative buoyancy of the Egyptian economy attracted many professional weavers, singers and dancers, and immigrant workers from Asia were a common feature of everyday Dynastic life. A few free-born Egyptians actually chose to enter voluntary slavery by executing a legal contract of self-sale or self-dedication, thereby extricating themselves from a burden of debt due to their now-owner; that free-born Egyptians were prepared to take this irrevocable step, binding on both themselves and their descendants, suggests that the life of the Egyptian slave was perhaps not quite as harsh as we might imagine.

Whether the female slaves, or indeed the female servants, were expected to provide sexual services for their masters and their house-guests is unclear, although we know that many unmarried slave women did bear children during their captivity. Similarly, it is not clear whether the brothels of Dynastic Egypt were staffed by free women or by slaves. Certainly all other slave-owning societies, past and present, have expected their female slaves to sleep with their masters as and when required, while the less conventional Greeks also expected pretty young boy slaves to be available to the men of the household. The case of Nenufer and Nebnufer who purchased a slave woman expressly for the purpose of breeding heirs has been discussed in Chapter 1. Under Egyptian law the children of such a union would be born into slavery, but could easily be freed and adopted by their owner/father. We must assume that this couple were not alone in choosing to use a slave as a surrogate mother, and the Bible suggests that this may have been a standard practice at this time:

Now Sarai, Abram's wife, bore him no children; and she had a handmaid, an Egyptian whose name was Hagar. And Sarai said unto Abram, 'Behold now, the Lord has restrained me from bearing; I pray thee, go in unto my handmaid; it may be that I may obtain children through her' . . . And Sarai took Hagar her maid and gave her to her husband Abram to be his wife.

Gen. 16:2

Ultimately, every Egyptian was a servant of the king, who could call upon the services of his people as and when he felt necessary. This he did under the long-established system of *corvée*, or conscripted labour, whereby all Egyptians were bound to donate their labour to royal projects such as the building of a public monument or the digging of irrigation ditches. Only those who were already employed on important projects, such as the higher-ranking servants of the local temple, were legally exempted from this conscription, although the administrators and those wealthy enough to pay a bribe or send along replacement labour quickly exempted themselves from their public duty. The heavy burden of the *corvée* therefore fell upon the poor, the uneducated and the peasants while the worst of the hard labour – a trip to the gold mines in the Sudan – was reserved for convicted felons and prisoners of war. All the *corvée* work was hard and highly unpopular and, to add insult to injury, paid only subsistence rations. The punishment for avoiding the work was, however, extremely harsh, and those tempted to desert could be faced with a lifelong prison sentence, interspersed with yet more periods of forced labour. Women were not automatically exempted from the *corvée*, and a Middle Kingdom register giving the names of eighty deserters includes the case of Teti, daughter of the Scribe Sainhur, who was found guilty and who suffered '. . . an order issued to execute against her the law pertaining to one who flees without performing his labour duty'.

On that day the workman Menna gave a pot of fresh fat to the chief of police Mentmose. Mentmose promised him 'I will pay you for it with barley obtained from my brother. My brother will guarantee the transaction. May Re keep you in good health.'

Ostracon from Deir el-Medina

Many women were able to make an important contribution to their family economy without actively seeking employment outside the home. Although tradition decreed that the work of men and women should be more or less separated, and that outdoor labour should be depicted as the prerogative of men, comparison with modern Egypt suggests that many women did, in fact, help their husbands with their daily work. For example, we know that the wives of fishermen were expected to gut and then sell their husbands' catch, and a few tomb illustrations show women labouring in the fields alongside their menfolk, picking flax, winnowing wheat and even carrying heavy baskets to the storehouses. Women are not conventionally illustrated ploughing, sowing or looking after the animals in the fields, but they are shown providing refreshments for the labourers, while gleaning was an approved female outdoor activity recorded in several tomb scenes; women and children follow the official harvesters and pick up any ears of corn which have been left behind. Of equal, or perhaps greater, importance were the small-scale informal transactions conducted between women, with one wife, for example, simply agreeing to swap a jug of her homemade beer for her neighbour's excess fish. This type of exchange, which formed the basis of the Egyptian economy, allowed the careful housewife to convert her surplus produce directly into usable goods, just as her husband was able to exchange his labour for his daily bread.

The few attendance records which have survived from Deir el-Medina indicate that this type of freelance trading by both men and women made an important contribution to the household budget. Officially the necropolis labourers worked a ten-day week, spending eight days in temporary accommodation in the Valley of the Kings and then returning home for a two-day rest. The full working day was eight hours long, with a midday meal break. However, the labourers were never unduly pressured to turn up for work on a regular basis and there were many holidays so that, as one ostracon shows, out of fifty consecutive days only eighteen were working days for the whole crew. Even on an official working day many labourers absented themselves with a variety of rather lame but apparently acceptable excuses ranging from the need to brew beer and weave to the need to build a house, and so relaxed were the authorities that the standard monthly grain ration was always paid over, regardless of the number of hours actually worked. Therefore, anyone wishing to increase his personal wealth was well advised to abandon any thought of working overtime at his official job and to concentrate instead on a spot of private enterprise which would bring an immediate reward. Not surprisingly, cottage industries flourished at Deir el-Medina, with enterprising weavers, brewers, dressmakers and potters supplementing their official income by supplying the immediate needs of their neighbours, while the skilled draughtsmen, artists and carpenters moonlighted by working unofficially to provide funerary equipment for the wealthy Theban aristocracy.

*

Fig. 22   Trading in the marketplace

Throughout the Dynastic period Egypt had no official currency. Barter, the exchange of one article or service for another, formed the basis of every transaction, no matter how trivial. Unfortunately, this reduces any modern attempt to calculate the true cost of dynastic living to little more than educated guesswork, as 'prices' were always both comparative and infinitely variable. It is quite simply impossible to state that a duck or a house or a funeral cost so much without understanding the full value placed on all types of commodities by a particular person at a specific time. Although the government, which acted as both the major employer and the major collector of surplus produce, was able to operate a crude price-control mechanism by regulating wages and the release of stored foodstuffs on to the market, there was no official policy of price-fixing, and the law of supply and demand was consequently paramount.

Despite the lack of coinage, shopping in Egypt was not always a totally haphazard experience as there was a universally recognized benchmark available as a point of reference for anyone wishing to conduct a serious transaction. This *deben*, a standard weight of copper, represented an intermediate stage between the use of money and true barter and allowed the Egyptians to develop a unique system of price referencing whereby any two commodities could be equated in value. Therefore, although the *deben* did not take the physical form of a note or coin, it was understood by everyone that, for example, at a given time during the New Kingdom a pig was priced at 5 *deben* of copper. Anyone wishing to buy a pig therefore had to find either 5 *deben* of copper or, more typically, a combination of other goods or services which were collectively also valued at 5 *deben*. It was then necessary to find a pig owner who valued the offered goods enough to make the swap. Some idea of the relative values placed on items at a given time can be gained from the study of surviving price lists. We know, for example, that during the New Kingdom the pig mentioned above was a pricey item when compared to a goat which was usually valued at two or three *deben*. This reflected the general scarcity of swine in Egypt at this time. In contrast a pair of shoes usually cost between one and two *deben* while a coffin, a very expensive item requiring both wood and skilled labour, was priced at over twenty *deben* of copper.[12]

The collector of taxes lands on the riverbank. He surveys the crops and assesses the tax payable, attended by menials who carry staves and Nubians wielding clubs. He orders 'give us grain', but there is none available to give. The farmer is beaten savagely, being tied up and ducked head first into the well. His wife is also tied up, as are his children. The neighbours all run away. And, after all this, there is still no grain to give.

New Kingdom *Wisdom Text*

The lack of currency did not mean that there was no taxation;

taxes in kind were levied on all the primary producers as a contribution towards the royal expenditure which could not be entirely matched by the income from the royal estates. The tax collector was one of the most feared of the Egyptian bureaucrats. He arrived regularly at harvest time, assessed the crops with an expert eye, and then extracted immediate payment from the farmers, using physical violence whenever necessary. Tax defaulters were summoned before the local magistrate and received summary punishment, while those who could not pay were conscripted into the forced labour gangs. A scene painted on the wall of the New Kingdom tomb of the vizier Rekhmira shows the tax man in action, accepting a diverse selection of goods and cattle from a local mayor; the items used to pay the tax include grain, cakes, rope, mats, goats, sacks, pigeons and metal ingots, and must have presented immediate storage problems for the official.

The recognized system of bartering meant that those householders who managed to acquire a substantial surplus of perishable foodstuffs, perhaps by producing a glut of home-grown vegetables or by making too much bread for family consumption, were able to offer their goods to a wider public by trading at the local market where they would in turn benefit from a more varied range of exchange goods. Here, every market day, local traders and visiting merchants spread out their temporary stalls to fill the crowded streets and alleys of the town, arranging their merchandise to best advantage in wide wicker baskets. Professional traders were in the minority, and the whole market was far more like a present-day garage or car-boot sale than a formal shopping centre. There was always an exciting variety of goods on offer, and the stands ranged from those of the professional jewellers who tempted potential customers with alluring and expensive displays of baubles, bangles and seals to the more humble stalls of the local peasants offering the most basic of market produce: bread, beer and gutted fish. Itinerant craftsmen took full advantage of the market crowds to sell their services, while small snack bars did brisk business serving delicious take-away food and reviving drinks to the jaded shoppers.

Several tomb scenes combine to provide us with a clear impression of the hustle and bustle of an Egyptian street market. On the walls of the Old Kingdom tomb of the officials Niankhkhnum and Khnumhotep at Sakkara a full-scale town market is in progress. Fruit, fish and vegetable stalls are all doing a roaring trade, two potters are competing to attract attention to their own wares and the haberdasher unrolls a bolt of his finest cloth to tempt a potential buyer. Over by the beer stand, at least one customer is already feeling somewhat tired and emotional. As the predominantly male shoppers stroll around with their practical shopping bags slung across their chests, a seller of lettuce and onion bargains with a man carrying a large jug of beer, 'Give me some of your product and I will give you sweet vegetables.' More excitingly, over by the vegetable stall, a trained security monkey is arresting a naked thief by biting him in the leg. One thousand years later, in the New Kingdom Theban tomb of Ipuy, the market ambience is virtually unchanged. Here, by the quayside, astute women traders have set up temporary stands to tempt the newly disembarked and newly paid sailors, helping them to convert their standard grain rations into a range of other goods. Bread, vegetables and fish are again on offer, and the ubiquitous beer stall is well stocked and ready for its first thirsty clients. Anyone who has ever enjoyed the cheerful bustle of a modern Egyptian village market will immediately recognize that, despite the presence of coinage and the absence of beer stands, there has been very little obvious change in the three thousand years since Ipuy's tomb was painted.

Make a holiday! And do not tire of playing! For no one is allowed to take his goods with him, and no one who departs this life ever comes back again.

                                        Middle Kingdom *Song of the Harpist*

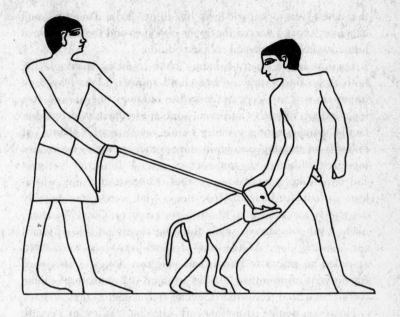

Fig. 23   Trained security monkey arresting a thief

The Egyptians were a people who knew how to make the most of their spare time. Whole families enjoyed spending the day together, and picnics at the tombs of the ancestors or boating expeditions on the Nile were always a popular treat. More exciting were the days spent hunting and fishing in the marshes when, as some tomb scenes suggest, the entire family squeezed into a light reed boat in order to watch the men of the household attempt to bring down birds with a traditional curved throwing stick. Given the fragile nature of these delicate boats it would appear that the artists must have employed a degree of artistic licence in their endeavours to portray a happy family day out; otherwise we would expect to see fairly frequent scenes of capsized boats and dripping-wet families. In contrast, hunting in the desert was acknowledged by all to be a dangerous and expensive sport, reserved for upper-class men and the professional hunters who accompanied each expedition.

Back at home, many a happy hour could be spent playing with the children and the household animals.[13] Pets played an important part in Egyptian family life and dogs and cats and, to a lesser extent, monkeys and even geese are frequently included in family groups, sitting proudly beside their owner's chair. The majority of the dogs shown in these scenes appear to be lovable mongrels, although the presence of several distinctive whippet and saluki-like animals suggests that deliberate breeding was at least partially successful. These dogs, who were given suitably descriptive names such as 'Ebony', 'Antelope' or 'Good Watcher', made loyal companions while fulfilling the useful role of guard and hunting dog. At the end of their lives they were often accorded an elaborate burial, and poignant doggy graves with expensively mummified bodies encased in miniature canine coffins have been recovered at several archaeological sites.

However, despite its useful work, the dog was not universally admired, and many Egyptians interpreted the dog's affectionate loyalty as a sign of cringing servility and weakness. Cats, with their mysterious aloofness and natural independence, attracted far more respect, becoming invested with several symbolic implications. In particular, as cats were customarily depicted sitting under a woman's chair and rarely depicted in association with a man, they became recognized as symbols of femininity and female sexuality. Several powerful female cat deities emerged, and the cult of the goddess Bast, centred on the town of Bubastis in the Nile Delta, became hugely popular during the Late and Graeco-Roman Periods. Cats were certainly a useful addition to any household; not only did they protect against snakes and vermin, but they also played an important role in hunting waterfowl.

After the hustle and bustle of the day, most married couples derived a great deal of quiet pleasure from simply sitting peacefully together; this evident enjoyment of each other's company is one of the most touching aspects of Egyptian married life. Wealthy families particularly enjoyed relaxing in the luxurious gardens of their villas, and this enjoyment was enhanced by watching the labour of others less fortunate. Home entertainments have left little trace in the archaeological record, and although we can guess that music and story-telling were important social events, we have no idea how often they occurred. In contrast, we do know that board games were hugely popular with all adults, and many tomb scenes show husbands and wives gently competing over the gaming board. It is perhaps surprising, given this evident enjoyment, that more such games did not develop. Indeed, during the entire Dynastic period there were only two universally popular games: 'senet', a board game for two players which was enjoyed from Predynastic times until the Roman Period, and its rival 'twenty squares', a game imported from the East, again for two players. Wooden boards for these two games are often found on either side of reversible gaming boxes designed to hold the necessary pieces, and these elaborate boxes were often included in the funerary equipment of the wealthy so that they could be used to while away dull moments in the Afterlife.

5

Good Grooming

Do not pamper your body: this will make you weak.
And do not pamper yourself in your youth, or you
will become weak in old age.

Late Period scribal advice

The importance attached to good grooming throughout Egyptian
society should never be underestimated. Both sexes paid great
attention to outward display and wealthy men as well as women
delighted in sporting the latest in fashions, hairstyles and makeup.
Cosmetics quickly became not a luxury but a necessity for daily
life and death so that, from Predynastic times onwards, ordinary
men and women chose to be buried with the carved palettes and
blocks of pigment used for adorning the eyes. At the opposite
end of the social scale, the elaborate fitted toilette sets placed in
royal tombs give us a clear indication of the value which their
owners attached to their cosmetics. As might be expected, there
was a corresponding well-developed commercial interest in
beauty treatments, while businesses dealing in cloth, false hair and
cosmetics thrived. Cleanliness was of equal, if not even greater,
importance. Herodotus, himself a Greek, clearly felt that the
Egyptians had become somewhat obsessive about their bodily
hygiene, in his view 'setting cleanliness above seemliness'. To the
Egyptians, living in the heat and ever-present dust of an arid
climate, personal cleanliness was essential both as a means of
promoting good health and, almost more importantly, as a sure
indication of breeding and rank. The poor, who lacked even the

most basic of sanitary facilities, and foreigners, who were believed to be dirty, were despised.

As a preliminary step towards personal hygiene fastidious men and women scrupulously removed all body hair by a constant and ruthless shaving and plucking. Hairy legs and chests were not greatly admired in either sex, and a quick review of the depilatory equipment recovered from women's tombs, including metal tweezers, knives and razors with tiny whetstones, indicates the extent to which some women were prepared to suffer to be beautiful. Less affluent members of the community had easy access to flint razors which could be flaked to form a very sharp cutting edge and, in the absence of soap, oil was cheaply available for use as a shaving lotion. The removal of body lice and other itchy nasties together with the hair was a welcome side-effect of body baldness.

... I was put in the house of a prince. In this house were luxuries including a bathroom and mirrors. In it were riches from the treasury; garments made of royal linen ... The choice perfume of the king and of his favourite courtiers was in every room ... Years were removed from my body. I was shaved and my hair was combed. In this way was my squalor returned to the foreign land, my dress to the Sandfarers. I was dressed in the finest of linen, I was anointed with perfumed oil and I slept on a real bed. I had returned the sand to those who dwell in it, and the tree oil to those who grease their bodies with it.

Middle Kingdom *Story of Sinuhe*

Frequent bathing of the hair-free body was considered essential. Soap was unknown but natron, ashes and soda made efficient if rather harsh non-lathering detergents, while linen towels were available for drying. A few privileged members of society were able to take full advantage of *en-suite* limestone bathrooms equipped with servant-powered showers; an attendant poured water over the head of the bather who stood in a special stone trough with a waterproof outlet. To preserve modesty the shower-servant stood behind a screen intended to obscure his or her view of the proceedings and this screen, like the bathroom itself, was stone-lined to prevent the inadvertent dissolution of the mud-brick house structure. For the vast majority of the population, however, bathrooms were unknown, and washing took place on the banks of the Nile or in the irrigation canals. Unfortunately the River Nile, which provided almost all the villages and towns with their daily drinking, cooking and washing water, also functioned as the main sewerage and waste disposal system of Egypt. The purity of the stagnant pools along the banks of the river must have been highly questionable, and evidence from mummies indicates that water-borne diseases such as bilharzia were rife.

If washing failed, and those embarrassing personal problems persisted, the *Ebers Medical Papyrus* could suggest various deodorants designed to restore self-confidence and facilitate a successful social life:

To expel stinking of the body of a man or woman: ostrich-egg, shell of tortoise and gallnut from tamarisk are roasted and the body is rubbed with the mixture.

Surviving lavatories are few and far between. The most universal model, modestly housed in a small cupboard-like room next to the bathroom, was a modern-looking carved wooden seat carefully balanced on two brick pillars and set over a deep bowl of sand which could be replaced as necessary. Extra sand was stored in a box beside the toilet and it was considered polite to cover the bowl after making use of the facilities. Presumably one of the more junior members of the household was given the unsavoury task of emptying the bowl whenever necessary. Stools with a wide hole cut into the seat have been recovered from several tombs and tentatively identified as ancient Portaloos, presumably again intended for use over a bowl of sand, and we may presume that chamber pots were frequently used. Universal access to an indoor toilet is, however, a relatively modern luxury, and one which has only become regarded as necessity in the west in the past fifty years. Most Dynastic Egyptians had no access to sanitary facilities of any description and would have regarded it as no hardship to make full use of the nearby fields and desert. Curiously, one of the strange and unprovable Egyptian 'facts' which fascinated Herodotus was the rumour that the women urinated standing up, while the men apparently sat or squatted for this purpose.

Menstruation was a subject of little interest to the men who wrote our surviving Egyptian texts. We therefore have no understanding of how women perceived this important aspect of their femininity and very little idea of how they approached the practical aspects of sanitary protection. However, laundry lists recovered from Deir el-Medina include 'bands of the behind': sanitary towels made from a folded piece of linen fabric which were used, sent to the laundry and then re-used. We do have certain indications that either menstruating women or the menstrual blood itself were regarded as ritually unclean; similar taboos are found in many primitive societies where the mechanics and function of menstruation are not fully understood. Blood is often perceived as both frightening and dangerous, and the fact that women regularly bled for days on end must have appeared unnatural and somewhat disturbing to the male members of society who could not bleed without an obvious wound. The term 'purification' or 'cleansing' was used to describe a menstrual period just as it was used to describe the lochia following childbirth, and the Middle Kingdom *Satire of the Trades* deplores the lot of the unfortunate washerman who has to handle women's garments stained with menstrual blood. Even coming into contact with a man whose female relations were bleeding could be considered undesirable, and at Deir el-Medina a labourer had a valid excuse to absent himself from work if either his wife or one of his daughters was having a period.

*

One of the customs most zealously observed by the Egyptians is this, that they rear every child that is born, and circumcise the males and excise the females as is also customary among the Jews, who are also Egyptians in origin.

Strabo

During the Old and Middle Kingdoms Egyptian boys were routinely circumcised at between six and twelve years of age. A male circumcision scene, shown in disconcertingly graphic detail in the tomb of the Royal Architect Ankhmahor at Sakkara, gives some indication of the importance attached to this ceremony.[1] The young boy is held tightly from behind while a Ka priest stands in front of him wielding a knife and ordering his assistant to 'restrain him firmly and prevent him from fainting'. Herodotus remarks, rather disapprovingly, that this operation was performed for reasons of hygiene although the fact that it was conducted by a priest rather than a doctor suggests that it may have had more ritual than practical significance. The Egyptians themselves looked down on uncircumcised, and therefore uncivilized, foreigners. There is no direct evidence that circumcision or clitoridectomy was ever inflicted on girls and, even though societies rarely make reference to this intimate female rite of passage, the fact that no circumcised female mummy has been recovered tends to confirm its absence. Contrary to popular belief there is absolutely no proof that the drastic pharaonic excision, or Sudanese circumcision as it is known in modern Egypt, actually originated in pharaonic Egypt.[2] It should, however, be remembered that those mummified bodies which have been examined belonged to upper-class women; whether or not the lower classes ever circumcised their daughters is unclear. Strabo, quoted above, certainly believed that they did, although he does not elaborate on his statement so we do not know whether he is referring to the removal of part or all of the external genitalia or to a less damaging token cut made in the clitoris. Nor does he indicate whether he was reporting a rumour or known fact.

Recipe for a tongue that is ill: bran, milk and goose grease are used to rinse the mouth.

Ebers Medical Papyrus

Oral hygiene did not play an obvious part in the daily toilette, although the Roman historian Pliny informs us that the Egyptians cleaned their teeth with a special toothpaste made from plant roots. In the absence of specific tooth brushes this dentifrice was applied by means of a chewed twig or stiff reed. For that extra feeling of confidence, women were specifically recommended to sweeten their breath by chewing little balls of myrrh, frankincense, rush-nut and cinnamon; advice presumably prompted by the high level of garlic, onion and radish consumption.

The unfortunate Egyptians were prone to a great deal of tooth disease as the fine desert sand which still seems to find its way into every corner of the Egyptian home became inadvertently included in their daily food and had a harsh abrasive effect on the teeth. Large and painful abscesses were very common and most Egyptians suffered from toothache at some time in their lives. The long-lived King Ramesses II, for example, died with a mouthful of badly worn teeth with exposed pulp chambers; these had clearly caused him a great deal of discomfort during his final years. In contrast, dental caries was far less of a problem than it is in modern Egypt as there was a shortage of sugary products; both refined sugar and sugar cane were unknown. It was the upper classes, the consumers of large amounts of date- and honey-sweetened cake, who were most likely to suffer from tooth decay. Loose teeth, however, seem to have been common throughout the entire population, and indeed almost half the dental references included in the medical papyri attempt to remedy the problem of missing teeth. Although there is some evidence for the construction of ingenious dental bridges using thin gold or silver wire and spare human teeth – presumably collected from the embalming house – the Egyptian dentists did not attempt to make a full set of false teeth.

*

Both men and women routinely completed their ablutions by massaging moisturizing oils into their skin. These reduced the ageing effect of the hot and dusty climate and the drying 'soap' whose main ingredient, natron, was the principal dehydrating agent used to desiccate dead bodies during mummification. The use of oils was believed to enhance skin condition and prevent wrinkles while partially concealing the after-effects of disfiguring diseases such as smallpox and leprosy; the *Ebers Medical Papyrus* certainly promoted their use with all the enthusiasm of a modern advertising campaign:

To remove facial wrinkles: frankincense gum, wax, fresh balanites oil and rush-nut should be finely ground and applied to the face every day. Make it and you will see!

While the lower classes had to be content with using simple castor or linseed oil, the upper echelons of society imported luxuriously scented unguents from the east; these had the added benefit of leaving the smooth body sensuously and expensively perfumed. As with many modern moisturizing creams, however, it would appear that the difference in actual effect would have been minimal, the difference in price and perceived value extreme, and it seems highly likely that the scent was added as much to mask potentially rancid smells as to delight the purchaser. No fashionable Egyptian man or woman would be caught dead without his or her preferred skin lotion, and Tutankhamen's funerary equipment included a large jar of his favourite brand. Similar oil-based unguents were used by pregnant women wishing to prevent the formation of disfiguring stretch-marks across the stomach, and these oils were often stored in special jars shaped like a naked pregnant woman holding her swollen stomach. That these luxury cosmetics could be very costly indulgences is beyond doubt. Indeed, Diodorus Siculus believed that the taxes paid by the fishermen licensed to fish in Lake Moeris, a huge annual income, was allotted to the queens of

Egypt to enable them to purchase their cosmetics, perfumes and other toiletry items.

Place myrrh upon your head, dress yourself in the finest of linens.

New Kingdom poem

A wide variety of perfumed conditioning oils was also available for rubbing into the scalp after shampooing, again with the aim of protecting the hair from the harsh climate. During the New Kingdom this practice was extended to include the fashion, rather bizarre to modern eyes, of wearing perfumed lumps or cosmetic cones of fat balanced precariously on the head during social occasions. These unusual party hats were made from tallow impregnated with myrrh, and were designed to melt slowly as the festivities progressed, releasing their perfume and allowing a thin and presumably refreshing trickle of wax to run down the hair and face. As the heat of the party made the fat melt away it was topped up by a servant. The cones appear to have been provided by the host for both his guests and the attendant servants, and tomb scenes indicate that no dinner party would have been complete without them. They are generally illustrated as white lumps with brown streaks running down the sides, while brown stains shown on the shoulders of white clothing may well represent the greasy drips. No actual examples of perfume cones have survived, and it is now difficult to determine how literally these party scenes should be interpreted.

My heart thought of my love of you when only half my hair was dressed. I came running to find you and neglected my appearance. Now, if you will wait while I plait my hair, I shall be ready for you in a moment.

New Kingdom love song

Many societies exert moral pressure to control the way in which both men and women are allowed to display their hair. Without any clear legal obligation both sexes are expected to observe the conventions of their time, which may for example decree that women must have long hair, that men must not have long hair, or that hair should not be revealed at all by either sex. Deviation from this norm may be seen as in some way threatening to society as a whole. If this view seems extreme it should be remembered that less than a hundred years ago in Europe 'bobbed' hair was regarded by many as a sign of extreme female depravity, while long hair in men is still regarded by some as a sinister modern development indicating that the wearer has chosen to opt out of conventional society. Within the conventions imposed by the community a woman's chosen hairstyle indicates to others the group to which that woman either belongs or aspires to belong. The punk and the hippy provide extreme modern examples: a tightly permed blue rinse or cascade of artificially golden curls send out equally clear social signals. It is unfortunate that, as with so many aspects of Egyptian life, our knowledge of female coiffure is confined to the more wealthy members of society and their servants, portrayed under idealized conditions. The effect of changing fashions on the village woman is simply not known.

We do, however, have some clear examples of rank or occupation influencing female hairstyles. Even when short hair was in vogue the most attractive dancers and acrobats wore their hair long, occasionally plaiting weights into the ends so that it gave a good swing when dancing. Pre-pubescent upper-class boys and girls are frequently represented sporting the 'sidelock of youth': an almost entirely bald pate with a single long thick curl worn on the side of the head. Hair charms were suspended from the base of the sidelock and brought good luck and protection to their wearer. Unkempt long hair was generally restricted to men and women in mourning, while women in labour are occasionally portrayed with a dishevelled-looking archaic hairstyle intended to ward off evil spirits by sympathetic magic; as the woman loosens her normally neat hair she also symbolically loosens the baby ready for birth.

To cause the hair to fall out: burnt leaf of lotus is put in oil and applied to the head of a hated woman.

Ebers Medical Papyrus

Women did not necessarily regard their natural hair as their crowning glory. Indeed, throughout pharaonic times it was common practice for upper-class men and women to wear their natural hair closely cropped or even shaved as a practical response to the hot climate and a means of avoiding uncomfortable tangles. Fashionable wigs, which protected the near-bald heads against the fierce Egyptian sun, were worn for aesthetic reasons on more formal occasions, and false hair developed into an important commercial industry. Most wealthy people owned at least one hairpiece, and the convenience of a convention which combined cool comfort during the day with elegance at night must have been much appreciated. The best and most natural looking of the wigs were made of over 120,000 human hairs woven into a mesh and glued into place with a mixture of melted beeswax and resin.[3] The worst and least natural were made entirely of coarse red date-palm fibre and must have presented a startlingly bizarre appearance.

Recipe to make the hair of a bald person grow: fat of lion, fat of hippopotamus, fat of crocodile, fat of cat, fat of serpent, and fat of ibex are mixed together and the head of the bald person is anointed therewith.

Ebers Medical Papyrus

Despite the evident popularity of shaved heads, mummies of all periods have been recovered with well-dressed heads of natural hair, and the surviving romantic poetry makes it clear that clean and shining tresses were much admired. Indeed, the mummified body of Queen Ahmose Nefertari, who died at an advanced age having lost most of her natural hair, wore a wig of human braids thoughtfully supplied by the embalmers who presumably wished

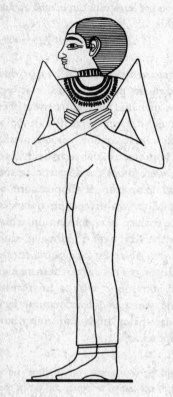

*Fig. 24   Old Kingdom queen
wearing a striking red and yellow wig
and perhaps the earliest shoulder-pads
in the world*

to save her from the indignity of being reborn bald in the Afterlife. The medical papyri supplied useful recipes to enhance the appearance by curing such social embarrassments as unwanted baldness and persistent dandruff, while helpfully suggesting that the fat of black snakes, the blood of black oxen or even a repulsive-sounding compound made from the pulverized genitals of a bitch could usefully be employed to disguise unsightly grey hair. A slightly more acceptable and presumably less smelly means of changing hair colour was the use of henna paste which could also be used to decorate finger and toe nails. Henna is still used as a skin and hair dye in modern Egyptian villages.

Women's hair and wig styles changed far more frequently than either clothing or jewellery fashions, graduating from the rather severe cuts worn throughout the Old Kingdom to the longer and more elaborate styles favoured at the zenith of the Egyptian Empire. It is tempting, although perhaps over-simplistic, to see a direct correlation between the wealth of Egypt and the time and money made available for hair and wig care. During the Old Kingdom the most trendy women sported a short, straight bob such as is frequently seen today. This style gradually became longer, until by the Middle Kingdom shoulder-length hair and heavier wigs had been adopted by all classes. The longer hair was either worn loose or dressed in the so-called 'tripartite style', with the hair at the back of the head hanging free and bunches of hair on either side of the head pulled forward to frame the face and expose the ears. This tripartite style was originally confined to females of low status in society, principally the unmarried, but its use gradually spread to higher-ranking married women. Indeed, a more intricate version, the 'Hathor-style', which involved binding the two sections of front hair with ribbons and wrapping them round a flat disk-shaped weight, became hugely popular and was the firm favourite of most 18th Dynasty queens. In contrast the Amarna royal ladies, who liked to do most things differently, favoured the rather more masculine 'Nubian'-style wig based on the short and curly haircuts of Nubian soldiers. As the New Kingdom progressed hair and wig fashions became less standardized, growing generally longer and far more exaggerated, perhaps due to the increasing foreign influence being felt throughout Egypt at this time. A 19th Dynasty vogue for fuller wigs and a corresponding increase in the use of supplementary hairpieces to pad out both wigs and natural hair led to the abandonment of the tripartite hairstyle, and the formerly simple strand wigs were rejected in favour of wild-looking wigs of curls and thin plaits ending in fringes.

The barber labours until dusk. He travels to a town, sets himself up in his corner, and moves from street to street looking for a customer. He strains his arms to fill his stomach, like the bee that eats as it works.

Middle Kingdom *Satire of the Trades*

Wealthy ladies did not dress their own hair or wigs, but were assisted either by a female servant or by a daughter, mother or friend.[4] There was no ancient Egyptian equivalent of the beauty salon, and barbers were either attached to the staff of the larger establishments or worked as itinerant tradesmen servicing the

Fig. 25   Girl wearing a fish ornament in her hair

less affluent members of society. Inscriptions dating to the Old Kingdom show that these professional hairdressers, who were invariably male, were regarded as people of some importance with a possible ritual function; the association of human hair with witchcraft and superstition has been a frequent one throughout the world and hair-cutting often forms an important part in rituals or rites of passage. Indeed, the cutting of male hair has even been regarded by some psychoanalysts as a symbolic form of castration, as genitals are apparently at a subconscious level invariably associated with hair. The biblical tale of Samson and Delilah, which tells how Samson lost all his male strength as a direct result of his unscheduled haircut, appears to lend some support to this rather ingenious theory. However, by the Middle Kingdom female hair and wig-dressers had become far more common and any ritual significance in their work had been lost. The hairdressers are usually depicted standing behind their mistress, who keeps a close eye on the proceedings through a polished metal mirror which she holds in her hand. A variety of specialized equipment was available to those wishing to enhance the hair, and tombs have yielded curlers, hairpins, and wooden and ivory combs all similar in design to their modern counterparts. Many women chose to weave fresh flowers into their newly dressed locks, while more formal ornaments – including diadems, circlets specifically intended for wear over wigs, hair-bands, hair-rings and hair-weights – provided the final touch to the elegant coiffure.

★

Western societies traditionally make a clear distinction between medicinal and beauty treatments, with health farms sitting uneasily on the fence between the two. An even firmer line is drawn between the many cosmetics used by women and those few considered socially acceptable for men, with cultural conditioning tempting us to view makeup as a rather trivial matter of purely feminine interest. The Egyptians approached this matter very differently, regarding their cosmetics as an important aid to health and enhanced good looks for both sexes, with magical and amuletic benefits providing an added bonus. A well-stocked cosmetic chest was a prized masculine possession at a time when a well made-up face conveyed a message of high social status rather than effeminacy.

I wish to paint my eyes, so if I see you my eyes will sparkle.

New Kingdom love poem

Both men and women adopted a dramatic 1960s-style makeup with heavy emphasis on the eyes. Kohl, or eye-paint, was used to enhance beauty while providing healing and protective powers against the fierce Egyptian sun. The paint was applied to the upper and lower lids, outlining, defining and exaggerating the eyes and lengthening the eyebrows; frequently a bold line drawn from the outer corner of the eye to the hairline completed the look. Even allowing for artistic exaggeration in tomb paintings and statuary, it is clear that the 'natural' look was not much admired. Two pigment colours were widely available from the Predynastic period onwards. Green (malachite) was by far the most popular colour during the earlier Dynastic period, but dark grey (galena) gained in popularity during the New Kingdom. The most fashionable ladies used the two colours in combination, with green applied to the brows and corners of the eyes, grey to the rims and lashes. Black kohl is still widely used as an eyeliner by Egyptian peasant women, as it is believed that it will decrease reflected glare from the sun and reduce the chances of eye infections. Other cosmetics were far less common, although some women used a powdered rouge made from red ochre. There is little indication of the use of lip paint by either sex, although the *Turin Erotic Papyrus* does show a prostitute painting her lips with the aid of a modern-looking lip brush and a mirror.

More permanent body decoration was demanded by those women – the professional dancers, acrobats and prostitutes – who relied on displaying the charms of their bodies to earn a living. This could be achieved by the tattooing of intricate patterns on the arms, torso and legs. Tattooing is a traditional Egyptian form of female adornment whose popularity has lasted from the Dynastic era until the present day, as Miss Blackman recorded:

The implement used in tattooing consists of seven needles fixed into a short stick, which is bound round the end and then plastered over to keep the needles firmly in position. Sometimes smaller needles, and only five in number, are used for tattooing children. Lamp black is the pigment employed, and this is usually mixed with oil, though some people say that water is used.

Unfortunately, tattooing is a practice which leaves little tangible trace, so that although female figurines with incised and painted body decorations have been found in Dynastic graves of all periods it is not until the Middle Kingdom that the mummified bodies of ladies tentatively identified as royal concubines confirm its use.[5] The tradition appears to have died out by the New Kingdom, although some New Kingdom entertainers and servant girls displayed a small picture of the dwarf god Bes high on each thigh as a good luck symbol and a less than subtle means of drawing attention to their hidden charms. It has been suggested that this particular tattoo may have been the trade mark of a prostitute, but it seems equally likely to have been worn as an amuletic guard against the dangers of childbirth, or even as a protection against sexually transmitted diseases. Tattooing seems to have been confined to lower-class women and to men, who were tattooed less extensively.

★

Although artistic conventions decreed that women should be depicted as fashionably gaunt, there is very little direct evidence to show whether Egyptian women struggled to lose weight. The loose untailored clothing could have been worn by women of any size, and we do not have the equivalent of ancient diet sheets or exercise routines, while the medical papyri remain tantalizingly silent in this area. Comparison with modern rural Egypt suggests that although women may have been expected to be thinner than men the almost skeletal appearance currently admired in western societies would not have been appreciated. It seems that only in societies where famine is unthinkable is this female body type greatly admired. Naked female figurines recovered from tombs generally have gently rounded figures with relatively wide hips and slightly prominent buttocks. These figurines were included among grave goods for men, women and children, not as models of individual women but as generalized fertility symbols representing the whole process of Egyptian family life including reproduction and child-rearing. They suggest that, perhaps above all, a good child-bearing physique would be the most widely admired female physical type.

Most Egyptians were very comfortable with their own bodies and were not offended by nudity in others. Nakedness in its correct place was not regarded as in any way shocking or indecent, and tomb owners showed no false modesty when depicting scenes of daily life which included fishermen or other workers whose occupations would have made the wearing of clothes inappropriate to their task. Nakedness could be used by the artists as a means of indicating low social status, and children were often illustrated nude although we know that they were normally dressed in clothes similar to those worn by their parents. During the New Kingdom female nudity, or semi-nudity, became common for those lower-status women whose employment was in some way related to their physical charms. Dancers and acrobats, for example, were depicted wearing either an eye-catching girdle or a practical short flared skirt, sometimes with narrow straps crossed over the breasts for purely decorative purposes. Servant girls at work wore a simple kilt with no blouse, and were frequently portrayed as either entirely naked but for ornamental bead collars and belts, or dressed in flimsy see-through garments. The trend for New Kingdom female nudity even extended to the gods, with a few naked foreign deities such as the Asian war-goddess Astarte developing cult followings in Egypt at this time.

It would, however, have been both inaccurate and inappropriate for the upper classes to be shown without their clothes. All indications are that those of high rank delighted in showing off their finery, and viewed elegant garments as a means of underlining their social position. It was only during the short-lived Amarna period, when all the old conventions were turned on their heads, that royal ladies allowed themselves to be depicted either naked or wearing casually unfastened robes which left nothing to the imagination. Whether nudity was, in fact, common in private life, 'off camera', we have no means of telling, although it seems reasonable to assume that nudity would not have been popular during the cool winters or in the chilly early mornings.

My lover, it is pleasant to go to the pond and bathe myself while you watch me. In this way I may let you see my beauty revealed through my tunic of finest white linen, when it becomes wet and clinging . . . I go down with you into the water and come out again to you with a red fish which lies beautiful on my fingers . . . Come and look at me.

New Kingdom love song

Clothes serve the basic function of protecting the naked body from the elements while preserving modesty by concealing those parts which society prefers to leave to the imagination. However, a quick glance down any high street shows that clothing, or more particularly fashion, also sends out clear social signals indicating such diversities as financial status, aspiration, occupation and even religious persuasion. The businesswoman, the student and the young mother may be wearing variants of the same shirt and skirt but differences in style and cut will be apparent to the most casual observer, while the individualistic punk dressed in torn plastic and bondage chains is wearing a uniform as indicative of group membership as the habit worn by the nun. Just as a modern Egyptian peasant woman can glean many accurate facts about a stranger by observing and analysing subtle variations in dress-style which pass unnoticed by the uninitiated western observer, so we can assume that the dress of the ancient Egyptian woman conveyed a wealth of information to her contemporaries. Unfortunately, without the cultural key necessary to decode the message we are unlikely to extract anything more than the most obvious inferences from any study of Egyptian fashion.

At first sight the Egyptians have provided us with a great deal of evidence for a study of their clothing.[6] We have a little written information, a few surviving garments and numerous statues, engravings and paintings which combine to provide an illustrated catalogue which may be used to chronicle changing styles throughout the dynasties. However, there are certain problems inherent in relying on this representational type of evidence. By their very nature the illustrations tend to depict the upper echelons of society recorded under atypical conditions. Just as today people prefer to be photographed in their best clothes, we must assume that those affluent enough to be recorded for posterity would choose to display their most elaborate or formal costumes. Clothing shown in depictions of the Afterlife may have had an additional ritual significance which is now lost to us. Given the strict conventions of Egyptian art it is highly likely that the artist chose to depict traditional or stylized garments indicative of femininity rather than those actually worn, and in many cases the subtle nuances of female dress may simply not have been recognized by the male artist who would have painted the majority of his portraits from memory or from a pattern book rather than from a live model. In fact, basing a discussion of garments solely on the types of evidence described above may well be analogous to basing a discussion of contemporary western styles on a collection of formal wedding portraits and ultra-fashion haute couture photographs taken from the pages of *Vogue*. Nevertheless, and despite inaccuracies in depiction, the clear message which reaches across the centuries from the tomb walls is the sheer delight with which both women and men pose to display their finery. Certainly clothes were important to the Egyptians.

Linen was the material most often used in dressmaking. Cotton and silk were both unknown in Egypt before the Graeco-Roman period and, despite the farming of large flocks of sheep, woollen clothes were apparently rare in pre-Roman times. Herodotus, who was the first to mention this aversion to wool, supposed that it must have been a ritual avoidance as 'nothing woollen is taken into their temples or buried with them as their religion forbids it'; his theory was echoed by Plutarch, who noted that 'priests, because they revere sheep, abstain from using its wool as well as its flesh'. However, it seems far more likely that woollen garments were relatively uncommon because of a scarcity of good-quality wool; the rather bald Egyptian sheep which were bred principally for their milk and meat were evidently unsuitable for full-scale wool production. Archaeological evidence is now beginning to indicate that Herodotus may have been writing under a mis-apprehension, and that although people preferred to be illustrated in their traditional linen garments, woollen clothes might have been a great deal more common than has been supposed. There is certainly no contemporary evidence for a strict taboo against wearing wool and, while linen is certainly an appropriate material for clothing in a hot climate, being both lightweight and comfort-able to the touch, the warmth of a woollen shawl or cloak would have been much appreciated on a chilly winter's evening.

Although it is relatively easy to dye woollen cloth successfully, linen requires a specialized two-stage dyeing process to make the new colour permanent. For a long time it was thought that, despite their obvious skills at the loom, the Egyptians had never developed the technology necessary to dye their linen. The few women who were depicted wearing coloured frocks with bright blue, red and yellow patterning were therefore interpreted either as foreigners or as servant girls dressed in imported foreign clothes. Egyptologists are now beginning to question whether, just as the popularity of woollen garments may have been seriously understated, the availability of dyed cloth has also been underestimated; certainly several dolls with gaily painted dresses have been recovered from working-class graves, indicating that multi-coloured and cheerfully patterned frocks were far more common than has ever been supposed. Whether these were dyed linen dresses or dyed woollen dresses is now not clear. White or off-white always remained the standard colour for all formal clothing, and the garments illustrated in tomb paintings are invariably bright white.

As colourful garments were something of a rarity the Egyptians developed the art of elaborate folding and pleating to decorate their cloth. This pleating grew finer and even more intricate as the standard of cloth production improved, and was accompanied by a parallel change in fashion from tight-fitting to more free-flowing dresses, designed to show off the expensive material to its best advantage. By the middle of the New Kingdom the style of the pleating was changing so rapidly that statues may now be dated with a considerable degree of accuracy by a consideration of the form of the pleats in the garments. We still have no idea how the ancient clothmakers managed to fix their pleats so firmly into the material that some still survive today, but it has been suggested that the long ribbed and grooved boards which have been recovered from several tombs may have played a part in the process. Some form of starch may have been applied to stiffen the material and hold the pleats in place.

Enough complete female outer garments have survived to confirm that throughout the Dynastic age the majority of women dressed in rather plain and crudely made variants of the long nightshirt-like djellaba which is still worn by the modern Egyptian peasant.[7] These simple clothes lack the style and elegance of the more extreme fashions included in the formal tomb scenes but they would have been easy to make and both practical and comfortable to wear while working. Several of the surviving dresses have sleeves, a refinement which is rarely depicted in paintings before the New Kingdom but which would have provided a welcome protection against the ever-present dust and mosquitoes. Detachable sleeves, designed to be removed in warm weather, were a clever way of making one dress comfortable all year round.

Sandals – soles of woven reeds or leather bound on to the foot by a thong – were worn throughout the Dynastic period with more elaborate leather slippers becoming fashionable in the 19th Dynasty. The basic sandals often formed a part of the workman's standard wage, even though artistic representations of daily life suggest that most activities were carried out barefoot as they are in many parts of the world today. Shoes were automatically discarded as a mark of courtesy on entering a house, and were removed in the presence of a socially superior person as a sign of respect. The honorary title of 'Sandal-bearer to the Pharaoh' was one of the highest regard, and it is highly unlikely that the holder of such a prestigious position actually had to do much ignominious shoe-carrying.

Simple shawls, again similar to those in modern use, were thrown over the dresses during the cool Egyptian nights. The 18th Dynasty tomb provisions of the Architect Kha and his wife Merit included not only shawls but also Merit's elaborately fringed dressing gown, neatly folded in its storage basket which also held her comb and a wig curler. Several ostraca give comparative prices for these garments, and we know that during the New Kingdom the value of one simple djellaba-like shift dress made of plain cloth was, at five *deben*, relatively expensive; it is difficult to translate this value into exact modern monetary terms, but the fact that a goat was valued at two *deben* at this time gives an indication of the value attached to cloth. It is clear that clothing was priced according to the quality and quantity of the material used, as a shawl made of good quality cloth was a luxury item valued as high as fifteen *deben*.

Not surprisingly, thefts of basic clothing were relatively common. Theoretically these petty crimes could be brought before the court, but it was more usual for the victim to consult the local oracle who could be relied upon to solve the mystery and name the culprit with the minimum of official fuss. The oracle, in the form of a statue of the local god, was placed on a litter which was in turn supported on the shoulders of qualified lay-priests. He or she was able to indicate the answers to direct yes or no questions by forcing the litter-bearers to move either forwards or backwards at the appropriate moment. In more complicated cases, where there was a range of suspects, the plaintiff recited a list of names and the god again moved to indicate the guilty party. Although many local deities provided an efficient oracle service, the deified Amenhotep I at Deir el-Medina was widely recognized to be one of the best.[8] One ostracon from this site tells how the draughtsman Kaha decided to consult the oracle when some of his clothing was stolen. Kaha read out a list of the suspect households, and the god twice gave a sign when the household of Scribe Imenhet was mentioned. Eventually the field of suspects was narrowed down even further, and the unnamed daughter of Imenhet was identified as the thief. There is no record of any subsequent punishment being meted out, but it would appear that adverse public opinion combined with a very real fear of divine retribution would force the guilty party to return the stolen goods promptly to their rightful owner.

His majesty said 'Indeed, I shall go boating! Bring me twenty oars of gold-plated ebony with handles of sandalwood plated with electrum. Bring me twenty women with the shapeliest bodies, breasts and braids, and who have not yet given birth. Also bring me twenty nets and give the nets to the women in place of their clothes!' All was done as his majesty commanded. They rowed up and down and his majesty's heart was happy seeing them row.

Part of the Middle Kingdom *Westcar Papyrus*

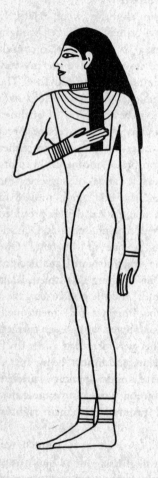

Fig. 26   Old Kingdom sheath dress

The dresses worn by the more up-to-date members of society were also very simple in design, but far less practical for everyday wear. Fashions naturally varied, but the basic garment was always a single length of cloth which was wrapped or draped sarong-style around the body and either tied in place with a belt or held with simple sewn shoulder straps. Such garments become almost unrecognizable when off the body, and examples recovered from tombs have frequently been misclassified as sheets. During the Old Kingdom the stylish woman wore a long, smoothly fitting white sheath extending from her breast to her shin. It was made from a length of linen folded in half, hemmed and stitched into a basic tube shape, and was held in place by two broad shoulder straps. Tomb-scenes suggest that this basic dress was very tight-fitting and worn so

as to reveal the form of the
body beneath, although it is difficult to take such an impractical garment literally as even the
most fashion-conscious girl
would have found the need to
be sewn into her dress and her
subsequent inability to walk
somewhat irksome. Presum-
ably this represents yet another
artistic convention, designed to
stress the femininity of the
wearer whose passive role in
life is subtly emphasized by her
totally impractical clothing. As
an alternative to the stark white
garment, decorated shoulder
straps and horizontal panels of
geometric patterning could
either be woven or embroi-
dered on to the dress. Tabards
of beaded or pearl network
worn over the plain dress gave
an exciting patterned effect,
and the *Westcar Papyrus* quoted
above records jaded King
Sneferu's lecherous delight in

Fig. 27   New Kingdom fashion

watching his crew of nubile female rowers wearing the 'fishing
net' beaded dresses without the customary modesty garment.

This rather understated Old Kingdom elegance eventually
gave way to a more elaborate style of attire, and the New
Kingdom lady was able to select her dress from a much wider
and less conservative wardrobe, with highly pleated and fringed
garments providing suitable accompaniments to the more elaborate wig-styles also in vogue at this time. The standard garment

was a flowing sari-like dress made from one long length of pleated cloth which was draped around the body and shoulders and tied under the bust to give an Empire-line silhouette. Finely pleated sleeves covered the upper arms to the elbow. The old-fashioned sheath dress continued to be popular, but was now covered by a shorter and more diaphanous flowing robe.

> With her hair she throws lassoes at me,
> And with her eyes she catches me,
> With her necklace she entangles me,
> And brands me with her seal ring.
>   New Kingdom love poem

The plain white garments provided the perfect background for the colourful and varied jewellery which was popular with men, women and children of all classes from Predynastic times onwards. Vividly coloured mass-produced beads were used in the manufacture of cheap and cheerfully eye-catching costume jewellery while, at the other end of the financial scale, valuable metals and semi-precious stones were transformed by master-craftsmen into exquisite designer pieces which are true works of art. The jewellery worn by the royal family was exclusively produced by the workshops attached to the king's palace which, with all the resources of the royal court at their disposal, were able to develop advanced and intricate techniques such as *cloisonné*, granulation and filigree work. The less wealthy purchased their simple trinkets from local craftsmen or the itinerant jewellers who could always be found at the village market. Generally, whatever the standard of workmanship, the materials used in the jewellery were opaque. In contrast to our modern jewellery, it was the colour and brightness of the whole rather than the purity of individual components which created the desired dramatic effect.

The Egyptian craftsmen did not have access to the precious stones which play a major role in our modern jewellery. However, amethyst, carnelian and jasper could all be found within Egypt's boundaries, while turquoise was mined in the Sinai desert and deep blue lapis-lazuli was imported from as far away as Afghanistan. Gold occurs naturally in the Egyptian desert both as pure seams running through quartz rock and as alluvial deposits which need to be panned; both these sources were exploited throughout the Dynastic period. Pure silver, however, was always imported from elsewhere in the Mediterranean. Silver does occur as an impurity in the native Egyptian gold, but it is very difficult to separate the two metals.[9] Silver was consequently more highly prized than gold, and is less frequently encountered in jewellery. Neither metal would have been easy for ordinary members of the public to obtain, and it is obvious that there was a thriving black-market trade in illicit gold excavated from the richly-endowed royal burials by enterprising tomb robbers.

The Egyptians loved to display their finery during life, and confidently expected to continue displaying it after death. They regarded it as essential that they should be interred with suitably impressive jewellery, appropriate to both their sex and their status in society. Consequently, much of the Egyptian jewellery now housed in museums throughout the world comes from funerary contexts, often looted by modern tomb robbers or amateur egyptologists who gave little thought to the archaeological importance of their booty. Some of these pieces were obviously well-loved and well-worn by their owners, but much of the remaining jewellery was specifically manufactured for the grave. Several of these pieces are made out of tissue-thin metal and could not have been worn without tearing, while several of the broad collars are lacking the counterpoise weight necessary to allow the collar to lie correctly. In the Afterlife this symbolic jewellery would be made functional and would be worn by the deceased. There is no indication that this funerary jewellery was anything other than an imitation of the jewellery that was being worn on a daily basis by living Egyptians, and specific types of death-jewellery only suitable for wearing in the Afterlife are unknown, although there were specific protective amulets designed to be included in mummy wrappings.

We broke open the tombs to the West of the No and brought away the inner coffins which were in them. We stripped off the gold and the silver which was on them and stole it, and I divided it between myself and my confederates.

New Kingdom trial transcript

Theft from the royal tombs, often by the very workmen who had been employed in their construction, was a constant headache as it was impossible to keep the location of such major building works secret for any length of time. At Thebes, the site of the New Kingdom royal tombs, a special necropolis police force was responsible for guarding the royal tombs, reporting directly to the vizier, the pharaoh's second-in-command. However, several 20th Dynasty papyri which deal with the arrest and subsequent trial of gangs of tomb robbers and the fences who received the stolen property indicate that this police force was perhaps not as efficient as it might have been; indeed, some of the necropolis officials were clearly implicated in the crimes. Any observed irregularities in the necropolis were reported directly to either the vizier or the other high-ranking administrators. A commission was then established to investigate the violated tombs, draw up a list of suspects and conduct a trial. Those found guilty were referred to the pharaoh for punishment; the official penalty for tomb robbery was a nasty lingering death by impalement on a stake.

In the western world we regard our jewellery as primarily decorative, a means of expressing our individuality and perhaps displaying our financial worth. There are, of course, certain exceptions to this rule. Pieces such as a crucifix, a St Christopher medal or a horseshoe charm may be worn for both ornamental and religious or superstitious reasons, while a wedding band or engagement ring is expected to function as a decorative indication of social status. The Egyptians, who felt themselves to be constantly under siege from evil spirits, demons and all the hazards of their harsh natural world, expected their jewellery to combine an ornamental function with the important practical role of warding off evil, attributing an amuletic effect to almost all their pieces. The prophylactic features of certain motifs are not always clear to us today, but as with many aspects of Dynastic life it seems safe to state that no piece of Egyptian jewellery should be taken at its face value. To be fully effective all these charms had to be kept close to the skin; they were usually worn suspended on a thong tied around the neck.

The hidden amuletic effect of some pieces has been passed down to us, and we can tell that many charms were particularly appropriate to women. For example, the head of Bat, a fertility goddess who could help the childless to conceive, is shown on some of the earliest recovered amulets which date from the dawn of the Dynastic age. Fish ornaments, worn in the hair or suspended around the neck, were believed to protect young girls against drowning, while oyster shell amulets were believed to bring general good health to all women. The Udjat Eye of Horus, representing the eye that was knocked out by the evil Seth, became a symbol of light which would ward off evil; as such it was a popular amulet with both men and women. Less obvious now are the protective powers attributed to certain colours – notably green which signified life and birth – and certain types of stone. The wearer of a green turquoise necklace would probably have felt herself to be adequately protected against all harm.

The most popular and least expensive jewellery consisted of simple beads, shells and charms threaded on to linen or leather cords. These beads, usually made from glazed steatite, faience or glass, came in many different shapes and colours ready to be made into necklaces, bracelets, and anklets. Some beads were highly sophisticated; the beaded girdles which were worn for purely ornamental purposes by dancing girls often included cowrie beads designed to rattle in an enticing manner as the dance progressed. It may well be that these cowrie shells, which bear a passing resemblance to female genitalia, were intended to be symbolic of fertility. Such rattling girdles were by no means confined to those who needed to display their physical charms, and they have been recovered from the tombs of elegant and presumably highly respectable royal princesses. While most people had to be content with simple bead pendants and necklaces, elaborate broad collars made from several interlinked strands of faience beads passing through broad terminals were worn by the middle and upper classes, ranging from low-ranking officials to the Royal Family. The pectoral, a wide pendant of inlaid precious metal worn across the chest, was also confined to the more wealthy members of society, and was usually, but not always, worn by women.

Bracelets, bangles and anklets were popular ornaments for women of all classes from the Predynastic period onwards, with one of the most prominent early bracelet-wearers being Queen Hetepheres, the mother of the 4th Dynasty pyramid-builder King Cheops. Hetepheres' portrait shows her arms loaded down with jewellery, and she was buried with a box containing twenty inlaid silver bracelets intended for wear during the Afterlife. Anklets are notoriously difficult to differentiate from bracelets unless they are recovered still encircling the limb of a dead body, and even the Egyptians found it necessary to add the words 'for the feet' when labelling boxes of foot jewellery. It would appear that many archaeologists, perhaps unused to the idea of anklets, have also been confused by the similarity of these pieces, as items recovered from disturbed graves have frequently been misclassified. Anklets were originally exclusively female ornaments, but by the Middle Kingdom were being worn by both men and women of all classes. The most chic coordinated look was achieved by those who sported a wide decorated bracelet and a slightly thicker matching anklet.

Finger rings are rarely shown in either paintings or sculpture but they were worn by both sexes from the Predynastic period onwards, growing in popularity until, by the New Kingdom, faience rings were being mass produced and worn as fashionable costume jewellery. These rings were worn on any finger of either hand though scarab-seal rings, which were indicative of high social status and consequently confined to male bureaucrats, were by convention worn on the third finger of the left hand. In contrast, earrings were almost unknown until the New Kingdom when, influenced by their foreign neighbours, women of all ranks pierced their ears and enthusiastically purchased a wide variety of styles. Gold hoops and glass studs, very similar in design to those worn all over the world today, became very popular. Decorated faience ear plugs, comparatively large flat discs with a grooved edge designed to permanently stretch the earlobe far beyond its natural size, were also highly prized. As today, the expensive and well-made gold and jewelled earrings worn by the ladies of the court were reproduced in cheaper materials such as pottery or glass, and became within the reach of everyone's pocket. High-ranking men also wore earrings and Tutankhamen's mummy had pierced ears even though he was not wearing his earrings when he was mummified. Earrings for men were not simply a form of personal adornment; they represented a badge of faithful service to the king and were only worn by those who had also been awarded a ceremonial gold necklace for their loyal work. The pharaoh traditionally used expensive gifts of jewellery, the 'Gold of the Brave', as a means of expressing his approval to both his distinguished soldiers and his loyal civil servants, somewhat as medals and knighthoods are awarded today. The lucky recipients of these tokens of esteem frequently recorded the presentation ceremony on the walls of their tombs.

The importance of an Egyptian woman's jewellery is very difficult for us to assess. We can see that it had an ornamental function, can assume that it acted as an indication of the wealth and social status of the woman and her family, and know that many of the pieces also had a perceived protective power.

Whether the woman also regarded her jewels as an investment for her future is less clear. In many societies where women's ownership of property is limited, jewellery and gold ornaments, often given by the husband at the time of the marriage, are traditionally held to be the property of the woman herself and act as her hedge against hard times. This is the case in the modern Egyptian village where gold is given to a girl by her fiancé to seal their engagement. It is the weight of the gold rather than the craftsmanship of the pieces which is of importance in this instance. The system functions because the jewellery given is precious, and has a recognized high financial value which may be redeemed at a later date. In contrast, the situation in Dynastic Egypt, where a woman's right to a share of joint property was recognized both by convention and by the law, and where the majority of the jewellery which has been recovered is not of particularly high value, is not directly comparable. All indications are that the jewellery was simply valued as an indication of social status and as a means of expressing personal taste.

She who once lacked even a box now had furniture, while she who used to see her face in the water now owns a mirror.

Admonitions of the Middle Kingdom Scribe Ipuwer

Sadly, there was no way that the Egyptian lady could get a head-to-toe view of herself dressed in all her finery as full-length mirrors were unknown; indeed, the less affluent members of society had to be content with viewing their reflections in the River Nile. For those of greater means, a hand-held mirror of polished metal, appropriately named a 'see-face', was very useful for examining the features and perfecting the makeup. The majority of the mirrors which have been recovered are made from bronze and are heavily tarnished with pitted and corroded surfaces, but experimental repolishing has confirmed that they would indeed have provided a true or even a slightly magnified image. As with many other everyday objects in Egyptian life,

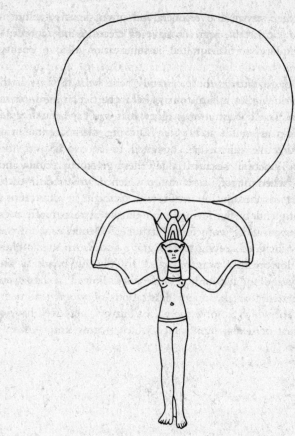

Fig. 28   Bronze mirror

mirrors came to be regarded as far more than a simple aid to achieving beauty. The oval mirror, with its inexplicable ability to show a virtual image and reflect and concentrate light, became associated with the religious concepts of life, creation and regeneration and, to a lesser extent, was also connected with the gods of the sun and the moon. The decorated handles of the mirrors reflected these mystical overtones, and often depicted either a papyrus or lotus stalk, representative of creation and reproduction, or the head of Hathor, the personification of love, beauty and fertility.

Even though mirrors must certainly have been used by both men and women they appear to have held a particular significance for women. Tomb illustrations suggest that wealthy ladies treated their mirrors as stylish accessories, carrying them around in a special protective mirror-bag designed to be worn over the shoulder. Tradition decreed that these women should be portrayed with mirrors carefully positioned underneath their chairs. Mirrors became an important element in illustrations representing childbirth, formed one of the standard offerings made by upper-class women to Hathor of Dendera, and were commonly included among female grave goods. All this implies that the mirror itself was regarded by the Egyptians as an obvious symbol of femininity or fertility. Indeed, it has even been suggested that the many illustrations of women at their toilette, all of which involve the use of mirrors, may well have a hidden ritual or sexual significance which is now unfortunately lost to us.

6

The Royal Harem

Beware of the woman who is a stranger in your town. Do not stare at her as she goes by, and avoid sexual intercourse with her. Such a woman, away from her husband, is like deep water whose depth is unknown.

Prudent advice from the New Kingdom Scribe Any

The harem is a concept largely unknown in both ancient and modern western culture. However, the image of the exotic Turkish-style seraglio, a secluded and closely guarded pleasure-palace filled with scantily dressed concubines idling away their days in languid preparation for their sultan's command, has become an integral part of our western fascination with the mysterious east, a fascination which stretches from the temptingly decadent orientalist paintings of the nineteenth century along the *Road to Morocco* and beyond. Most inappropriately, it is this vision of a haven of oriental hedonism and secret sensual delights which has heavily influenced our interpretation of the evidence for and against the role of the harem in Egyptian society.

Early excavators fully expected to find Ottoman-style harems in Egypt and so find them they did, ruthlessly classifying almost all single and otherwise unexplained females as either concubines or courtesans in need of male protection. On this shaky basis of dubious identifications and outright guesswork the concept of the wildly polygamous Egyptian society grew to become firmly entrenched in the public imagination, influencing the interpretation of new archaeological finds. It is only in the past few years that egyptologists, aided by new archaeological, linguistic and

anthropological research, have come to realize that their understanding has been seriously warped by these preconceived ideas
and ingrained assumptions. We now know that there was no
direct Egyptian equivalent of the traditional seraglio described
above and no widespread tradition of either polygamy or
concubinage; the royal harem of the pharaohs certainly did exist,
but as a very different place to the high-class brothel of our
imagination.

If you wish to retain the friendship of the household which you enter
either as a master, a brother or a friend, whatever you do, beware of
approaching the women.

                                        Old Kingdom scribal advice

Although the overwhelming majority of Egyptian men
remained monogamous, officially restricting themselves to one
wife at a time, all householders could find themselves in the
position of providing a home for a varied assortment of unmarried or widowed sisters, daughters, aunts, mothers-in-law and
mothers. Consequently, the private women's quarters of any
sizeable household or palace could reasonably be classified as a
harem, the term being used in its modern sense to refer to either
the group of ladies or to their accommodation without any
necessary implication of sexual bondage. The king, in his role as
head of the royal family, had the duty of supporting a relatively
large group of queens, princesses and concubines together with
their numerous children, nurses and personal attendants. This
group of women constituted the royal harem.

Unfortunately, we do not know how the Egyptians themselves
referred to these households of women. During the Old and
Middle Kingdoms the term *ipet nesut* was used to describe a
vague but obviously female-based royal institution. This term is
now conventionally translated as 'Harem of the King', although
the exact meaning of *ipet* is by no means certain and it may well
prove equally valid to interpret the *ipet nesut* as the 'Royal

Women's Quarters', the 'Royal Apartments' or even the 'Royal Granary' or the 'Royal Accounts Office'.[1] Following the traditional translation, various male officials have been identified as 'Overseer of the Harem'; as this identification rests solely on the interpretation of the word *ipet*, it may be incorrect. In a similar fashion, the ladies of the royal court who bore vague and non-explicit titles such as 'Royal Ornament' or 'Sole Royal Ornament' have conventionally been interpreted as royal concubines. However, this is a translation which again reflects the preoccupations of the early egyptologists; it is now clear that the 'Sole Royal Ornaments' were eminently respectable First Intermediate Period ladies who were often also priestesses of Hathor, while the more general title of 'Royal Ornament' was used to describe the ladies-in-waiting attached to the 13th Dynasty court.

The earliest direct evidence for an entourage of women 'belonging' to the monarch is provided by the subsidiary burials which are associated with the royal tombs of the Archaic Period 1st Dynasty at Abydos. These graves were allocated to men and women who had been closely attached to the king in a personal and subservient capacity, rather than to high-ranking court officials and ministers. They therefore include servants and minor mortuary priests, together with dwarfs, favourite dogs and, of course, favourite women.[2] The number of subsidiary burials accompanying each monarch varied but was invariably large; for example, the burial-complex of King Djer included the graves of over three hundred associated retainers. Ninety-seven private stelae have survived from Djer's secondary burials, and it is striking that seventy-six (78 per cent) of these graves were occupied by women. Many of these ladies had been interred with high-quality grave-goods suggesting that they had been people of some importance in court circles; it is by no means a foregone conclusion that they were all royal concubines.

Unfortunately, most of the subsidiary burials have been badly plundered and their human remains dispersed, so that in many cases it is now only the names and rather vague titles carved on the surviving gravestones which give an indication of the sex of the interred. We therefore have no scientific evidence to suggest how the occupants of these graves met their end. It may be that as the king made detailed preparations for his own death he also made provision for his loyal retainers, allocating plots of land for their subsidiary graves and thereby ensuring that, at the end of their natural lives, they could be interred in the shadow of their master's far more impressive tomb. Alternatively, it must be considered at least possible that the graves were dug for servants who were either killed or forced to commit suicide following the death of their master. Professor Emery, the excavator of the subsidiary graves around the Sakkara burial associated with Queen Meryt-Neith, had the opportunity of observing the position of some of the human remains as the graves were opened, and he remarked that:

No trace of violence was noted on the anatomical remains, and the position of the skeletons in no case suggested any movement after burial. It would therefore appear probable that when these people were buried they were already dead and there is no evidence of their having been buried alive. The absence of any marks of violence suggests that they were killed by poison prior to burial.[3]

The harsh tradition of automatically sacrificing loyal retainers and even wives following the natural death of their master or husband is one which is occasionally found in strongly feudal and patriarchal societies both ancient and modern. Indeed, the now illegal Indian custom of suttee, which requires a widow to throw herself on to her husband's blazing funeral pyre, is still surreptitiously practised in remote parts of rural India today. The most relevant contemporary parallel to the archaic Egyptian burials comes from Mesopotamia. The Sumerian Royal Cemetery of Ur has been dated to approximately 2650 BC. Here, both kings and queens shared magnificent tombs with their personal attendants and a wealth of treasure, while the associated burials included a mass grave, now known as the Great Death Pit, which yielded the bodies of six men and sixty-eight elegantly dressed women. All these courtiers had apparently entered their grave willingly, taking poison to the accompaniment of music provided by the musicians whose fingers were still resting on their harp strings four thousand years later. The Sumerian Royal family, like the Egyptian, enjoyed semi-divine status and was perceived as the mortal parallel to the heavenly gods. It would appear that their servants and attendants were happy enough to exchange a certain earthly existence for the chance to continue to serve their gods in the next world.[4]

Although it is possible that either voluntary or involuntary human sacrifices were made during the Archaic Period, there is absolutely no evidence to suggest that this wasteful tradition extended into the Old Kingdom. However, the Old Kingdom monarchs did continue the custom of maintaining a relatively large group of women attached to the court, and the more important of these women, the principal wives, daughters and mothers of kings, were eventually buried in the subsidiary tombs constructed around the royal pyramids. Herodotus believed, incorrectly, that at least one Old Kingdom princess had earned the wealth to build her own pyramid:

The wickedness of King Cheops reached such a pitch that, when he had spent all his treasures and wanted more, he sent his daughter to the brothels with orders to earn a certain sum for him – how much, I don't know. She earned the money, but at the same time she asked each of her clients to give her one stone as a contribution towards building a monument which would perpetuate her own memory. With these stones she eventually built the pyramid which stands in the middle of the three which are in front of the great pyramid.

More direct evidence for the existence of the Middle Kingdom royal harem comes from *Papyrus Boulaq 18*, a day-book which

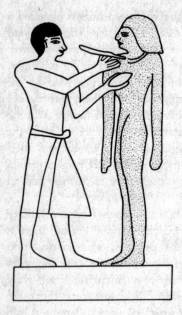

Fig. 29   Sculptor working on a statue of Queen Meresankh

lists all the business undertaken by the 13th Dynasty court at Thebes and so provides us with details of the composition of the immediate royal household at that time. Thanks to this document we know that the king's personal entourage was made up of eight to thirteen male court officials plus the royal family (one queen, one prince, three king's daughters and nine king's sisters) together with the 'house of nurses': nineteen nurses and associated groups of children. All these high-ranking ladies were crammed together in rather basic accommodation within the royal residence, generally occupying a stark suite of rooms built around a courtyard close to the king's private quarters. This lack of ornate or richly decorated apartments was typical of all Egyptian palaces. Throughout the Dynastic age it was customary for the court to move around the country on long tours of inspection and, consequently, the royal palaces were not necessarily designed for permanent occupation. Instead, they were built to be used as short-stay rest houses and the fact that most were named 'Mooring Place of Pharaoh' accurately reflects their rather sporadic occupation. Only the New Kingdom palace at Amarna seems to have been intended for a more settled family life.

By the beginning of the New Kingdom the royal harem had expanded to encompass a far wider range of women, including

numerous concubines and secondary wives of foreign origin.
Polygamous royal marriages had always been acceptable in Egypt
but during the New Kingdom, perhaps due to greater foreign
influence, there was a clear increase in the number of royal
brides, with a corresponding increase in the number of royal
children. The long-lived King Ramesses II, who died when over
ninety years old, was perhaps unusually well-blessed; he proudly
claimed to have fathered at least seventy-nine sons and fifty-nine
daughters by various women – all of these would have spent at
least their earlier years within the crowded harem. At this time
the phrase *per khenret* was used to denote a community of
women; *per* clearly means house, but *khenret*, which is generally
translated as harem, is highly similar to the words used to mean
prison and fortress. All three words seem to come from the same
root, meaning 'to restrain', hinting, perhaps misleadingly, that
there may have been an element of compulsion about membership of the royal harem. An alternative suggestion, that *khenret*
should be translated as 'establishment of musicians', is still the
subject of intense debate among egyptologists.[5]

A miracle brought to His Majesty Kirgipa [Gilukhepa], the daughter of
the prince of Nahrin Sutarna, and the members of her harem, some
317 women.

Marriage scarab of Amenhotep III

The kings of Egypt did not like to use their women as pawns
in tactical marriages with neighbouring monarchs. When the
King of Babylon, whose daughter was married to Amenhotep
III, requested an Egyptian princess for his own harem he was
curtly told 'Since the days of old, no Egyptian king's daughter
has been given to anyone.' In contrast, they had absolutely no
objection to welcoming foreign women into their own household
when it suited their diplomatic ambitions. Marriage with the
daughter of a neighbouring monarch ensured that the two kings
became relations, and therefore friends, strengthening alliances

and reducing the chances of conflict. Consequently, although diplomatic royal marriages were unknown during the Old and Middle Kingdoms, from the time of Tuthmosis IV onwards there was a slow trickle of foreign princesses entering Egypt in order to marry the king. These women travelled to their weddings with large dowries and considerable numbers of female attendants. They were received with all due pomp and ceremony and were then established in the harem-palace, where they took an Egyptian name and the honourable title of secondary wife[6] before sinking into obscurity.

Gilukhepa, a princess of the Asian kingdom of Mitanni, was sent by her father to marry King Amenhotep III. Their marriage agreement was the subject of a lengthy diplomatic correspondence which was fortuitously preserved on clay tablets in the Amarna state archives, while their eventual union was commemorated on the marriage scarab quoted above.[7] Amenhotep was clearly happy with the new addition to his household, for several years later he started to negotiate for the hand of Tadukhepa, another princess of Mitanni, the daughter of King Tushrata and the niece of Gilukhepa. In these new marriage negotiations Tushrata stipulated that his daughter should be acknowledged as a principal queen and 'Mistress of Egypt', providing a huge dowry to support his daughter's claim. In return, Amenhotep presented his new father-in-law with an even larger amount of gold. Unfortunately, the elderly groom died soon after the marriage contract was completed and his entire harem, including Tadukhepa, Gilukhepa and the daughter of the King of Babylon, was transferred to his son and heir, the future King Akhenaten.

Then His Majesty saw that her face was beautiful, like that of a goddess. The daughter of the prince of Khatti was beautiful in the heart of His Majesty. He loved her more than anything else . . . He had her named Queen Maatnefrure.

King Ramesses II on meeting his Hittite bride

Over a hundred years later, a Hittite princess left her home to become the bride of the 19th Dynasty King Ramesses II. The distant Hittite kingdom had entered into a diplomatic treaty with Egypt in Year 21 of Ramesses' reign, with both sides pledging to respect each other's territory and agreeing to act as allies in the event of attack from a third party. To mark the onset of cordial relations between the two lands Ramesses wrote personal letters to both the Hittite King Khattasulis and his queen, Pudukhepa, while the Queen of Egypt, Nefertari, also sent formal letters to the Hittite court. After years these friendly relations were still in place, and to add strength to the alliance Ramesses married the daughter of Khattasulis and Pudukhepa, giving her the Egyptian name of Maatnefrure and uniquely, for a foreigner, allowing her to assume the title of 'King's Great Wife'.

The large increase in the numbers of royal women and their associated households now made it logistically impossible for the entire harem to travel around the country with the court. Instead, a select band of women accompanied the king, and permanent harem-palaces were built to house the surplus ladies and their retinues. These harem-palaces were independent, both physically and economically, of the main royal residence. The archaeological site of Medinet el-Ghurab, lying near the village of Kahun, is the best surviving example of such a harem-palace. This settlement, known in ancient times as *Mer-Wer*, was founded during the reign of Tuthmosis III and remained in constant use until the Late New Kingdom.[8] It consisted of a group of mud-brick buildings contained within an enclosure wall. Included in the complex was a central block of living rooms and lofty pillared halls, several narrow storerooms, and even a small mud-brick temple, while extensive cemeteries were situated in the nearby desert sands. Although it was primarily home to a community of women, their children and their servants, men were by no means barred from *Mer-Wer*, and we know that at least eleven male administrators were seconded to the harem-palace throughout its

life. These administrators, who were married men rather than
eunuchs, were not guards but scribes and accountants charged
with the task of helping to control the considerable business
interests of the royal women. As the New Kingdom *Wilbour
Papyrus* confirms, *Mer-Wer* quickly became an important financial
institution, owning all the surrounding land and its crops and
with clear rights over the labour of the local peasant farmers.

Beware of loyal subjects who do not really exist! For you will not be
aware of their plotting. Trust neither a brother nor a friend and have
no intimate companions, for they are worthless.

Extract from the *Instructions of King Amenemhat I*

Mer-Wer, situated at the mouth of the Faiyum, was obviously
isolated from the main centres of Egyptian government. Was this
an attempt to provide a stable background for the royal women
and their children, away from the bustle of the court? Or should
it be interpreted in a more sinister light, as a deliberate attempt to
keep royal women out of political life? Certainly the harem-
palace, housing ambitious royal wives and their even more
ambitious sons, always had the potential of becoming a focus of
civil unrest and political intrigue. Treason within the royal
household was a very serious matter which was generally
hushed-up by government officials as it contradicted the official
doctrine of divine kingship. However, we do know of three
palace plots which at different times threatened the stability of
the country. The first and possibly the least serious of these
occurred during the 6th Dynasty rule of King Pepi I. The long
autobiography carved in the tomb-chapel of the official Weni
tells how the deceased, a favourite of the king, had been asked to
adjudicate in a top-secret case of unrest within the women's
quarters. We are not told of the outcome of this trial, although
we do know that Weni received royal assistance with the furnishing of his tomb as a reward for his loyal services to the
throne:

When there was a secret charge in the royal harem against Queen Weretkhetes, His Majesty made me hear the case alone, without any judge or vizier, because I was firmly planted in His Majesty's heart and in his confidence. I put the matter in writing, together with an Overseer, even though I was merely an Overseer of the Tenants myself. Never before had anyone in my position heard a secret of the royal harem, but His Majesty asked me to hear it because he regarded me as worthy beyond any official of his, beyond any noble of his and indeed beyond any servant of his.

The theme of royal assassination forms the basis of the 12th Dynasty *Instructions of King Amenemhat I* to his son Senwosret I, in which the spirit of the king speaks directly to his successor, begging him to be aware of the potential treachery of his disloyal subjects. Experts originally believed that this piece had been composed by the king himself in the wake of an unsuccessful coup, but it is now thought to have been written by the royal scribe Khety following the assassination of Amenemhat in his thirtieth regnal year. The rhetorical questions 'Has any woman previously raised troops? And has rebellion previously been raised in the palace?' strongly imply that this was a plot hatched within the harem. Precise details of the fatal assault upon the king are included within the text, and it is made clear that he was killed by those whom he had previously trusted while alone and off his guard:

It was after supper and night had fallen. I was lying on my bed and resting, for I was very weary. As I began to drift into sleep, the very weapons which should have been used to protect me were turned against me . . . Had I been able to seize my weapon I would have beaten the cowards back single-handed. But no one is strong at night. No one can fight alone, and no success can be achieved without a helper.

Equally serious was the 20th Dynasty intrigue which threatened and possibly ended the life of Ramesses III. The 20th Dynasty

was a period of sporadic civil unrest with high inflation leading
to a succession of wildcat strikes in the Theban necropolis. The
internal discontent was made worse by constant troubles along
the western border and a spate of abortive invasions by the so-
called 'Sea Peoples' who attempted to enter Egypt via the
Mediterranean coast. A group of conspirators led by the royal
concubine Tiy and the supervisor of the harem, Paibekkamen,
attempted to capitalize on the mood of dissatisfaction by inciting
a national uprising with the ultimate aim of placing Tiy's son
Pentawert on the throne. The plot was hatched in the 'harem of
the accompanying', presumably the small harem which escorted
the king in his travels, and involved many trusted officials
including the deputy overseer, six inspectors and even the wives
of the doorkeepers. We don't know whether or not the conspirators succeeded in assassinating Ramesses III,[9] but we do know
that the planned national uprising failed and that Ramesses IV,
the rightful heir to the throne, became the next king. The leaders
of the plot were caught and sentenced to death either by execution
or suicide, while the more minor participants had their noses and
ears cut off.

The Prince of Nahrin had only one child, a daughter. He built for her
a house whose windows were seventy cubits from the ground. He sent
for all the sons of all the Princes of Syria, and said to them 'Whoever
leaps up and reaches my daughter's window shall have her as a
bride . . .'

From the New Kingdom *Tale of the Doomed Prince*

Although all Egyptian kings were polygamous, routinely marrying several women and maintaining a succession of royal
concubines, only one wife was chosen from the harem to act as
the official queen-consort and be the acknowledged queen of
Egypt. Her name and image were linked with those of the king
in the official records, she was the mother in the royal nuclear
family and it was her children who would rightfully inherit the

throne. The secondary wives and mistresses played a far more peripheral role in court life; although their presence added to the monarch's prestige and, we must assume, provided him with an interesting diversion, they only became important at times of national crisis when the consort was unable to provide the king with a suitable son and heir.

Unfortunately, we have no idea how the principal queen was selected although it is clear that, as a general rule, the honour went most often to ladies of royal birth. Indeed, at least during the 18th Dynasty, the queen was often a full or half-sister of the king. However she was chosen, the 'Great Royal Consort' or 'Great King's Wife' was undoubtedly the most important woman to reside within the royal harem. In private, she was likely to be a lady of considerable personal wealth and breeding who was able to use her feminine influence over one of the most powerful monarchs in the ancient Near East. In public, she was set apart from other wives as the companion and consort of a semi-divine ruler, and the potential mother of future semi-divine kings. Her political position was reinforced by her numerous honorary titles and by the granting of impressive privileges, such as the right to write her name in a cartouche[10] or the right to be buried in a pyramid, which were otherwise reserved for the king alone. Given that the pharaoh was accepted as a living god, it is not surprising that the role of the queen-consort became very closely identified with several goddesses, principally Hathor and Maat, hinting at a divine origin for the queen herself and offering a further link between the secular and the sacred aspects of the monarchy.

It is very frustrating that we have virtually no information concerning either the private lives or the public duties of the queens of Egypt, and consequently no real understanding of the perceived role of the queen-consort. Although we can see that the queen's titles, her official regalia and even her religious affiliations slowly evolved as the Dynastic period progressed, we can only draw the most tentative of conclusions from this

combined evidence.[11] We can see that the queens of the Old
Kingdom, who did not adopt a standard diadem or crown, often
served as priestesses for the cult of Hathor. This Hathoric tradition
had died out by the end of the 11th Dynasty and the later Middle
Kingdom queens, who are seldom mentioned in any official
capacity, were rarely associated with any particular cult. Where
they are depicted, these shadowy ladies wear a distinctive headdress of two tall feathers. The queens of the New Kingdom
emerged from this relative obscurity as fully formed personalities
wearing a complex range of royal insignia apparently intended to
stress the links between the potentially divine queen and the
gods. These New Kingdom queens did not as a rule serve as
priestesses although the queenly title of 'God's Wife of Amen'
became very important at this time. By the Late Period, queens
were again functioning as priestesses, but the suggestions of a
connection between the queen and the gods had become
somewhat muted.

Official illustrations almost invariably present the queen as a
dutiful wife providing loyal but entirely passive support for her
husband. In the approved Egyptian tradition the queen was
literally expected to stand by the king, and indeed Queen Merytre,
consort of the New Kingdom ruler Tuthmosis III, earned high
praise as 'one who is never absent from the side of the Lord of the
Two Lands'. This essentially inactive role is constantly reinforced
by the numerous scenes which show the queen observing her
husband as he performs a royal duty, just as non-royal tomb scenes
depict more humble wives watching their husbands at work. In
the vast majority of these scenes the queen is totally static. She
keeps her hands by her sides and, although she may carry an ankh
sign symbolizing life or a sistrum to stress her link with Hathor,
she has no formal role to play at the official function. It is not until
the 18th Dynasty that we see a queen actually shake her sistrum,
while only in very specialized and female-orientated scenes such as
those depicting royal births, or those included on the walls of her
tomb, do we see the queen acting independently of her husband.

The individual queens of the turbulent and unsettled Archaic Period are now very remote figures, better known for their funerary monuments than their deeds. However, four prominent women have emerged from the mists of historical obscurity to suggest that royal females played a far more prominent role in the unification of their country than the present dearth of evidence would suggest. Three of these women (Neith-Hotep, Her-Neith and Meryt-Neith) bear names compounded with that of the goddess Neith, the patron deity of the town of Sais in the Nile Delta, and this strongly implies that all three may have been born into prominent northern families; an important distinction at a time when Upper and Lower Egypt were still very much separate entities. One of these women, Queen Meryt-Neith, may have been a queen regnant rather than a queen-consort; the evidence for and against her reign is therefore considered in detail in Chapter 7.[12]

Queen Neith-Hotep may well have been the first queen-consort of the newly unified Egypt; the evidence recovered from her tomb certainly suggests that she was an important element in 1st Dynasty political life. We know that in spite of her northern name Neith-Hotep was buried at the southern site of Nagada, where her enormous tomb (measuring over 53 x 26 metres) contained objects inscribed with the names of both King Aha and his predecessor, King Narmer. Aha has been very tentatively identified as King Menes, the traditional unifier of the country, while we know that Narmer was a highly successful southern warrior king. It is perhaps not stretching the available evidence too far to suggest that Neith-Hotep, a princess from the north, was married to the southerner Narmer in order to add strength to his ambition to rule over both north and south. Aha, or Menes, would therefore be the son of both Neith-Hotep and Narmer, and a man with an impeccable right to claim the throne of a united Egypt. This suggestion of a dynastic marriage is supported by a decorated mace-head recovered from Hierakonpolis which shows Narmer participating in an unidentified ceremony while wearing the distinctive crown of Lower Egypt; this may well represent the celebration of his marriage with Neith-Hotep. History shows that such calculating alliances are certainly not unknown and, for example, some 4,500 years after Neith-Hotep's marriage King Henry VII followed exactly the same line of reasoning when he married Elizabeth of York, the daughter of his defeated enemy, in order to emphasize his right to the throne of England and Wales.

The following queen-consort, Her-Neith, has been tentatively identified as the wife of the 1st Dynasty King Djer, the successor of Aha. Although we know little about her life, Her-Neith's large and impressive Sakkara tomb is of considerable architectural and historical importance as it consists of a traditional rectangular mud-brick superstructure built over a pyramid-like mound of earth which is itself faced with brick. Experts disagree on the precise implication of hiding one tomb-type within another, but it is at least possible that this represents a rather unsatisfactory attempt to combine the tumulus-style burial mounds of the south with the linear tombs of the north, again hinting at a dynastic marriage between the two warring provinces. The last queen-consort of the Archaic Period, Queen Nemaathep, has also left little trace in the archaeological record. We know, however, that she was the wife of the last king of the 2nd Dynasty, Khasekhemwy, and was required to act as regent for her young son Djoser, the first king of the 3rd Dynasty. In recognition of her services Nemaathep was accorded the prestigious title of 'Mother of the King', and she was later worshipped as the ancestress of the kings of the 3rd Dynasty.

The queens of the Old Kingdom, living under more settled conditions, played a less obtrusive role in matters of state than their Archaic Period predecessors. The most prominent Old Kingdom consort was probably Queen Ankhes-Merire, the second wife of the 6th Dynasty King Pepi I. She acted as regnant for her son Pepi II who succeeded his half-brother to the throne

at six years of age. Ankhes-Merire was actually the full sister of
the first wife of Pepi I, also named Ankhes-Merire, who was the
mother of his immediate successor Merenre. These sisters were
the daughters of a local hereditary prince named Khui and,
although not themselves of royal blood, they clearly belonged to
an influential family as their brother Djau eventually became
vizier of Egypt. Tradition decrees that the Old Kingdom ended
with the rule of the Queen Regnant Nitocris.

With the exception of the 12th Dynasty Queen Regnant
Sobeknofru, we know surprisingly little about the lives of the
individual queens of the Middle Kingdom. This sudden disappear-
ance of women from royal statuary and art coincides with a
definite decrease in higher-ranking female job titles, and lends
weight to suggestions that the women of the Middle Kingdom
were expected, or forced, to play a far less conspicuous role in
public life than had hitherto been accepted. Our main evidence
for the queens of this time therefore comes from the royal
burials. As in the Old Kingdom, the queens and princesses of the
Middle Kingdom were traditionally interred close to their king,
and the impressive 11th Dynasty funeral temple of Nebhepetre
Mentuhotep at Deir el-Bahri appears to have been fairly typical
in including provision for the burial of six royal ladies, including
a five-year-old girl, in addition to his two queens. The sarcophagi
recovered from two of these subsidiary tombs have provided us
with a series of delightful reliefs showing events in the daily life
of the royal women; these include the performance of the daily
toilette and preparations for a dinner party.[13]

By the 12th Dynasty the more important royal women were
allocated their own small pyramids, and the pyramid-complex of
Senwosret I at Lisht provides us with a good example of a king
providing for the proper burial of important royal females. The
major pyramid, a small dummy pyramid which also belonged to
the king and part of the main mortuary temple were all surrounded by a stone wall. Nine much smaller pyramids allocated

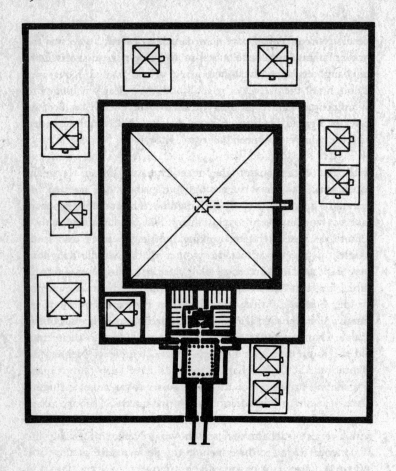

Fig. 30   The pyramid-complex of Senwosret I

to female members of the royal household were built around the
outside of this wall, each having its own small mortuary temple,
offering chapel and enclosure wall. The whole, together with the
entrance to the main mortuary temple and a cloistered court, was

enclosed by a substantial mud-brick outer wall. Seven of the female pyramid owners are now nameless, but we know that the two remaining tombs belonged to the principal queen, Neferu, and a princess named Itakayt.

During the New Kingdom, queens became more visible than they had ever been before, with an increasing emphasis being placed on both the individuality of each queen and the divinity of the role of the queen-consort. Queen Tetisheri, the commoner wife of the 17th Dynasty King Sekenenre Tao I, was the first of a succession of particularly forceful consorts which extended to include the queens of the 18th Dynasty, a remarkable group of women who managed to play a prominent role in the political life of the country at a time of economic and military expansion. These 17th and 18th Dynasty consorts were accorded more titles than their predecessors, becoming more firmly associated with the goddess Hathor in her role as both a divine consort and the mother of a king. At the same time, depictions of Hathor and Isis show them starting to wear the traditional queen's regalia of uraeus, double feathers and vulture crown, so that the precise distinction between the mortal queens and the immortal goddesses becomes deliberately blurred.

This increasing prominence encouraged early egyptologists, already heavily influenced by the fallacious theory of a matriarchal origin for the Egyptian state, to speculate about an 18th Dynasty tradition of female royal descent with the right to rule being passed directly along the female line. Under this system it would not be enough that the rightful king should be the son of the previous monarch; he had to reinforce his claim to the throne by marrying the heiress who was ideally a daughter of the previous king and queen-consort and therefore either his full or half-sister. Through this predestined marriage the heiress transmitted the right of kingship to her husband-brother, herself becoming the principal queen. This so-called 'heiress-princess' theory neatly explained away all the complexities of 18th Dynasty royal family life, and had the added attraction of providing an explanation for the brother–sister and father–daughter incest which was otherwise both unnatural and abhorrent to early egyptologists. However, it is now largely discredited as being based on incorrect assumptions.[14]

We now know that by no means all of the principal queens of the 18th Dynasty were of royal descent, and that the sons of these less exalted unions were not in any obvious way handicapped by their non-royal mothers. Indeed, the consecutive kings Tuthmosis I, Tuthmosis II and Tuthmosis III all had non-royal mothers while Queen Tiy, daughter of the commoners Yuya and Thuyu and 'Great Wife' of Amenhotep III, was widely respected both at home and abroad throughout the reigns of both her husband and her son. Nevertheless, all evidence suggests that although a blood-tie with the royal family was not a prerequisite of queen-ship, it was a relationship which was fully exploited whenever it occurred. Titles such as 'King's Daughter' or 'King's Wife', indicating a close relationship with the ruler, were certainly very important. They had a definite cumulative effect, with a succession of royal titles conveying increasing prestige. Therefore, the woman who started out in life as a mere 'King's Daughter' and progressed to become 'King's Sister', 'King's Wife' and finally 'King's Mother' was undoubtedly a powerful lady. These titles expressed the relationship of the woman with the kingship rather than an actual monarch, so that when the dowager queen Ahmose-Nefertari was described as 'King's Daughter' during the reign of her son (Amenhotep I), the king in question was her royal father.

... His sister was his guard ... The mighty Isis who protected her brother, seeking him without tiring, not resting until she found him ... She received his seed and bore his heir, raising their child in solitude in an unknown hiding place ...

New Kingdom hymn to Osiris

The prevalence of brother–sister marriages within the New

Kingdom royal family, a custom in obvious contrast to contemporary non-royal marriage patterns, appears to have been an attempt to reinforce the links between the royal family and the gods who themselves frequently indulged in brother–sister unions. Often, the gods were forced to make their incestuous matches through an undeniable lack of eligible marriage partners; for example, when Geb (the earth) wished to reproduce the only available female was his sister Nut (the sky). Together they produced Isis, Osiris, Nephthys and Seth. Isis and Osiris again had little choice but to mate with each other, while some legends state that Nephthys and Seth also married. Since Osiris had married Isis, albeit for a very practical reason, it was considered highly suitable that the king should follow the divine example and marry his sister. This custom certainly had the additional benefit of restricting entry to the royal family, thereby preserving the purity of the dynastic line, preventing the dissipation of the royal estates and reducing potential squabbles over the succession. It also provided a suitably royal husband for the higher-ranking princesses who, by tradition, were not married into foreign royal families but who may not have wished to marry an Egyptian man of less rarefied descent.

Four queen-consorts of the 18th Dynasty are worthy of special consideration as powerful women who had a profound influence on the development of the Egyptian state, while two further queens, Hatchepsut and Nefertiti, are discussed in Chapter 7. Queen Ahhotep was the first of these dominant consorts. She was the wife, and possibly the sister, of King Sekenenre Tao II and the mother of Ahmose, the southern warrior who defeated the Hyksos and founded the 18th Dynasty. She appears to have been a clever and courageous woman who had a profound influence on her son; in a curious stela recovered from Karnak Ahmose urged all his people to give due reverence to his mother as she had at one time rallied all the troops of Egypt and so prevented civil unrest from spreading throughout the land. Ahhotep lived to be at least eighty years old, and was given a magnificent burial by Ahmose. Her tomb was excavated at the end of the nineteenth century, and her mummy is now housed in Cairo Museum.

The succeeding queen-consort, Ahmose Nefertari, 'King's Daughter' and 'King's Sister', was the wife and possibly niece of Ahmose, the mother of the succeeding pharaoh Amenhotep I and the granddaughter of Tetisheri; the mummified bodies of both these ladies show that they shared a family tendency towards unfortunately prominent front teeth. After her death she became the patron goddess of the Theban necropolis, an unprecedented honour reflecting her exalted position. She was eventually worshipped as the 'Mistress of the Sky' and 'Lady of the West'.

All the words which I have spoken to your father, your mother knows them. No other person knows them, but you can ask your mother, Tiy, about them.

You know that I lived on friendly terms with your husband, and that your husband lived on friendly terms with me. You know, just as my messenger knows, the words that I have written and spoken to your husband, and the words which he has written back to me. You yourself know best all the words which we have spoken together. No one else knows them.

> Letters of condolence written by King Tushrata of Mittani
> to the new King Akhenaten and the Dowager Queen Tiy
> on the death of Amenhotep III

Queen Tiy – 'Like Maat following Re, she is in the following of your Majesty' – was the wife of Amenhotep III and the mother of his successor Amenhotep IV/Akhenaten. She was not herself of royal blood, but came from a prominent and wealthy Egyptian family who lived at Akhmim on the east bank of the River Nile opposite the modern town of Sohag. Despite the suggestions of some early egyptologists, there is no proof at all that Tiy was not a native Egyptian although it is just possible that her father Yuya was of foreign extraction as his name is unusual and does not have a consistent Egyptian spelling. Yuya bore the prestigious titles of 'God's Father', 'Prophet of Min' and 'Overseer of the Horses' while Tiy's brother or half-brother Anen was a Second Prophet of Amen and her mother, Thuyu, was a well-respected lady. Both Yuya and Thuyu were eventually buried in a rock-cut tomb in the Valley of the Kings; a very great honour for a non-royal couple.

Although Amenhotep III maintained a considerable number of women in his harem, including Gilukhepa, Tadukhepa and the daughter of the King of Babylon who were mentioned earlier, Tiy remained a powerful figure throughout her husband's reign. She had a very high public profile, being the first queen to be regularly depicted with her husband and the first queen whose name was constantly linked with that of her husband on official inscriptions. Her obvious political skills were widely recognized both within and outside Egypt, and Tushrata's letters of condolence quoted above indicate just how widely the queen's influence had spread. Throughout her life Tiy collected numerous titles; she was even, uniquely, represented in the tomb of Kheruef as a female sphinx trampling two female enemies (one Nubian and one Asiatic) underfoot. Although the sphinx was not an unusual motif in Egyptian art, this was the first time that a queen-consort had been shown in a typically (male) kingly role, while the depiction of female rather than male enemies is also highly unusual. Tiy, who was always closely identified with Hathor and who was the first queen to adopt the cow horns and sun disc in her headdress, gradually became regarded as the female counterpart of the semi-divine king, until eventually a temple was dedicated to her at Sedeinga in Nubia, the complement to her husband's temple at nearby Soleb.

Amenhotep III and Tiy had four daughters – Sitamen, Henuttaneb, Isis and Nebetah – whose images are frequently depicted alongside those of their mother and father. Sitamen is even accorded the title of 'Great King's Wife', and it is possible that she eventually became one of her father's wives. In contrast the

two sons of the marriage, Tuthmosis and Amenhotep, were
rarely depicted in association with the king. Tuthmosis, the elder
son, died young, and it was Amenhotep IV who succeeded his
father to the throne.

My husband has died and I have no son. But you, so they say, have
many sons. If you would give me one of your sons I would make him
my husband. I could never select one of my servants and make him my
husband.

> Letter written by the widowed Queen Ankhesenamen
> to King Suppiluliuma of the Hittites

The last of these remarkable 18th Dynasty queen-consorts was
Ankhesenamen, wife and possibly half-sister to the boy-king
Tutankhamen. Ankhesenamen, who was originally named
Ankhesenpaaten, was the third of the six daughters born to King
Akhenaten and Queen Nefertiti, and therefore a granddaughter
of the great Queen Tiy. She appears to have enjoyed a very
happy if brief married life, and as a typically loyal Egyptian wife
she is shown supporting her husband in several conventional
scenes, either watching him vanquishing the traditional enemies
of Egypt or handing him arrows as he shoots in the marshes.
After Tutankhamen's untimely death, however, the teenage
queen was faced with a constitutional crisis. As she had no
children and neither she nor her husband had a living brother,
there was no obvious and undisputed legal successor to the
throne. Ankhesenamen did not attempt to follow the precedent
set by Hatchepsut and rule Egypt alone. Instead, she wrote an
extraordinary letter to King Suppiluliuma of the Hittites, explaining her predicament and begging for a suitable husband who
would automatically become the next pharaoh. Not surprisingly,
Suppiluliuma was highly suspicious of this unprecedented request.
However, control of Egypt was too rich a prize to dismiss
without further inquiry, and so he despatched an ambassador to
ascertain whether or not Ankhesenamen was in earnest. A young

prince did eventually set out to be married; unfortunately the groom was murdered on the way to his wedding, provoking a small war between the two countries. The husbandless queen eventually married the commoner Ay, a former general and 'Overseer of all the Horses of His Majesty' and sank into relative obscurity. Her new husband became the next pharaoh of Egypt.

The queens of the succeeding dynasties were far less conspicuous than their 18th Dynasty predecessors, and only the wives of the 19th Dynasty King Ramesses II managed to make any real impact on Egyptian history. Ramesses had many wives, including his younger sister Hentmire, but his chief queen was Nefertari, who is featured on the temple of Hathor built by her husband at Abu Simbel. Although Nefertari was given the title 'Great Royal Wife' so was the Lady Istnofret, so we have the very unusual situation of having two major royal consorts at the same time. Nefertari bore Ramesses his eldest son Amen-hir-Khapshef and his daughter Meryt-Amen, while Istnofret produced his second son Ramesses, his elder daughter, Bint-Anath, and his twelfth son Merenptah, who eventually succeeded his father to the throne. Both Nefertari and Istnofret were buried in the Valley of the Queens; Nefertari's painted tomb is acknowledged to be a particularly fine one.

Over the years Ramesses' domestic arrangements grew even more eccentric as his two Great Royal Wives were succeeded by their daughters Meryt-Amen and Bint-Anath; the title 'Great Royal Wife' seems to have had a very literal meaning, and we know that Bint-Anath bore her father at least one daughter. A third 'Great Wife' was appointed in Year 34 when Maatnefrure, the daughter of the King of the Hittites, was also made a principal wife; at roughly the same time Maatnefrure's sister married Ramesses II and joined the royal harem. Meryt-Amen either died or fell from grace, and her place was taken by Nebet-Tawy who was yet another of Ramesses' daughters – this time by an unknown woman – the last of the Princess-Queens.

★

The one queen's title which became very important towards the end of the Dynastic era was that of 'God's Wife of Amen', a title which should not be confused with the less specific accolade of 'God's Wife' which had been used by several royal women during the Middle Kingdom. The god Amen and his influential Theban priesthood first came to national prominence during the Middle Kingdom. At the start of the New Kingdom they managed to consolidate and extended their power, ensuring that the victorious defeat of the Hyksos invaders became attributed to the direct intervention of Amen. It was at this time that the title God's Wife of Amen was first employed, lasting in popular use for a period of approximately eighty years. The title reflected the mythological idea that the mothers of kings were impregnated by the god Amen; this reinforced the dogma that the king was indeed the son of Amen. The God's Wife was not originally, as might be supposed, a young virgin dedicated to the service of the state god. Instead, the title was awarded to high-ranking ladies in the royal family – not always women of royal birth but usually the wife, mother or eldest daughter of a king. Its rarity shows that it was regarded as a position of some distinction and, indeed, several queens used it as their only or major title. The first 18th Dynasty holder of the title was Ahmose Nefertari, and contemporary illustrations show her dressed in a distinctive, short, Middle Kingdom-style wig and archaic-looking clothes, performing a range of public religious duties including processing in public with the priests of Amen. In return for her efforts, she received a generous endowment of land. The title slowly declined in popularity at the end of the 18th Dynasty.

During the troubled Third Intermediate Period Egypt was effectively split into two independent provinces; much of the north was ruled by the royal family living at Tanis in the Nile Delta while the south remained under the control of the influential High Priests of Amen based at Thebes. In a repetition of the north–south diplomatic marriages seen during the Archaic Period, it became customary for northern princesses to marry the High Priests of Amen, an arrangement which allowed the northern kings to assert a degree of long-range control over the wealthy and powerful Theban priesthood. The role of God's Wife of Amen was revived at this time and conferred on an unmarried daughter of such a union who was formally consecrated to the service of the god. The position was now politically very important as the current God's Wife held theoretical control over all the estates owned by Amen; rather than attempt to remove the powerful priests, the kings had sought to trump their influence by appointing a higher-ranking God's Wife. Naturally, it was important that such a political figurehead should remain a virgin as the insecure kings could not risk the establishment of a new and powerful dynasty.

Year 4 of Apries, 4th Month of Shomu, day 4. The God's Wife of Amen, Niacin, the justified, was raised up to heaven and united with the sun's disk, the divine flesh being merged with him who made it.

Stela, Cairo Museum

Following the breakdown of relations between the north and the south the system of diplomatic marriages was abandoned. The title God's Wife of Amen was, however, too important to lose, and it was continued and handed down to successive kings' daughters by adoption, a useful means of ensuring that the position was always held by a politically suitable woman. The most famous God's Wife of this time was Nitocris, the daughter of the Late Period King Psammeticus I, who held the position for over sixty years, using her influence in the south to help her northern family. By this time the nature of the position had obviously changed. The God's Wife was now a very powerful figure who dressed in the uraeus and other royal insignia, was accorded regal titles and who even wrote her name in a royal cartouche. With the help of trusted stewards and a large bureaucracy she controlled a political office of immense wealth and prestige, including the ownership of over 2,000 acres (about 810 hectares) of fertile land in both Upper Egypt and the Nile Delta. Indeed, the God's Wife eventually took over all the duties of the male First Prophet of Amen becoming, under her more popular title of Divine Adoratrice, one of the most influential women in the country. Locally, her influence exceeded that of the king in the north. Ankhnesneferibre, the daughter of Psammeticus II and niece of Nitocris, was adopted as Nitocris' successor eight years before her death; she was also created 'First Prophet of Amen', an honour not accorded to the other God's 'Wives'. Unfortunately Ankhnesneferibre proved to be the very last God's Wife of Amen, as the tradition was discontinued during the period of Persian rule which started during her 'reign'.

The Royal Succession:
Tuthmosis I to Tutankhamen

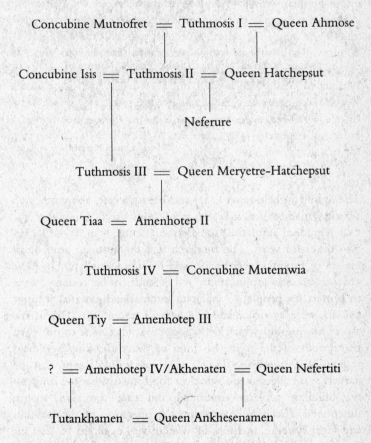

Concubine Mutnofret ══ Tuthmosis I ══ Queen Ahmose

Concubine Isis ══ Tuthmosis II ══ Queen Hatchepsut

Neferure

Tuthmosis III ══ Queen Meryetre-Hatchepsut

Queen Tiaa ══ Amenhotep II

Tuthmosis IV ══ Concubine Mutemwia

Queen Tiy ══ Amenhotep III

? ══ Amenhotep IV/Akhenaten ══ Queen Nefertiti

Tutankhamen ══ Queen Ankhesenamen

7

Female Kings

The Heiress, Great in the Palace, Fair in the
Face, Adorned with the Double Plumes, Mistress of
Happiness, Endowed with Favours, at hearing whose
voice the King rejoices, the Chief Wife of the
King, his beloved, the Lady of the Two Lands,
Neferneferuaten-Nefertiti, may she live for ever and
ever.

Titles of Queen Nefertiti

The Egyptians held remarkably consistent theories about kingship
which remained generally unvaried from the beginning of the
Old Kingdom until the Late Period, a time span of well over
two thousand years. The monarch was the absolute head of all
aspects of Egyptian secular life, and his word was law. His most
obvious tasks, as administrator and defender of his country, were
to protect his people, to maintain internal and external security
and to preserve order and the general status quo. This is the
aspect of kingship which perhaps approaches closest to our own
perceptions of the term. In times of peace the king was held
responsible for ensuring that all went well within Egypt, that the
harvest was collected and sufficient food stored, that the impressive building projects continued and that the civil service
functioned efficiently, overseeing the operation of the taxation
and legal systems. In times of war he was expected to lead his
troops bravely into battle, successfully defending his land against
invaders and routing traditional enemies with spectacular
victories. To help him achieve these ends the king employed a
large and efficient bureaucracy and an equally large and efficient

army, surrounding himself by
loyal and trusted advisors who
were often members of his immediate family.

The importance of the pharaoh was not, however, limited
to the performance of his secular obligations as the nominal
head of a well-organized civil
service and army; that was a
function which could be done
by any competent official. It
was the very presence of a recognized king on the throne of
Egypt which ensured the stability of the country. *Maat*, a
broad concept which may be
translated literally as justice or
truth, was the term used by the
Egyptians when referring to
the ideal state of the universe.[1]
Maat had been established at
the beginning of the world but
was not permanent and could
never be taken for granted;
chaos or disorder was always
lurking as an ever-present
threat to stability. The king was
personally responsible for the
operation and maintenance of
maat throughout the land, and

Fig. 31   *The goddess Maat*

indeed this formed an essential part of the contract drawn up
between the king and his gods. The gods established the king on
the Horus throne and endowed him with 'life, stability and
dominion'. They also controlled all natural phenomena, ensuring

that the Nile continued in its annual inundation cycle and that the sun never failed to shine. In return, the king pledged to rule Egypt wisely, establishing temples for the gods and making sure that the offering tables were well provisioned with offerings. Thus was *maat* established. In lawless or kingless times the coming of a ruler would bring *maat* or order, while conversely there could be no *maat* without a pharaoh on the throne. The Egyptians could no more conceive of their country surviving without a king than they could imagine their agriculture surviving without the annual inundation.

How the gods rejoice – you have strengthened their offerings. How the people rejoice – you have established their frontiers. How your forebears rejoice – you have enriched their offerings. How Egypt rejoices in your strength – you have protected her customs.

From a Middle Kingdom cycle of hymns to King Senwosret III

The king of Egypt was no mere mortal, he was a god incarnate. His divinity was universally and unquestioningly accepted by both himself and his people, and he was treated by all as the living embodiment of the god Horus and the son of Re or Amen-Re. He was divinely appointed by the gods, was the high priest of every temple in the land and, by observing the required daily rituals, he provided an earthly link between his people and the more inaccessible deities. This acceptance of divine kingship played an important part in the maintenance of stability throughout the Dynastic period. It both confirmed the absolute right of each monarch to the throne and reinforced the strength of the royal line by stressing the need for the correct dynastic succession. The survival of the kingship was seen by all as vital to the maintenance of the good relationship between Egypt and its gods, without which the country would founder, while the divinity of the monarch had the added bonus of making the king head of all religious practices, thereby preventing individual religious factions from gaining too much power. However, it was clearly understood that the king's divinity was not absolute; he was subordinate to his fellow gods and did not himself hold their miraculous powers. He was expected to show them due respect, and the piety of the king was considered essential for a prosperous and successful reign: as Queen Hatchepsut wrote in an attempt to stress her divine links with her god-father Amen, 'I am in very truth his daughter who serves him and knows what he ordains.'

Throughout the Dynastic period the position of king of Egypt was always perceived as a man's role. There seems to have been no specific ban on women succeeding to the throne but, with the exception of Manetho who records a King Binothris of the 2nd Dynasty during whose reign 'it was decided that women might hold kingly office', nowhere is it even briefly admitted that such a possibility could arise. The traditional stately duties of diplomat, soldier and priest were by convention masculine duties; any intentional disturbance of this natural order would certainly be going against *maat*. If, as often occurred, the king nominated his successor as his co-regent before his death, it would be seen as extremely unreasonable for him to select a daughter in preference to a son, particularly as the tradition of royal brother–sister marriages could involve the promotion of a wife above her husband. One of the practical aspects of polygamous royal marriages was to ensure that each king enjoyed the optimum circumstances in which to beget at least one male heir.

I know that I have the body of a weak and feeble woman, but I have the heart and stomach of a king, and a king of England too.

> Queen Elizabeth I rallying her troops
> at the approach of the Spanish Armada

There are few societies which will allow a woman to accede to the throne in preference to a man. Nor have there ever been many such societies. The handful of women who have been permitted by their communities to rule have generally been tolerated because of the absence of a suitably qualified male candidate and they have therefore been perceived as acting, at least ostensibly, on behalf of a male relative. There have certainly been powerful women in the histories and legends of past societies – for example, the Greeks Antigone and Clytemnestra and the Romans Livia and Agrippina – but these women were exceptional, often forced beyond their normal circumstances to act in an atypical and unfeminine manner. Even in countries where the monarch is merely a figurehead and not expected to make important decisions of state, kings are regarded as the norm, queens regnant a deviation from the norm. Thus, in almost all the monarchies of present-day Europe the first-born son succeeds to the throne, automatically taking precedence over his elder and possibly more suitable sisters; although this may be regarded by some as unfair it is nevertheless accepted by all the countries concerned. The ability to rule, no matter how nominally, is almost universally perceived as a male attribute, and in this respect females are definitely accorded a secondary role in the royal family. The explanation for this blatant discrimination is usually found within the society's interpretation of the function of kingship and its view of the proper role of women.

As a general rule societies accord women the right to rule at times when there is no clear male heir to the throne, although in a well-established royal family this situation is less common than might be imagined: in England, for example, only six queens in the past five hundred years have inherited either their father's or uncle's crown.[2] Women are also accorded the right to assume positions of leadership at times of national unrest or disturbance, often replacing or avenging a deposed or murdered husband, son or father. Although royal women are generally consigned to a passive role and are expected to act via men, such strident behaviour in a good cause generally meets with the approval of society. In almost all cases ruling queens come from within the existing royal family. Non-royal men have managed to claim thrones by aptitude, cunning or force, but this is virtually unheard of for non-royal women who rarely have either access to wealth or control over troops.

Only three remarkable women are definitely known to have ruled Dynastic Egypt as kings, each one taking the throne, as might be expected, under highly unusual circumstances. Three further women may have acted as queens regnant, although the evidence relating to their reigns is both flimsy and inconclusive in all three cases. The biographies of Queens Meryt-Neith, Nitocris, Sobeknofru, Hatchepsut, Nefertiti and Twosret are given below.[3] Unfortunately, our understanding of all six women is very patchy. Only Hatchepsut reigned for long enough to make a clear impact on the archaeological and historical record; unluckily she also made a strong impact on her people to the extent that much of the evidence relating to her rule was deliberately effaced and destroyed after her death. The earliest putative queen regnant, Meryt-Neith, ruled at the start of the Dynastic age and is known principally from her funerary monuments, while the memory of her 6th Dynasty successor, Nitocris, has become entangled with many romantic myths and legends to the extent that the truth behind her reign is difficult to ascertain. The remaining two queens, Sobeknofru and Twosret, ruled only briefly at times of civil disruption and were followed by periods of near anarchy, leaving us with few monuments and written records with which to reconstruct the events of their reigns. The Egyptian king lists have provided some confirmation of the surviving archaeological evidence relating to these ladies while later historians, such as Manetho, Herodotus and Strabo, have all made interesting, if occasionally rather unlikely, contributions to our understanding of their reigns.

Two important facts connect these six queens: they were each queen-consort and therefore probably of royal blood and, with the possible exception of Meryt-Neith, as far as we are able to tell, they each failed to produce a son. All six women, no matter how dominant their personalities, must have had the support of male members of the establishment. Three of the queens followed a very similar career track. Nitocris, Sobeknofru and Twosret all took the throne during periods of disruption when *maat* was absent from the land and there was no obvious male successor, and all three reigned for less than three years before being followed by periods of lawlessness and a change of dynasty. History has generally regarded these three reigns as brave attempts to perpetuate the royal succession against all odds. Hatchepsut's long rule is more of a puzzle as she proclaimed herself co-ruler with the acknowledged heir to the throne at a time when there was no clear or obvious need for a woman to assume power. The reasoning behind this action is now obscure. She is, however, the only queen regnant whose solo rule was not followed by a period of lawlessness. Queen Nefertiti presents us with even more of a conundrum. There is no incontrovertible evidence that she ever ruled Egypt but several intriguing clues hint that she may have been a co-regent with her husband either under her own name or under a name which has also been attributed to a young prince. Between them the stories of these six women contain elements of intrigue, mystery, power and death.

Queen Meryt-Neith – 1st Dynasty

We have no direct proof that Meryt-Neith ever ruled as king, and she is not included on any of the surviving king lists. However, Meryt-Neith lived at the very dawn of Egyptian history, a time whose written records are both sparse and somewhat obscure. There is certainly a strong body of circumstantial evidence which suggests that she may have actually taken the throne; evidence which, if related to a man, would surely be accepted as confirmation of her reign.

The problem of Meryt-Neith first came to light in AD 1900 when Petrie, excavating an impressively spacious tomb included among the burials of kings at the royal necropolis of Abydos, recovered a large carved funeral stela. This bore the name 'Meryt-Neith' and, although it lacked the customary royal Horus name, was unquestioningly accepted as a male king's funerary stela. On the basis of this evidence Meryt-Neith was identified as a king, possibly the third ruler of the 1st Dynasty. Only later did it become apparent that the name is actually female, literally meaning 'Beloved of [the goddess] Neith', and that the hitherto unremarkable king was, in fact, a woman. Instantly, on the basis of cultural expectations rather than sound archaeological evidence, Meryt-Neith was re-classified as an unusually powerful queen-consort.

We now know that Meryt-Neith was provided with an additional funerary monument at the northern royal burial ground of Sakkara. Here she also had a solar boat which would enable her spirit to travel with the god of the sun in the Afterlife, an honour normally reserved for the king. The curious custom of building two tombs, one in Lower Egypt close to the capital of the newly unified state and one in Upper Egypt, the homeland of the ruling dynasty, was peculiar to the early kings of Egypt; although logic dictated that they could only ever be interred in one tomb they seem to have felt the need to have two funerary monuments, one serving as an actual tomb and the other as a dummy tomb or cenotaph.[4] At the moment Meryt-Neith is the only woman known to have been commemorated in this way, and this again strongly suggests that she may well have been a ruler or at least a co-regent rather than a consort. Following contemporary custom, each of her tombs was surrounded by the subsidiary graves of at least forty attendants while a further seventy-seven servants were buried in a neat U-shape – presumably around three sides of a now-vanished building – near her Abydos monument. The attendants buried at Sakkara were all interred with objects symbolizing their trade, so that the shipbuilder was provided with a model boat while the artist was buried with several pots of pigment.

Queen Nitocris – 6th Dynasty

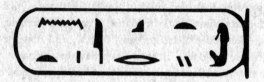

Fig. 32   Cartouche of Queen Nitocris

Nitocris presents us with exactly the opposite problem to that posed by Meryt-Neith. Tradition records that the good and beautiful Queen Nitocris was the first woman to reign as king over Egypt, and many fantastic and romantic legends have become entangled around her name. However, although selected details of her life were preserved by the historians Manetho and Herodotus, and despite the fact that her name is clearly included among the Old Kingdom monarchs of the *Turin Canon*, there is no definite archaeological evidence to show that a Queen Nitocris ever existed. She has left us no inscribed monuments, and has no known tomb. Experts are generally divided over her life, some declaring her to be a true king, while others classify her as a mere legend.

The 6th Dynasty King Pepi II is reputed to have ruled Egypt for over ninety years. His long reign was marked by a gradual decline in the stability of the country and when, following his death, there was no obvious successor to his crown, there was a phase of general unrest which eventually degenerated into the unruly First Intermediate Period. During this unstable episode the throne was occupied by a succession of little-known kings with very short reigns – a clear indication that all was not well within Egypt. The *Turin Canon* records that 'Nitokerti' was the second or third of these kings after Pepi II, reigning for precisely 'two years, one month and a day' at the end of the 6th Dynasty. Manetho describes Queen Nitocris as 'the noblest and loveliest woman of her time, rosy-cheeked and of fair complexion'. Confusing his Queen Menkare-Nitocris with King Menkaure of the 4th Dynasty, he believed that she had completed the construction of the third pyramid – presumably at Giza – and had at the appropriate time been entombed within it. He assigned to Nitocris a reign of twelve years. Eretosthenes, translating Nitocris's name into Greek as 'Athena is victorious', allotted her a shorter reign of six years.

The Queen's much admired rosy complexion (*rhodophis* in Greek) has led to a certain amount of confusion between Nitocris and a beautiful but infamous courtesan of the 26th Dynasty; a woman named Rhodophis or Dorchia who lived in the Egyptian city of Naukratis. Many improbable stories have been transferred from Rhodophis-Dorchia to 'Queen Rhodophis'. One such Cinderella-like tale recorded by Strabo tells us how, while the beautiful Rhodophis was bathing in the Nile, an eagle snatched away her discarded sandal and flew with it to the royal residence at Memphis. The king was sitting in the palace gardens as the bird passed overhead, and the sandal dropped from the eagle's grasp directly into his lap. On examining the sandal the king became so enchanted by its delicate shape and perfume that he at once started a nationwide search for its owner. Eventually Rhodophis was discovered at home in Naukratis and was given a royal escort to Memphis. There the impetuous king fell head over heels in love with his beautiful subject and at once made her his wife. After her death the grieving king buried his queen in a great pyramid. A second and considerably less romantic legend affirms that the evil Queen Rhodophis haunts the third Giza pyramid, appearing naked and beautiful to drive demented all who are unfortunate enough to behold her.

Herodotus, for once more down-to-earth than Strabo, was scornful of those ignorant enough to believe that a woman of Rhodophis' alleged profession could ever become rich enough to build herself a pyramid, but rather wistfully reflected that 'Naukratis seems somehow to be the place where such women are most attractive.' Of Queen Nitocris he wrote:

After Menes there came 330 kings whose names the priests recited to me from a papyrus roll. Included in these generations were eighteen Ethiopian kings and one queen, a native of the country; the rest were all Egyptian men. The name of the queen was the same as that of the Babylonian princess Nitocris.

He then recounted the tradition of the tragic and dramatic death of the queen, which may be summarized as follows:

Nitocris was the beautiful and virtuous wife and sister of King Metesouphis II, an Old Kingdom monarch who had ascended to the throne at the end of the 6th Dynasty but who had been savagely murdered by his subjects soon afterwards. Nitocris then became the sole ruler of Egypt and determined to avenge the death of her beloved husband-brother. She gave orders for the secret construction of a huge underground hall connected to the River Nile by a hidden channel. When this chamber was complete she threw a splendid inaugural banquet, inviting as guests all those whom she held personally responsible for the death of the king. While the unsuspecting guests were feasting she commanded that the secret conduit be opened and, as the Nile waters flooded in, all the traitors were drowned. In order to escape the vengeance of the Egyptian people she then committed suicide by throwing herself 'into a great chamber filled with hot ashes' and suffocating.

Queen Sobeknofru – 12th Dynasty

The life of the next Egyptian queen regnant, Sobeknofru, is far better documented than that of Nitocris, but there are still unfortunately large gaps in our knowledge of her reign. We know that Sobeknofru held power briefly as the last ruler of the 12th Dynasty, ascending to the throne in approximately 1789 BC

Fig. 33   Cartouche of Queen Sobeknofru

and ruling, according to the *Turin Canon*, for a period of precisely three years, ten months and twenty-four days. The 12th Dynasty had been a period of over two hundred years of Egyptian peace and stability, presided over by one of the longest continuous royal lines ever to rule Egypt. However, Sobeknofru's short reign occurred in a far less secure political climate; the succeeding confused and badly documented 13th Dynasty heralded the end of the Middle Kingdom and a rapid decline into the disorder of the Second Intermediate Period.

We are told by Manetho that Sobeknofru was a royal princess, the sister of her predecessor, King Amenemhat IV. This suggests that she was the daughter of the previous king, Amenemhat III, and indeed a stone block recovered from his pyramid at Hawara specifically mentions this fact. It is not clear whether as a royal princess she was married to her brother the king: a 'Queen Tanefru', also a daughter of Amenemhat III, whose name appears in regal cartouches and who bears the title 'King's Wife', was possibly the consort of Amenemhat IV but, as the two names are very similar, it may be that they belong to the same woman, or perhaps to royal sisters. Although blocks have been recovered engraved with the names of both Sobeknofru and her father it is unlikely that these two monarchs ever shared a co-regency. Nor was Sobeknofru ever a co-regent of Amenemhat IV, who had himself been a co-regent of Amenemhat III and who had enjoyed a brief and unremarkable solo reign after his father's death.

The reasons behind Sobeknofru's ascent to the throne are now lost to us. There have been suggestions of a dramatic feud within the Royal family, with Sobeknofru plotting successfully to wrest power away from her male relations. However, it would be far more realistic to assume that there was no more suitable male claimant to the throne, and that Sobeknofru was required to become king in an attempt to continue her dying royal line. There are certainly no indications that her role as pharaoh was resented, and she has never been regarded by later historians as a usurping or scheming woman as were both Hatchepsut and Twosret. Indeed, Sobeknofru seems to have been perfectly acceptable as a female ruler, and is recorded as a female monarch in the major king lists. A number of statues of the queen, recovered from Tell Daba in the Nile Delta, clearly show her as a lady dressed in woman's clothing and, again unlike Hatchepsut, she appears to have made no effort to be portrayed symbolically as a man. The end of Sobeknofru's reign is obscure, although it is generally assumed that she died a natural death while in office. It is possible that she owned one of the two badly ruined pyramids at the site of Mazghuna, not far from the other 12th Dynasty pyramids.

Queen Hatchepsut – 18th Dynasty

Fig. 34   Cartouche of Queen Hatchepsut

Amen, Lord of Thrones of the Two Lands caused me to rule the Red Land and the Black Land as a reward. No one rebels against me in all my lands . . . I am his daughter in very truth, she who serves him and knows what he ordains. My reward from my father is life-stability-dominion on the Horus-throne of all the living, like Re forever.

Obelisk inscription of Queen Hatchepsut

Princess Hatchepsut, the eldest daughter of King Tuthmosis I and his consort, Queen Ahmose, was born into a time of unprecedented Egyptian wealth and prosperity. Unfortunately, this was also a time when the royal family was being plagued by a shortage of sons. Tuthmosis I was not himself of royal birth and his mother, the Lady Senseneb, was always known by the simple descriptive title of 'King's Mother'. He had achieved his dramatic rise to power by becoming a general in the army of his immediate predecessor, Amenhotep I. Amenhotep, impressed by his soldier's obvious abilities and lacking any more suitable heir, selected him to become the next pharaoh. To add strength to Tuthmosis' position he married him to his daughter, Ahmose, and announced a formal co-regency with his new son-in-law. In due course of time, Tuthmosis became the sole ruler of Egypt.

Sadly, the sons of Tuthmosis and Ahmose all died in infancy and, like Amenhotep before him, Tuthmosis I was forced to look outside the immediate royal family for a successor. He chose a young man also named Tuthmosis, his natural son by a concubine named Mutnofret, and married him to his daughter Hatchepsut, thereby reinforcing his son's right to inherit the throne. Mutnofret may herself have had royal blood in her veins as she was possibly the daughter of Amenhotep I and therefore either the full or half-sister of Queen Ahmose. Much later Hatchepsut was to distort the sequence of these events, claiming that Tuthmosis I had actually associated himself in a co-regency with his daughter with the intention that she should eventually become king. It seems highly unlikely that this was ever the case, particularly as contemporary monuments show that Hatchepsut continued to receive only the lesser titles of princess and queen-consort after her father's death. Her public announcement of the co-rule was apparently an attempt to explain and reinforce her hold on the throne; indeed, her reign is characterized by her constant need to justify her actions both to her people and for posterity.

Tuthmosis II followed his father to the throne and, as his consort, Hatchepsut became queen. She appears to have behaved in a modest and totally conventional manner throughout the new king's short reign, accepting the standard titles of 'King's Daughter, King's Sister, God's Wife and King's Great Wife' and allowing herself to be portrayed lending wifely support to her husband. She even started to build herself a suitably discreet consort's tomb in an out-of-the-way area to the south of Deir el-Bahri on the west bank of the Nile at Thebes. Hatchepsut was clearly a dutiful wife, and bore her half-brother two daughters, Neferure and Meritre-Hatchepsut, although she had no son. Once again there was no legitimate male heir to the throne and, like his father before him, Tuthmosis II was forced to turn to the son of a concubine for his successor. Isis, the mother of Tuthmosis III, was later described by her son as 'King's Great Wife, Mistress of South and North, Great Heiress, God's Wife and King's Mother' but there is no evidence that she was ever a principal wife of equal status with Hatchepsut.

Having ascended into heaven Tuthmosis II became united with the gods. His son, having succeeded in his place as king of the Two Lands, ruled upon the throne of his father while his sister, the God's Wife Hatchepsut, governed Egypt and the Two Lands were under her control. People worked for her, and Egypt bowed her head.

                              Recorded by the government official Ineni

The young Tuthmosis III succeeded to his father's throne under the direct supervision of his stepmother and aunt, the formidable Dowager Queen Hatchepsut. He does not appear to have felt the need to consolidate his position by marrying either of the two royal princesses, and it would appear that his right to rule was widely recognized. Hatchepsut herself accepted the

Top: The morning toilette of the early Middle Kingdom Queen Kawit, shown on her sarcophagus.

Above: Bronze razor with a handle in the form of a duck's head and neck.

Right: Bronze mirror with lotus-shaped handle.

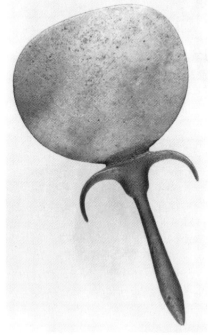

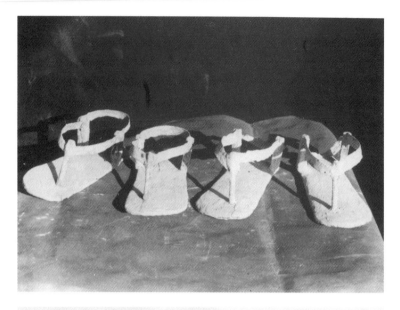

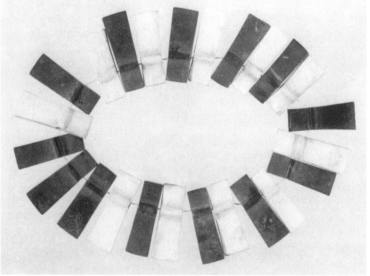

Top: Model sandals from a Middle Kingdom tomb.

Above: Ivory and slate bracelet from Nagada tomb of Queen Neith-Hotep.

Right: Middle Kingdom cosmetic pots, cosmetic grinder and applicators.

Left: Queen Nefertari representing the Goddess Hathor on the façade of her Abu Simbel temple.

Top: Queen Hatchepsut receives the Royal *ibs*-crown from the god Amen-Re.

Above: The mortuary temple of Queen Hatchepsut at Deir el-Bahri, Thebes.

Left: The 'God's Wife of Amen', possibly Amenirdis I.

Above: The goddess Hathor and the falcon-headed god Re.

Above: The mummy of the Lady Ray.

Left: Tomb of a rich New Kingdom lady.

accession of her young stepson, and throughout the first year of
the new regime she was content to remain the dutiful and
inconspicuous 'God's Wife and Great Royal Wife'. However,
towards the end of his second regnal year she was starting to
develop a higher profile; by his seventh year she had acquired
definite power, had announced herself co-regent and had been
crowned as a king of Egypt. The construction of her massive
mortuary temple at Deir el-Bahri and the building of a more
suitably regal tomb started at about this date. From this period
onwards Hatchepsut is uniquely depicted both as a conventional
woman and, in an attempt to symbolically emphasize her kingly
role, as a man wearing men's clothing and accessories down to
the artificial beard: her royal title, however, almost always has
the feminine ending attached and there is no suggestion that she
ever actually dressed up as a man. There is no confusion over
Hatchepsut's sexuality as there is over the heretic King Akhenaten,
and no suggestion that she was either a lesbian or a transvestite.

We have no idea what suddenly caused Hatchepsut to defy
convention and proclaim herself a king, and speculation on this
subject has been rife. Was it simple greed, or a lust for power on
the part of the queen? Was she unwilling to accept that as the
daughter, sister and wife of a king she could be passed over in
favour of her stepson? Was there some unrecorded national
emergency, or was the young Tuthmosis III initially too weak to
rule alone? Did Tuthmosis hate his stepmother, or welcome her
help? The fact that Hatchepsut was content to share her kingship,
however nominally, with her stepson, and the indications that
Tuthmosis accepted this co-regency even when he had reached
an age to rule alone, hint that the whole situation was far more
complex than is often supposed. The conventional explanation,
that Hatchepsut was a woman hungry for power, is certainly
unconvincing. If this was the case why wait so long to seize
power? And how did she manage to attract the steady support
which she undoubtedly received? It is certainly one of the greatest
puzzles of Egyptian history that the rightful king, Tuthmosis,

Fig. 35   Hatchepsut as a man

who might have been expected to react angrily and decisively to
Hatchepsut's unprecedented activities, seems to have accepted the
new situation, appearing content to remain in the background
and ruling alone only after his stepmother's death. Two major
but opposing views may be suggested to explain this conundrum,
but the truth almost certainly lies somewhere between these two
extremes.

   The conventional and most widely held belief is that Tuthmosis
did not like the situation but was incapable of doing anything

about it. As he came to the throne as a young and inexperienced boy he may well have needed the support and advice provided by the queen; by the time he grew old enough to resent his loss of authority the reins of power were firmly gathered in Hatchepsut's obviously capable hands. If Hatchepsut controlled the treasury and had the full support of the civil service Tuthmosis would have been powerless against her. The desecration of Hatchepsut's monuments after her death has often been taken as indirect proof of Tuthmosis' hatred of his co-regent. However, archaeological evidence indicates that this defacement may not have occurred until at least twenty years after Hatchepsut's death, a long time for Tuthmosis to hold his grudge before taking action.

The second explanation is that Tuthmosis did not feel that he had any grounds for complaint against his stepmother. He may even have actively welcomed Hatchepsut's guidance at a time when he was too young to rule alone effectively, and may have preferred to show his gratitude by waiting for her death rather than demoting her when he came of age. After all, although there were well-established precedents for co-regencies these invariably ended with the death of one of the partners, not with an abdication, and Tuthmosis could have reasonably expected to outlive his aunt and then enjoy a solo reign. Hatchepsut clearly made no attempt to depose Tuthmosis from the throne or to have him permanently put out of the way, and this suggests that she did not regard him as a threat to her security. Although contemporary illustrations almost invariably depict Hatchepsut as the dominant partner taking precedence over her co-ruler, Tuthmosis was always scrupulously accorded his correct royal regalia and, indeed, towards the end of the joint reign the two rulers are shown acting almost as equals. Certainly it would seem that Tuthmosis could have attempted to put an end to the situation had he so wished. He was by no means a weak or ineffectual man as his performance as pharaoh later proved.

Then His Majesty said to them, 'This daughter of mine ... I have
appointed as successor upon my throne. She shall sit on this marvellous
dais. She shall direct the commons in every sphere of the palace. It is she
who will lead you. Obey her words and unite yourselves at her
command.'

> Text carved on the wall of Hatchepsut's
> mortuary temple at Deir el-Bahri[5]

A number of what can best be described as propaganda texts –
records full of self-justification – survive to provide an official
explanation of Hatchepsut's unprecedented assumption of power.

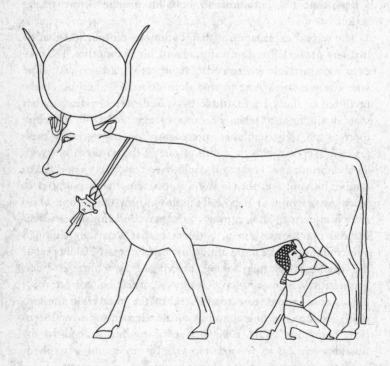

Fig. 36   Hatchepsut being suckled by the goddess Hathor

These texts stress both her relationship with her earthly father, the pharaoh, and her divine link with the gods, emphasizing over and over again her temporal and spiritual right to rule. The most explicit of these is the record of her 'divine birth', preserved on the wall of her Deir el-Bahri temple. Here, in a series of cartoons and brief captions, Hatchepsut reveals to the world that she is actually the natural daughter of the great god Amen, who had predestined his child for the crown. Amen, cunningly disguised as Tuthmosis I, is shown visiting Queen Ahmose in her chamber where, in an appropriately restrained scene, he fills her nostrils with the breath of life. The resulting pregnancy of the queen is made discreetly obvious, and the god Khnum is shown modelling the body and soul of the infant Hatchepsut on his potter's wheel, promising her anxious father Amen, 'I will shape for you your daughter . . .' Hatchepsut's miraculous birth, and the goddess Hathor's introduction of the baby to the proud father, are made clear. Finally Hatchepsut is presented before all the gods, who accept her as a future king of Egypt. A filial devotion to the god Amen was emphasized throughout Hatchepsut's life: 'I am truly His daughter, the one who glorifies Him.'

I was promoted before the companions, knowing that I was in Her favour. They set me to be the chief of Her house; the Palace – may it thrive in health in prosperity – was under my supervision. I was the judge of the whole land and the Overseer of the Granaries of Amen, Senenmut.

> Part of a long text of self-justification
> carved on the base of a statue of Senenmut

Hatchepsut must have been supported in her rule by many loyal male civil servants, several of whom had already served under her father and her husband. The enigmatic 'Steward of Amen' Senenmut stands out as being the most important and able administrator of this period.[6] Originally a man of relatively low birth who started his career in the army, Senenmut remained a bachelor and devoted his life to Hatchepsut's service. His precise relationship with the queen is unclear, although he seems to have been accorded unusual privileges for a non-royal male and it is difficult to determine exactly how much of his meteoric rise to prominence was due to his personal relationship with the widowed queen. He certainly made an impact on the bureaucracy, managing to acquire at least twenty important secular and religious posts in the course of his varied life, and his titles attest his role as effective controller of the state finances. He himself rather immodestly claimed responsibility for the construction of the most important of the queen's monuments at Thebes, although there is no proof that he was actually an architect. He is most frequently depicted in what was probably one of his most prestigious roles, as tutor to the young Princess Neferure, heiress presumptive to the Egyptian throne. Egyptologists originally believed that Neferure, 'Lady of the Two Lands, Mistress of Upper and Lower Egypt', had died in childhood, but new evidence suggests that she probably lived to survive her mother, and may even have been the first 'Great Wife' of her half-brother Tuthmosis III.

Senenmut managed to acquire enough wealth to build himself two expensive tombs, a relatively conspicuous gallery tomb at Gurnah and a more secret and secure chamber near the northern edge of Hatchepsut's temple courtyard where he intended to be buried; a number of ostraca show that he actually diverted the workmen away from the official temple-project to build the latter. He seems to have either fallen from grace or died before the end of Hatchepsut's reign, and he was never interred in his splendid but unfinished tomb. The memory of Senenmut was persecuted after his death, when the majority of his reliefs and statues were defaced and his tomb was desecrated. This destruction may have been ordered by Hatchepsut as the result of the bitter quarrel which ended their relationship, although it may equally well have been performed by those who later damaged Hatchepsut's monuments in the same way.

The general emphasis of Hatchepsut's long reign was on civil affairs, particularly on an intensive programme of building which included the restoration of temples and the erection of impressive monuments, all high-profile activities calculated to recall Egypt's former glories and to install confidence in her people. As the gods themselves had instructed their daughter, 'You shall refound the land, you shall repair what is in ruins in it, you shall make your chapels your monuments.' There was a diminution in military activity at this time, possibly due to the fact that the female Hatchepsut would have been unable to physically lead her troops in battle without creating a certain loss of confidence, but trade flourished and there was a memorable Egyptian expedition to the exotic and far-away land of Punt during her Year 9. Full details of this mission, and the wondrous sights encountered, have been preserved as a wall-scene at Deir el-Bahri, where the curiously tall round huts of the natives, the comical appearance of the ruler of Punt and his amazingly fat wife and the marvellous goods brought back to Egypt, are all faithfully recorded. There is further evidence for a punitive expedition in Nubia towards the end of the reign, and it may well be that the lack of evidence for military campaigns may be giving a misleading impression of Egyptian insularity at this time.

We do not know how Hatchepsut's long rule ended, although it seems likely that she died a natural death aged between fifty-two and seventy-two in her twenty-second regnal year. There is certainly no evidence to suggest that she was either murdered or in any way deposed by her co-ruler. Signs of her reign were destroyed after her death when an attempt was made to efface both her name and her memory, one of the worst punish-ments that could be inflicted on a dead pharaoh. Her portraits and cartouches were defaced and her monuments were either destroyed or re-named. This was, however, by no means an attempt at complete obliteration, and the destruction seems to have been conducted in a rather haphazard way. Hatchepsut's name was omitted from all the king lists, which record the

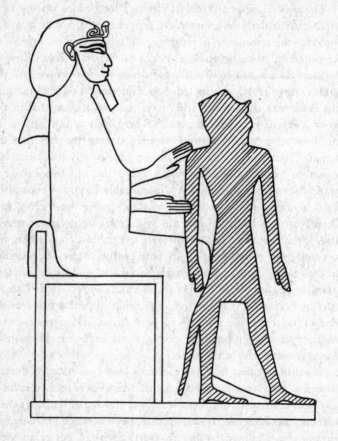

Fig. 37   Hatchepsut (now erased) with Tuthmosis I

simple succession of Tuthmosis I, II and III, and only Manetho
preserved the memory of a female ruler named Amensis or
Amense as his fifth sovereign of the 18th Dynasty.

Queen Nefertiti – 18th Dynasty

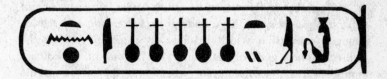

Fig. 38   Cartouche of Queen Nefertiti

As my heart rejoices in the Great Royal Wife and her children, and old age be granted to the Great Royal Wife Neferneruaten-Nefertiti, living forever in these millions of years, she being in the care of the pharaoh. And old age be granted to the Princess Meretaten and the Princess Meketaten, her children, they being in the care of their mother the Queen.

Amarna Boundary Stela

Nefertiti is the one queen of Egypt whose appearance is familiar to us today, thanks to the fortuitous preservation of the carved and painted head which now has pride of place in the Berlin Museum. We can therefore see that, as her name 'A Beautiful Woman has Come' implies, she was a strikingly attractive lady with a calm and slightly ironic smile. It is tempting to imagine that Nefertiti is perhaps having a private laugh at the attempts still being made by egyptologists to gain a sensible understanding of her confused life and even more enigmatic death.

Nefertiti rose from obscure origins to become the chief wife of the 18th Dynasty Pharaoh Amenhotep IV, the fifth king to succeed Hatchepsut. Given the 18th Dynasty fondness for incestuous royal marriages it is likely, but not proven, that she would have belonged to a minor branch of the royal family. The rule of the new king began in a conventional enough manner with Amenhotep succeeding his father to the throne in about 1358 BC, and we have enough surviving portraits of the new king and queen to see that they behaved very much in traditional royal style with Nefertiti acting as a passive support to her husband. However, a short time into his reign Amenhotep appears to have undergone a dramatic and sudden religious conversion which led him to completely reject the well-established gods of his country in favour of an obscure monotheistic religion requiring worship of the power of the sun, or the Aten. Amenhotep was not a man to do things by halves and, although the concept of one god who was the sole creator of all things must have been very strange to his fellow Egyptians who were used to worshipping a multitude of deities with different attributes, soon his entire court was also venerating the Aten. The king himself stressed his conversion by changing his throne name to Akhenaten, 'Spirit of the Aten', and it is under this name that he has become infamous as Egypt's first and last 'heretic' king.

We have no idea of the part that Nefertiti played in her husband's dramatic change of faith. However we do know that she accepted the new state religion with all the zeal of a recent convert; not only did she expand her name to the rather cumbersome Neferneruaten-Nefertiti — literally 'Beautiful are the Beauties of the Aten, A Beautiful Woman has Come' — but she was seen to participate enthusiastically in the new religious ceremonies, taking a highly prominent role which a less unconventional queen might more properly have left to her husband. Indeed, as the cult of the Aten developed, the royal couple themselves became gradually more and more involved not just as worshippers but as objects of worship, until all three received the regular prayers of the faithful with the king and queen continuing to acknowledge the superior power of the Aten. The ambitious building of a new capital city, Akhetaten or 'Horizon of the Aten' (present-day Amarna), sited well away from the cult centres of Amen and the other displaced deities, reinforced the dominance of the new religion and reduced the power of the old established priesthoods which were based in the traditionally important cities.

At this time there was a striking change in the type of clothing worn around the court. In all previous phases of Egyptian history there had been a clear distinction between the garments worn by men and those worn by women. However, during the Amarna period there was a curious blending of styles with both Akhenaten and his queen adopting long unisex pleated gowns. If contemporary illustrations are to be believed, Nefertiti occasionally wore hers completely unfastened to display all her womanly charms. The more fashionable ladies of the court completed their toilette by donning short masculine-style wigs based on the curly haircuts worn by Nubian soldiers. This change in fashion was accompanied by a radically different approach to art, with the rigid conventions of the preceding centuries being discarded in favour of a more free and easy naturalistic style. Informal Amarna scenes of the royal couple relaxing as they play with their little daughters in the palace gardens are some of the most charming vignettes of Egyptian daily life to have survived the ravages of time.

There was a definite blurring of sexual identities in this new-style artwork. The convention of portraying women with lighter skin was dropped, and the formal regal pose of the king, which showed a most powerful and masculine aspect intended to strike fear into the hearts of his enemies and inspire the confidence of his people, was abandoned. Many of the statues of Akhenaten depict him as sporting the traditional accessories of kingship, the crook and flail, crown and beard, but he is portrayed as a virtual hermaphrodite, with a curiously feminine face, well-developed breasts and what appear to be good child-bearing hips. Why the king should have allowed himself to be immortalized in a way that seems perversely calculated to strike fear into the hearts of his people while inspiring his enemies is not clear. It may be that this was actually how the poor man looked, in which case he must

Fig. 39   Queen Nefertiti

have been suffering from some medical disorder, although it is worth remembering that he did father six daughters with Nefertiti, and she was by no means the only woman to bear his children. It has been suggested that at least some of the more sexually

ambivalent statues actually represent Nefertiti in the role of the
goddess Tefnut, although this would not quite explain why she
was carrying the royal regalia and, indeed, why there should be so
many statues of the queen and so few of the king. It may even be
that Akhenaten was attempting, under the influence of his new
religion, to deliberately and symbolically depict in himself both
masculine and feminine aspects of nature. The mummified body
of Akhenaten, which could go a long way towards answering
some of these fascinating questions, has never been properly
identified and would appear to have been destroyed.

Nefertiti was clearly a woman to be reckoned with in matters
of state and religion. Queens and dowager queens had always
played an important part in royal life and were often included on
monuments supporting their husband or son, but Nefertiti was
accorded a far higher profile than her predecessors, being depicted
at all times by the side of her husband and taking an active role in
proceedings rather than simply looking on. She gradually grew
in status until she was regularly shown wearing a monarch's blue
crown and performing tasks normally reserved for the king, and
she was even illustrated in the ritual act of smiting the foes of
Egypt, a traditional male role hitherto exclusively reserved for
the pharaoh. To all intents and purposes it would appear that
Nefertiti was regarded as co-regent with her husband, although
this was never formally announced. The reasons behind her rise
to prominence are unknown. Was she a scheming woman able to
impose her will on her husband? Or did her unique role owe
more to the change of religious thought which perceived her as a
parallel to Tefnut, the wife and daughter of the sun god?

Although the life of Nefertiti presents us with some intriguing
problems, it is with her death that we meet the true enigma. The
last clear view that we have of the queen is of her weeping over
the lifeless body of her thirteen-year-old daughter, Meketaten,
who died in childbirth in Year 14 of her father's reign. After this
family tragedy Nefertiti fades out of the picture. The obvious
inference is that she died at this time and was buried in the

Fig. 40   Cartouche of Smenkhare

normal manner, although it is surprising that Amarna does not furnish any reference to her demise as we would expect her obviously doting husband to be devastated by such a loss. Nefertiti's mummified body has never been recovered. Alternatively, she may have continued her life as before, retiring from prominence at the death of her husband a few years later. A third, and slightly less plausible explanation, is that she somehow fell from grace and retired to live out the remainder of her life in relative seclusion. However, archaeologists do not necessarily favour the obvious solutions to their problems, and the far more dramatic suggestion has been made that Nefertiti may, from this point onwards, have become officially known as Akhenaten's co-ruler, the enigmatic Prince Smenkhare.

There is some evidence that towards the end of his life Akhenaten followed royal tradition and took as his co-regent his heir, Smenkhare. The identity of this shadowy young man is obscure, although he may have been either the king's younger brother or his son by his favourite secondary wife, the Lady Kiya. The identification of Smenkhare with Nefertiti is based on the fact that he appears for the first time in the archaeological record at precisely the moment that Nefertiti disappears. If Akhenaten had wished to make his wife co-ruler would he have considered it necessary to 'convert' her into a man first? There is the dubious parallel of Hatchepsut assuming male attire as pharaoh, although this was a symbolic transvestism and there is no evidence that Hatchepsut wanted to be regarded as anything other than a woman. The actual evidence relating to Smenkhare is both scanty and ambiguous, although it does appear that a person of that name did exist. A damaged illustration once believed to represent Smenkhare and Akhenaten relaxing together is now widely accepted as showing Nefertiti with her husband, the artistic conventions of the time making the precise identification of the genders difficult. Smenkhare did not follow Akhenaten to the throne and so may be presumed to have died before his mentor. The body of a royal young man of this period, which was recovered encased in a coffin originally intended for a high-born woman, has been tentatively identified as that of Smenkhare, although as it has suffered from both desecration and unbelievably bad excavation, this is now unprovable. As with many aspects of egyptology, the theory that Queen Nefertiti may have become Prince Smenkhare is one which waxes and wanes in popularity as new shreds of evidence come to light.

Queen Twosret – 19th Dynasty

Fig. 41   Cartouche of Queen Twosret

The final female king known to have taken the throne of Egypt, 250 years after the reign of Hatchepsut, was Queen Twosret, who took full advantage of a period of near-anarchy at the end of the 19th Dynasty to seize power for herself. The 19th Dynasty had started well as a time of relatively stable and effective rule following the religious disruptions at the end of the 18th Dynasty, and had flourished during the prosperous and well-documented reign of Ramesses II when the completion of great monuments and the success of extensive foreign campaigns had confirmed the presence of *maat* throughout the land. Following the deaths of Ramesses and his son and successor Merenptah, law and order disintegrated and there was a confusing succession of brief and badly attested pharaohs. Contemporary documents use standard phrases to record a time of turbulence and unrest and there are vague allusions to a war although this may simply be a reference to the internal conflicts. Trouble in the Theban necropolis – a standard indication of weak rule – was endemic at this time, with bribery, theft, and even murder rife among the chief workmen. Unfortunately, this period of disruption, which provided the typical conditions necessary for the emergence of a female ruler, has left few royal documents, and we are left with tantalizing glimpses of palace plots and intrigues which we may never be able to fully understand.

Merenptah was almost certainly succeeded on the throne by his son Seti II. Seti ruled for only six years and died in middle age to be succeeded in turn by his young son Ramesses Siptah who also ruled for only six years, for some unknown reason changing his name to Merenptah Siptah part way through his reign. Although Siptah was Seti's son and principal heir his mother was not the 'King's Great Wife' Twosret but a relatively unimportant secondary wife named Sutailja who appears to have been of Syrian origin. Twosret was therefore the new king's stepmother. There is no evidence that Twosret herself ever bore a child, and it certainly seems inconceivable that she would have tolerated Siptah taking the throne had she a rival son of her own. The origins of Queen Twosret are somewhat obscure; she did not bear the title of 'King's Daughter' and was possibly not of royal blood. In her tomb she is accorded the title 'Mistress of all the Land', a courtesy which she would have received as the consort of Seti II.

As might be expected from a young boy, Siptah was a weak and ineffectual monarch who left few monuments and who was soon forgotten after his early death. His weakness may have had a purely physical cause as examination of his preserved mummy, which has one distorted foot and an atrophied lower leg, suggests that he suffered from either a club foot or, more likely, the after-effects of childhood polio. Throughout his short reign Siptah was guided, or controlled, by his forceful stepmother, who gradually took over the role of consort and joint ruler. Whether Twosret actually married her young stepson in order to increase her power by becoming queen-regent is not clear; paintings in her tomb show her standing behind Siptah in a typical wifely posture as he offers a dedication to the earth god, Geb. Siptah's name has, however, been erased from the tomb and that of Seti II substituted, and it would appear that, after the death of Siptah, Twosret preferred to be associated with the memory of her prestigious first husband rather than her less than impressive stepson.

There was another dominant character playing an active part in the struggle for power at this time. The 'Great Chancellor of the Whole Land', Bay was a shadowy figure with an Asiatic name whose unique title emphasized his great influence over the boy-king. He was depicted standing behind his ruler's throne in an unusually important position for a non-royal person, and was even allowed the high honour of a tomb built near to that of his master in the Valley of the Kings. The epithet 'Who Establishes the King on his Father's Throne', attributed to Bay in two inscriptions, hints at Bay's role in maintaining the young king in his somewhat precarious position of authority while resisting the growing ambitions of the queen. It would appear that Bay ultimately failed in his mission to restrict Twosret's power, as he faded mysteriously out of the political scene during Siptah's fourth year of rule.

Following Siptah's untimely death a wave of civil unrest swept through the country. With no obvious male successor to the throne, Twosret was able to take full advantage of the chaos to extend her rule as co-regent and hold on to the crown, reinforcing her claim by adopting the full titulary of a male King of Upper and Lower Egypt. It is clear that she did achieve her ultimate ambition and reign alone for a brief period; she counted the years of Siptah's co-regency together with hers while distinguishing the rule of her husband, Seti II. Twosret's highest preserved year date is Year 8, while Manetho records that a 'King Thuoris, who in Homer is called Polybus, husband of Alcandara, and in whose time Troy was taken' ruled for seven years at the end of the 19th Dynasty. As Siptah ruled for at least six years, Twosret may have enjoyed a solo reign of less than two years. There is very little archaeological evidence for her brief rule, although her name has been found as far afield as the Nile Delta, the turquoise mines in Sinai, and even Palestine. Her major monuments are her tomb and a funerary temple which she started to build to the south of the Ramesseum but which was never completed. The end of Twosret's reign is shrouded in mystery, and we do not know whether she was deposed or indeed whether she died a natural death. She was succeeded by the obscure pharaoh Sethnakht, the founder of the 20th Dynasty.

Twosret was clearly a forceful woman with a driving personal ambition which allowed her to rise from relatively humble origins to the highest position in the land, despite the considerable handicap of her sex. Perhaps the best indication of her character is given by a consideration of her decorated tomb, which the Theban workmen began to prepare in the Valley of the Kings either at the end of Seti's reign or at the start of Siptah's rule, an unprecedented honour for a queen who should have expected to be interred in the neighbouring Valley of the Queens. The tomb was initially a relatively modest construction, but as Twosret gained in power she gradually extended and improved her tomb, until at the height of her power it had truly become a resting place fit for a king. The building work was never completed, but it is clear that the various building phases correspond closely to the various stages of Twosret's political life. Unfortunately Twosret was not able to enjoy the luxury of lying in her tomb undisturbed; her successor Sethnakht usurped the tomb and attempted to efface both her name and her image from its walls. We do not know what happened to her body, although a mummy in Cairo Museum has been attributed to Queen Twosret.

8

Religious Life and Death

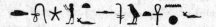

All know the monstrous worships that defile the
    Egyptians.
They adore the crocodile and the ibis gorged on
    snake,
While in awe they gape before the golden image of
    an ape.
    . . .
The leek's taboo! Don't chew an onion head!
O holy people, whose gods are garden-bred,
They spare the woolly race and won't permit
The throat of any goatbitch to be slit,
Yet unrebuked, at meals of human flesh they sit.[1]

The theology of ancient Egypt, with its awesome pantheon of
animal-headed deities, its imposing temples and its idiosyncratic
preparations for death, has fascinated observers from the end of
the Dynastic period onwards. Juvenal's largely inaccurate religious
satire quoted above – far from being taboo the onion was a staple
of the Egyptian diet, while there is certainly no evidence to
support claims of bloodthirsty acts of priestly cannibalism –
indicates how even to the peoples of the classical world the gods
of Egypt were a powerful and exciting mystery, the subjects of
endless superstition and rumour. Two thousand years later tourists
continue to flock in vast numbers to gaze in wonder at the
pyramids and there speculate on the faith which inspired such
extravagant building projects, while the mystical names of Isis,
her husband–brother Osiris and her son Horus, have retained
their power to conjure up vivid images of ancient beliefs and
dark, intriguing rituals.

It would certainly not be possible to make any valid study of Egyptian society without giving some consideration to the religion which played an important political role within the Egyptian state, and which may be supposed to have influenced the thoughts and daily actions of her people. However, any such consideration must be taken with a suitable degree of caution. It is extremely difficult for us, looking back over a vast span of historical events, to evaluate the precise influence of past beliefs. Although we are fortunate enough to have both written and archaeological evidence for a variety of religious and superstitious rituals it must always be remembered that we are able to observe only some of the outward or material signs of inner faith. It may be very tempting to impose our own expectations and preconceptions on the Egyptians, to the extent of imagining that we might actually be able to understand how they thought and felt, but this would clearly be wrong. We only have to consider the problems of a twenty-second-century archaeologist trying to identify all aspects of Christian doctrine, based on the excavation of a few churches plus a study of the Bible, to see how difficult an attempted interpretation of past religions can be.

The conventional phrase 'Egyptian religion', with its implication of one single creed enshrined in holy writings and accepted by all, is actually very misleading. Throughout the Dynastic period there were several distinct but related aspects of Egyptian spiritual life which were able to co-exist happily, each gradually evolving and developing through time while always overlapping with the others. The two extremes which may easily be both recognized and classified were the official or major tradition, represented by the formal state theology and its associated bureaucracy, and the unofficial or minor tradition which included the less respectable arts often lumped together under the headings of magic, superstition and witchcraft. Between these two distinct poles lay the respectable semi-official religions; the regional and family cults which were very important in the lives of individual households and their members but of relatively little interest to the state. There was no obvious cut-off point between any of these religious approaches, and each influenced the ordinary man and woman to a greater or lesser extent. For example, the women of Deir el-Medina, living very close to the centre of the cult of the state god Amen, participated in the annual festivals of the major tradition but officially worshipped the more local patron deities of the Theban necropolis, the deified king Amenhotep I and his mother Ahmose Nefertari together with Meretseger ('She-Loves-Silence'), the snake goddess of the Theban mountain who was also known as the 'Peak of the West'. Evidence recovered from their houses, however, suggests that more personal family-based cults with a heavy emphasis on the gods and spirits associated with pregnancy and childbirth were at least equally important in their lives, while belief in the awesome powers of superstition and magic was widespread.

Fig. 42   Woman praying

This diversity of religious approach is by no means unusual. Indeed, it is widely recognized that where there is a highly focalized official religion with an intricate theology less sophisticated grassroots cults will often develop, adapting and reinterpreting certain facets of the mainstream belief while completely disregarding others. This is particularly common where the major tradition is primarily a male-oriented religion, controlled by an élite of upper-class educated men and therefore remote from the daily life of most women. In these circumstances men are often able to satisfy their religious needs by adherence to the state theology while women, excluded from fully participating in the rituals of their official faith and often unable to fully understand the intricacies of doctrine due to a lack of religious teaching, find their spiritual fulfilment by developing the minor traditions, or 'woman's superstitions', without feeling that they are in any way deviating from the demands of their major religion.

This religious duality is still seen to a remarkable degree in present-day Egypt, where both Moslem and Christian peasant women retain a deep-rooted belief in the malignancy of certain spirits and the awesome powers of the evil eye. A village wife wishing to conceive a child, for example, is far more likely to call upon the spirits of her dead children or to obtain a spell from the local magician than to pray to Allah, and would not see this as a betrayal of her 'official' faith. Many modern village women feel that the ancient monuments of Egypt themselves possess magical or spiritual powers, and while walking across an archaeological site it is not unusual to find evidence for modern fertility rites – usually small heaps of recently broken pottery – associated with the ancient statues and images. Winifred Blackman observed this same phenomenon in an Egyptian village in the 1920s, where she attempted to help childless women conceive by enlisting the aid of ancient relics and modern Egyptian-style charms:

The ritual was as follows. The women first repaired to one of the ancient decorated tomb-chapels, conducted thither by one of our servants who had the key. On entering they each stepped seven times backwards and forwards over what they supposed to be the mouth of the shaft admitting to the subterranean burial chamber. When this performance was over they returned to the undecorated tomb-chapel in which I lived. Here I produced the charms, two of which were placed on the ground at a time. Then each woman solemnly stepped over them backwards and forwards seven times. Four charms in all were used, representing the head of Isis, a mummified divinity, a scarab and a cat. When this was accomplished the lower jaw-bone of an ancient Egyptian skull was placed on the ground. The same ceremony was yet again performed, being repeated with two complete ancient Egyptian heads, one a well-preserved mummified head, the other a skull. A glass of water was then brought, into which the blue glazed charms were dropped. Each woman drank some of the water, and then picked out the charms and sucked them, and some rubbed their bodies with these magical objects, and also applied the water to their persons.

Happily, Miss Blackman was able to report that at least two of the ladies helped in this way became pregnant soon after receiving their unorthodox treatment.

The state religion of ancient Egypt evolved with the unification of the country and remained relatively consistent throughout the Dynastic era, although it was at all times receptive to new ideas and flexible enough to accept foreign influences. Before unification each town or village simply worshipped its own omnipotent totem who provided a rational explanation for the puzzling and often frightening natural phenomena which would otherwise have worried the whole community. Everyone understood that neighbouring areas respected different gods, and people were happy to accept the polytheistic concept of many deities existing simultaneously while retaining their personal loyalty to one particular being. Following unification, several specific cults started to rise to prominence and, although individual communities continued to worship their own local gods, major national deities began to emerge. In particular, the cults of Re, the sun god, and Horus, the god associated with royalty, became politically very important due to the increased patronage of the king.

You are Amen, the Lord of the silent, who pays heed to the voice of the poor. When I call to you in my distress you come to rescue me.

You give breath to me in my wretchedness and release me from my
bondage.

New Kingdom stela from Deir el-Medina

It was not until the New Kingdom that some of the more
conspicuous national gods started to take on particular specialized
attributes and characteristics, a change which led directly to the
development of Egyptian mythology. Meanwhile, the smaller
regional cults continued to flourish under the supervision of local
priestly families. Local temples and shrines were endowed with
land and property by the monarch and their gods and goddesses,
who were also included in the wider state pantheon, continued in
their role as regional omnipotent deity. This dual role is
somewhat confusing to modern observers but was perfectly
acceptable to the Egyptians. For example, at Hermopolis Magna
in Middle Egypt the ibis- or baboon-headed god Thoth, state
god of writing and learning, was worshipped not simply because
of his impressive educational skills but as the supreme deity of the
region; the two distinct aspects of Thoth were certainly not felt
to be mutually incompatible. The local versions of the gods and
goddesses were generally far less specialized than their
counterparts in the state pantheon, being more strongly associated
with nature and the annual cycle of the Nile inundation which
played an important part in day-to-day life.

Throughout this time the relationship between the ordinary
people and the principal gods was conducted, in theory at least,
exclusively through the monarch. The king, as a god himself,
was the only person able to communicate with his fellow deities,
and he automatically became the chief priest of all Egyptian
cults. However, as he obviously could not be physically present
to serve every god in every temple, priests were appointed from
upper-class families to deputize for the king and perform all the
necessary rituals. The monarch would normally choose to deleg-
ate much of his routine work to these deputies but would wish
to be seen officiating during the important annual festivals of the

major national gods, especially the Opet festival for Amen, the
state god of the Egyptian Empire, when the statues of the god,
his consort Mut and their child Khonsu were taken in a lengthy
procession from the Luxor temple to the nearby temple of
Karnak. This ritual journey was a great public spectacle, and the
banks of the Nile were lined with Egyptians eager to get a
glimpse of their god.

Fig. 43   The sky goddess Nut

This Egyptian state religion was clearly very different to the
major faiths of the present day. Not only was it polytheistic, it
was also a theology without a creed, with no real moral
undertones and no tradition of pastoral care. Indeed, it was
generally more important as a source of continuing unity and
stability throughout the country than as a means of spiritual
enlightenment. Although it was generally accepted that men and
women should choose to lead a good life rather than a bad one,
this moral code evolved more for the convenience of society than
the gratification of the gods. Virtue did not necessarily reap any
heavenly reward, and only the king was required to act in a

fitting and proper manner to ensure the preservation of *maat* throughout the land. The gods themselves showed remarkably little concern over the behaviour of the ordinary Egyptians, although when directly provoked they could retaliate with a vengeance; the New Kingdom testimony of Neferabu, a draughtsman working at Deir el-Medina who had offended Ptah by swearing a false oath, tells us how he was struck blind as a punishment for the lies which had been interpreted as a lack of proper respect for the god:

I am a man who swore falsely by Ptah, Lord of *maat*, and he made me see darkness by day. I will announce his might to both those who are ignorant of him and those who know him, to both the small and the great. Beware of Ptah, Lord of *maat*, for he does not forgive anyone's lapse! Refrain from using the name of Ptah falsely, for he who utters it falsely, will fall.

Priests were appointed simply to serve the god on behalf of their king, and consequently had absolutely no interest in the spiritual or other welfare of the people. The temples of Egypt should not be regarded as the ancient equivalent of cathedrals or mosques; they were built simply to be the homes of the gods, housing the cult statues within which the deities were thought to dwell. As such they had no congregation and, indeed, were usually out of bounds to the ordinary people. Access to the back part of the temple, which can be equated with the family rooms at the rear of the private houses, was restricted to the priesthood and the king who serviced the cult by providing food, drink and clothing and burning incense; the front part, which was decorated with scenes of royal propaganda, was thrown open to the general public only on special festival days, therefore there was no Egyptian equivalent of the Friday mosque, Saturday synagogue or Sunday church service.

The ordinary people were allowed to view the religious festivals which occurred throughout the year, although they were denied any ritual participation in these great events. The Opet festival, held at Thebes during the second month of the inundation, has already been mentioned. This ceremony, marked by a state holiday of at least eleven days, was clearly an occasion for national rejoicing; at Medinet Habu the celebrations were made extra special by the free distribution of over 11,300 loaves and 385 large jugs of beer. Later in the year the residents of Thebes enjoyed yet another public holiday as the statue of Amen made a second official journey from his Theban home, crossing the Nile to visit the mortuary temples of the past rulers of Egypt.

The Abydos equivalent of the Opet festival was the procession of the statue of Osiris from his temple at Abydos to his tomb at the Umm el-Qaab, the traditional site of the burials of the archaic kings of Egypt. The ritual of this procession seems to have re-enacted the myth of the death and burial of the god in a dramatic form which must have been quite similar to the English medieval passion-plays, and the reconstruction of the murder was followed by the triumphal return of the resurrected god to his home. It is best known from the description left to us by the Middle Kingdom official Ikhernofret, who had been sent to Abydos in order to oversee the refurbishment of the god's processional paraphernalia. Ikhernofret left a commemorative limestone stela at Abydos detailing both his own important activities and the highlights of the religious drama:

I conducted the Great Procession, following in the god's steps. I made the god's boat sail, with Thoth at the helm . . . Decked in his beautiful regalia, he proceeded to the domain of Peqer . . . I followed the god to his house.

At Edfu the annual festival included a drama commemorating the victory of Horus over Seth, his justification before the tribunal of the gods, and the dismemberment of his former adversary. By re-performing these events, their beneficial effect was reinforced and the king used the play as a means of deflecting some of Horus's triumph on to himself, ensuring a continuing prosperous reign. Not all the annual state festivals were so solemn, however; the Late Period celebration of the cat-headed goddess Bast held at the Delta town of Bubastis was clearly a more cheerful occasion. Herodotus has described how bands of excited pilgrims travelled by boat to the city, passing the journey by drinking, singing, more drinking, clapping, drinking again and playing musical instruments. Whenever they approached a town they steered their tipsy cargo towards the river bank and:

. . . while some of the women continue to play and sing others call out to the females of the place and hurl abuse at them, while a certain number dance, and some even stand up and expose their private parts. After proceeding in this fashion all along the river course they reach Bubastis, where they celebrate the feast with abundant sacrifices. More grape wine is consumed at this festival than in all the rest of the year.

The gods and goddesses of the New Kingdom pantheon were perceived as behaving in a remarkably human fashion, falling in love, marrying, quarrelling and indeed displaying many of the foibles and failings of their mortal counterparts. The goddesses therefore reflect, to a limited extent, the role of women within the community, providing us with one of our few opportunities to examine the behaviour of females – albeit mythological – outside the home environment. Within the pantheon there developed a natural hierarchy, and included among the more important of the gods were some impressively powerful goddesses. There was, however, no goddess as powerful as the most mighty of the gods, Osiris, Re and Amen, and initially no specific 'earth mother' particularly associated with the mysteries of fertility and creation. Although all the goddesses had originated as local deities capable of independent thought and action, in their state-goddess personae they followed Egyptian convention by marrying neighbouring gods of roughly equal stature and assuming the more passive woman's role within the marriage.

Typically, they bore a male child, thereby becoming associated with the approved feminine traits of fertility, motherhood and domesticity.

Fig. 44   Isis

Isis, perhaps the best known and most forceful of the goddesses, displayed decisive action only when attempting to protect and defend her husband, an admirable activity for a loyal Egyptian wife. Following Seth's betrayal and dismemberment of Osiris, Isis and her sister Nephthys travelled to the ends of the earth to gather up his scattered remains so that he could eventually became whole again: 'Rise up, Osiris, for Isis has your arm and Nephthys has your hand.' Following this remarkable resurrection,

Isis conceived a son, hiding in the marshes until she could safely present Horus before the tribunal of the gods where he was acknowledged as heir to his father. Motherhood slowly became an important part of the cult of Isis and, particularly during the Late Period, she was frequently illustrated breastfeeding the baby Horus. These depictions marked the transition of Isis from her relatively restricted role as a member of the Egyptian pantheon to more universal recognition as a mother goddess or earth mother. Isis remained an important goddess beyond the collapse of the Egyptian empire as her cult, carried by visiting sailors, first travelled to Rome and then spread throughout the Roman Empire, attracting mysterious rituals and doctrines. Within Egypt, it was only the gradual spread of Christianity which caused her adherents to dwindle, and her cult was still being practised on the Island of Philae, Upper Egypt, in the fifth century AD. The cult of Isis was always particularly important to women as she was variously perceived as being the patroness of marriage, a protector during childbirth and even the inventor of weaving. The major attraction of her cult in the Roman world, however, seems to have been that worshippers of both sexes were allowed to take an active part in the ceremonies rather than being forced to observe the rituals of the official priests.

The other highly influential Egyptian goddess was Hathor, 'Lady of the Sycamores' and mistress of love, music and drunkenness. Hathor was already a well-established goddess at the start of the Old Kingdom, as her prominent role on the Narmer Palette confirms, and she was still being worshipped in various forms during the Saite period some two thousand years later. She enjoyed a widespread popularity among women, and was depicted on many popular day-to-day female items such as mirrors, which were symbolically linked with both fertility and childbirth. Hathor's role as a nurturer or provider was emphasized by her identification with the cow; she was either depicted as a cow-goddess or as a lady with obviously rounded cow's ears and horns. Her cult, based at the Upper Egyptian town of Dendera, was served by a large number of female priestesses, often of high birth, who were supervised by relatively few male administrators. Hathor of Dendera was believed to be the wife of the nearby Horus of Edfu, and mother of Harsomtus, while the 'Seven Hathors' were connected with Hathor as a goddess of death.

There were, however, clear exceptions to the general rule of the goddess as a loyal wife preoccupied with approved feminine pursuits such as fertility, childbirth, music and love. Neith, the patron deity of the Delta town of Sais, had a slightly androgynous quality. Although she was always depicted as a woman she was linked with the undeniably masculine concerns of war and hunting, and she was often depicted carrying a bow or crossed arrows, so that eventually she became identified with the Greek warrior maiden Athene. Neith may be compared with Sekhmet, the bloodthirsty lion-headed goddess of war and sickness, who was only narrowly thwarted in her mission to destroy all of mankind by the cunning intervention of Re.[2] In her less dramatic moments, Sekhmet was the consort of Ptah and the mother of Nefertum at Memphis, and she had a more benevolent counterpart in Bast, the cat-headed goddess of Bubastis.

Several warlike goddesses were imported into Egypt during the New Kingdom, and it says much for the flexibility of the religious system that they were able to find a niche in the official pantheon without any undue fuss. The Canaanite goddess Astarte, who is also identified with the Assyrio-Babylonian goddess Ishtar, is either depicted as a lion-headed goddess driving a chariot over her vanquished enemies or as a naked goddess riding a horse and wielding a dangerous-looking sword and battle-axe; in her more gentle persona of Ashtoreth she is again shown as a beautiful naked woman, often identified with Hathor in her role as goddess of love. Anath was the Syrian war-goddess who in Egypt became 'Lady of Heaven' and 'Mistress of the Gods', the daughter of Re and the consort of Seth. Although she usually dressed in a conventional feminine style, she carried a battle-axe and spear to indicate where her real interests lay.

*

Behold, I will announce to the great and the small who are in the troop: Beware of the Peak, for there is a lion within her! The Peak pounces with the movement of a savage lion, and she goes after him who offends her.

New Kingdom stela from Deir el-Medina

Everyday religious life was very much centred around the cults of the family past and present. Bonds with living relatives were crucial to the family-centred Egyptians, and there was at all times a deeply felt and permanent link with the dead relations who were in many ways still regarded as family members. Paying honour to immediate ancestors was therefore regarded as a particularly important religious requirement. Those who were affluent enough to build their own private tombs made sure that they included an integral above-ground chapel in the plan. This allowed the living to visit the tomb and make offerings to the spirit dwelling in the body of the deceased family member who was interred at the bottom of a shaft dug within or in front of the chapel. Separate shafts were excavated for the husband, wife and young unmarried children, and each succeeding generation hoped to build a new tomb to house their own nuclear family.

Tomb ownership was, however, a luxury denied to most Egyptians who were forced to express their reverence either at the graveside or, more usually, at the family altar or shrine. In poorer houses this shrine was a simple decorated niche or cupboard set in the wall of the main room directly opposite a doorway. More wealthy families were able to build elaborate free-standing chapels in the gardens of their spacious villas. The shrine usually held a small sacred image, a carving or statue which represented a composite of the patron god or goddess, the king and the souls of all the deceased family members. The function of the family shrine or chapel extended beyond that of the tomb-chapel, being concerned not only with the welfare of the recently departed but also with the worship of a mixture of local cult gods and goddesses, minor deities and the king. The

*Fig. 45   The cobra goddess
Renenutet*

private votive chapels which were built on the outskirts of the Amarna workmen's village developed their own priesthood, and each chapel had its own guardian or curator who actually lived within the chapel precincts. Many of these chapels included images of Renenutet, the cobra-goddess of harvest and fertility, while the comparable votive chapels at the workmen's village of Deir el-Medina showed a definite bias towards the female-orientated goddesses Renenutet, Meretseger and Taweret. Although not particularly influential within the state pantheon, these three goddesses personified events and locations which were very important in the daily lives of their worshippers.

A particularly strong domestic cult evolved around the cobra goddess Renenutet who was firmly identified with household and family life and was also the patron goddess of nursing and the harvest. The snake, who at first sight might be regarded as an unwelcome guest in any home, protected the stored food from vermin and was therefore perceived as both helpful and friendly. Renenutet, Meretseger and Edjo, the cobra goddess of Lower Egypt and protector of the king, were all

widely revered female snake-deities, while the only wholly evil
snake was the male Apophis, a serpent who was despised as the
enemy of the gods. As the goddess of the Theban mountain,
Meretseger (the 'Peak of the West') was particularly important to
the workmen of Deir el-Medina, and was frequently depicted in
association with Ptah, the mummiform patron of craftsmen.

Snakes became very closely linked with women, fertility and
childbirth to the extent that Isis, holding the baby Horus, was
often depicted under the protection of two snakes. Further
evidence of a connection between the snake and femininity is
provided by a series of New Kingdom female-fertility figurines
which are modelled lying on beds decorated with red and black
stripy snakes, while both ostraca and wall paintings recovered at
Amarna and Deir el-Medina depict snakes in close association
with dancing Bes figures, Taweret and trailing foliage and
flowers.[3] These scenes may be literal depictions of a 'birth
bower', a particular room or even a separate hut reserved for the
use of women during their delivery and subsequent period of
purification, or they may be more symbolic representations
intended to give protection to the mother and child and to
ensure the continued prosperity of the whole family. Whatever
their purpose, they certainly emphasize the importance attached
to childbirth by the community as a whole.

The dangerous mysteries associated with the creation of a new
life led to the development of a female-orientated domestic cult
centred around fertility, pregnancy and, more specifically,
childbirth. The whole process of delivery was not only physically
hazardous for the mother and child, it also seemed to bring the
participants, indeed, the whole household, into contact with
forces of creation far outside human control. Medicine could be
of very little help at such a time, so women naturally turned to
the comfort of superstition and magic ritual to ward off evil and
assist them through their labour. A small hoard of private votive
material recently discovered in the cupboard of an abandoned
Amarna house includes a stela showing a woman and a girl

worshipping Taweret, two broken female figurines and two model beds; this poignant collection, symbolizing the hopes and fears of an unknown mother and her daughter, allows us a glimpse of the hidden rituals of childbirth. Three thousand years later the Egyptian village women were still treating their confinements as a matter for magic intervention rather than medical aid. As Miss Blackman dispassionately observed:

On many different occasions women have brought their babies to me with the request that I would spit into their mouths, in order to make them live long. Also I found that many of my old clothes that I had thrown away were torn up, and many small pieces of them given to various mothers in the village, who hung them on their babies as charms to prolong life. One expectant mother came and begged me to let her have one of my old frocks, in order that her child might be born on to it! She, poor thing, did not get her request granted, and I regret to say that her baby died very soon after the birth!

The most popular charms and amulets associated with childbirth were those of Taweret ('The Great One'), the hippopotamus goddess who was always depicted standing upright to display her large and presumably pregnant belly, and who protected women throughout their pregnancy and labour. Although a kindly goddess, Taweret's power should not be underestimated; the hippopotamus is a large and dangerous animal and even today more Africans are killed each year by hippos than by lions. Charms portraying Hekat, the frog-headed goddess, and Bes, the ugly dwarf god, were also associated with the mysteries of birth; indeed, both Taweret and Bes were occasionally painted on to the inner walls of the village houses to provide a degree of extra protection for the whole family.

All the items associated with childbirth developed a special ritual significance and became invested with particular magical powers, so that even the birthing-stool or birthing-bricks became personified in the form of the goddess Meskhenet, an idiosyncratic-looking lady occasionally illustrated as a tile or brick with a human head but more often shown as a woman sporting a cow's uterus as her divine headgear.[4] Meskhenet was entrusted with the task of protecting the new-born infant, and it is perhaps significant that the determinative sign of a snake was often written at the end of her name. Special care was taken to guard the birthing-bricks themselves, as these would later be used as tablets by the god Thoth when he wrote the future of the new-born child. During the Middle Kingdom magical boomerang-shaped batons or wands played an important but unfortunately obscure role during the delivery. Over one hundred of these batons have been recovered, and almost all are carved from hippopotamus teeth, stressing the link with Taweret. Many carry engraved images of the protective spirits, Taweret and Bes, while some even have inscriptions 'we have come to give protection to this child' and the name of the baby or

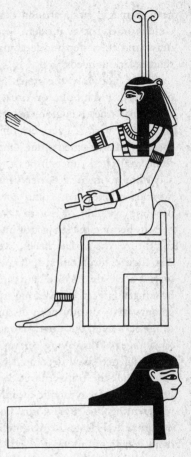

Fig. 46   The two forms of Meskhenet

the mother. These items were first identified as magical knives, although as they are all blunt it seems more likely that they had some other less obvious function. The most credible suggestion which has been made as to their use is that they were used to draw a magic circle around the bed to protect the mother and child, somewhat as modern witches are popularly supposed to draw and then step inside a magic pentagon while performing their nefarious deeds.

It was not only the items associated with childbirth which developed a symbolic or ritual meaning beyond their obvious functional role. Religion, or superstition, had become so much an integral part of everyday life that almost every item used by the Egyptians carried some underlying magical message or had some associated superstitious ritual. Even the days were graded according to magical portents into good, bad and indifferent, and nervous businessmen could consult the official calendar before deciding whether or not to take momentous actions. Similarly, dreams became the subject of intense study as a means of divining the future; the *Dream Book* gave a long list of common dreams and their interpretations: 'If a man dreams that he is drinking warm beer, this is bad and suffering will come to him.' The beneficial effects of wearing specific charms or even specific colours have already been discussed in Chapter 5. Less apparent to modern eyes, but clearly important to the Egyptians, were the advantages of displaying certain decorative devices. For example, a blue faience bowl decorated with a lotus-blossom pattern may have been a beautiful object to have in the house or the tomb, but it also had a symbolic meaning to its owner. The lotus motif, representing the blue lotus flower which opens its petals at daybreak and closes them at night, was closely associated with the daily rebirth of the sun god, and by extension became symbolic of rebirth after death. Similarly, a cosmetic dish or spoon in the shape of a fish would not only be an amusing and practical trinket, it too would represent rebirth and fertility to its owner.

As for the person who knows this spell, he will become like Re in the eastern sky and like Osiris in the Netherworld. He will go down into the circle of fire, without the flame ever touching him.

Part of a spell taken from the Middle Kingdom *Coffin Texts*

In marked contrast to the somewhat scanty evidence for the everyday religious practices of the ordinary people, the rituals associated with death have made a significant contribution to the archaeological record. The Egyptians were a joyful and vibrant people who enjoyed life and its pleasures to the full and who were tireless in their pursuit of happiness. It is therefore somewhat ironic that their idiosyncratic and highly materialistic approach towards the Afterlife has so fascinated modern observers that the uninformed visitor to an egyptological museum or specialist bookshop might be forgiven for imagining that the Egyptians themselves held an unhealthy and overwhelming obsession with all aspects of their own demise. To a large extent this misrepresentation is a direct result of the archaeological bias mentioned in the Introduction to this book, as the tradition of constructing permanent tombs of stone while living in relatively fragile mud-brick houses has naturally led to the disproportionate conservation of funerary remains. It has, however, been exacerbated by the fact that many observers, including trained egyptologists who should perhaps know better, exhibit a passionate interest in studying funerary rites to the virtual exclusion of other less bizarre but equally valid aspects of Egyptian existence. Could it be that this almost voyeuristic interest in the burial habits of others is a reflection of our own deep-seated insecurity which has made death a semi-taboo subject in the western world? It is certainly rare to find a modern people who can accept and even plan for their own departure with the equanimity of the ancient Egyptians.

Although the Egyptians did not allow persistent morbid thoughts to spoil their enjoyment of life they were very much aware that their earthly existence could be abruptly terminated at any moment. Indeed, their very love of life probably masked a very understandable fear of death and the unknown. The lack of some of the most basic of medical skills combined with ever-present natural dangers such as flood and famine to make death a constant threat to family security, and most Egyptians would have experienced the loss of one or more loved ones at a very early age. The official state theology did not attempt to provide any rational explanation or justification for death, and dying seems to have been accepted as an inexplicable fact of life. Rather than wasting time in endless speculation about the meaning of existence, the Egyptians preferred to make practical preparations for their own end. The prudent and the wealthy planned ahead, ensuring that their wishes would be fulfilled by supervising the construction of their own tombs and the collection of their own grave goods. However, this forward thinking should not be interpreted as a longing for death, and surviving texts give no indication that the planners ever anticipated their own demise in the way that traditionally devout Christians look forward to leaving the Vale of Tears and passing through the Pearly Gates of Heaven.

I asked the Majesty of my Lord that a white limestone sarcophagus might be brought for me from Tura. His Majesty caused the seal-bearer of the god and a crew under his direction to ferry over in order to bring for me this sarcophagus from Tura. He returned with it, in a great transport-boat of the Residence, together with its lid . . .

Inscription from the Old Kingdom tomb of Weni

Just as childbirth is almost universally perceived as a female rite so, in many cultures, it is women who are expected to supervise dying, while men assume control over the funeral rites of the dead. Birth and death therefore become inextricably linked together as contrasting sides of the same coin – one representing a passage into the light and the other a passage into the dark. It would appear that death is even in some obscure way perceived as polluting and that women, with their already impure bodies, are seen as the more appropriate sex to handle this transition. However, this rather neat anthropological theory may well represent the over-analysis of a basically simple situation; it is certainly equally valid to state that as women are conventionally at home all day, they are naturally the ones who are called upon to nurse the terminally ill. Whatever the reason, it is undeniable that most people regard death as a frightening event involving direct contact with unknown and uncontrollable forces. Even those with the advantages of modern medical knowledge regard the phenomena of birth and death with some awe and, until relatively recently, men have generally tended to avoid immediate contact with either of these mysteries. In practical terms this means that the care of the dying is generally perceived as female work, with men expecting women to preside over the deathbed and perhaps the laying out of the corpse before taking over with the more formal burial rituals which often cannot be adequately performed by a woman.

Egypt was no exception to this general rule, and it is no coincidence that the goddesses Isis and Nephthys were strongly connected with both the rites of birth (acting as midwives) and death (divine mourners). As there was no Dynastic equivalent of our hospital system to remove the sick from their home environment, nursing became the duty of the women of the household. Under these intimate circumstances no member of the family could hope to avoid contact with the dying or recently dead and, indeed, most women would expect, throughout their lives, to assist at the deathbeds of close relations. Death was therefore neither an abstract nor a sanitized concept to the Egyptian woman. It was a simple fact of life, albeit one to be avoided as far as possible by the appropriate use of prayers, amulets and charms.

Rise up, O Teti. Seize your head and collect up your bones. Gather your limbs together and shake the dust from your flesh. Take your bread which will never rot and your beer that will never sour, and stand before the gateway that excludes the common people. The gatekeeper comes out to you. He takes you by the hand and leads you into heaven, into the presence of your father, Geb.

Speech from the *Pyramid Texts* of the Old Kingdom Pharaoh Teti

Although death was inevitable it was not necessarily final.

Throughout the Dynastic period the Egyptians retained a firm belief in the possibility of life after death, a belief which had a deep influence upon the development of both art and architecture. This belief slowly evolved through time, so that the dying of the Archaic Period held a very different set of expectations from their Late Period descendants. During the Old Kingdom, it was widely accepted that only the king would be able to pass on to a new world outside the tomb, becoming himself a god and living with the other gods. He achieved his transformation by one of three main routes: by travelling with the sun god, Re, in his solar boat, by being reborn as an undying or circumpolar star, or by becoming identified with Osiris, the god of the dead. The spirits of less exalted Egyptians could also continue to exist after death, but they were forced to dwell in close proximity to the body interred in its tomb or grave – a belief which led the upper classes to build the largest and most comfortable tombs possible. After all, no one would wish to live for all eternity confined to an uncomfortably cramped and dirty pit-grave.

Gradually, following the collapse of central authority at the end of the Old Kingdom, many of the hitherto exclusively royal religious prerogatives were taken over by the ordinary people. As a result, survival in the next world for everyone during the Middle Kingdom depended on the identification of the deceased, male and female alike, with the dead Osiris. Now everyone was eligible to become a subject in the Netherworld, the kingdom of Osiris which was a direct counterpart to the living world ruled by the pharaoh, the living Horus. This rather restricted image of heaven slowly expanded to become the New Kingdom Afterlife, the 'Field of Reeds' or the 'Field of Offerings'; a land of pleasure and plenty again ruled by Osiris. This Afterlife was an almost exact replica of earthly rural life but was much, much better. Here the crops grew taller, the cattle grew fatter and the fish in the river simply begged to be caught. The residents were all young, fit and attractive as,. dressed in clean white linen and adorned with sparkling jewels, they enjoyed mouthwatering meals in a land where beer and wine flowed like Nile water. Life in the Field of Reeds was clearly very desirable. Unfortunately, admission to these delights was not automatic, nor could it be secured by living a virtuous or devout earthly life. Entrance to the Afterlife was by examination only, and there was a strict pass or fail system. Those who flunked got no second chance.

'I will not let you enter through me,' says the jamb of the door, 'unless you tell me my name.'
'Plumb-bob in the Place of Truth is your name.'

Extract from the New Kingdom *Book of the Dead*

After death the spirit of the deceased embarked upon a long and fantastic journey, voyaging through a surreal maze of halls, chambers and gates where he or she was repeatedly challenged by a series of intricate questions posed by either the gatekeepers or, more bizarrely, by the gates themselves. Those who safely negotiated this labyrinth entered before a tribunal of the gods where a strict *viva voce* examination allowed the traveller to make a series of formal speeches justifying his or her life: 'I have given bread to the hungry and water to the thirsty, clothes to the naked and a boat to those who have no boat.' As a final test the heart of the deceased was weighed in a balance against the feather which symbolized *maat*, in order that the gods might determine whether or not he or she was true of heart. Only those who triumphed over all these hazards could pass on to perpetual life in the Field of Reeds. Those who were found wanting were doomed to die a second, frightening and permanent, death.

Entry into the Afterlife was not, however, merely dependent upon good examination technique. As has already been noted, the Egyptians were an intensely practical people who preferred to leave nothing to chance. They therefore took care to equip their tombs with a complete set of those questions and answers which they knew would be posed on the journey after death, effectively providing themselves with a passport to the delights of the next world. As the gods did not disapprove of this rather blatant form of cheating, rebirth in the Field of Reeds became assured for the wealthy. During the Middle Kingdom, this guide to the Afterlife took the form of spells and incantations which had evolved from the Old Kingdom *Royal Pyramid Texts*, and which were either engraved or painted on the sides of the coffins. By the New Kingdom the deceased were provided with their own personalized copy of *The Chapters of Coming Forth by Day*, an illustrated papyrus scroll containing a lengthy collection of spells, rituals, questions and answers which is now known more familiarly as *The Book of the Dead*.[5] Affluent members of society had their individual copy of *The Book of the Dead* custom-written, while the less wealthy purchased mass-produced male or female scrolls which had gaps left at appropriate intervals so that the correct name and titles could be inserted. Occasionally there were mix-ups, and several women were buried with scrolls which were originally written for men.

The following is the way in which they conduct their mourning and their funerals. On the death in any house of a man of consequence, forthwith the women of the family plaster their heads, and sometimes even their faces, with mud. Then, leaving the body indoors, they sally forth and wander through the city with their dress fastened by a band and their bosoms bare, beating themselves as they walk. All the female relations join in and do the same. The men too, similarly dressed, beat their breasts separately. When these ceremonies are over, the body is carried away to be embalmed.

Herodotus

The Egyptians were by no means the only people of the ancient world to envisage an Afterlife. Indeed, there is an almost universal reluctance to accept that death might be the absolute end of all things. However, they were the only people to believe that the survival of the physical remains of the deceased was a virtual prerequisite for the survival of the spirits or life-force.

Two spirits, the Ka and the Ba, would be released from the body at death; the Ka stayed close to the corpse in the tomb while the Ba was free to leave the tomb in the form of a human-headed bird. At the same time a third and entirely different aspect of the soul embarked upon the lengthy journey to the Afterlife. Both the Ka and the Ba, however, needed to be able to return to the body. If the corpse was destroyed these spirits were also destroyed and there could be no further hope of continuing life, although in an emergency they could take up residence in a substitute body such as a statue or even an illustration on the tomb wall. It was this deeply held belief which led to the development of elaborate mortuary rituals, including mummification, which were all designed as a practical means of preserving the body for all eternity.

Ironically, it was those who tried hardest and paid the most to protect their bodies who faced the greatest threat of decomposition. The poorer people, who throughout the Dynastic periods continued to be buried without coffins in the simple graves of the desert cemeteries, became naturally desiccated in the hot sand and were relatively well-preserved in a lifelike, if somewhat shrivelled, form. It was the introduction of the wooden coffin and the wood- or brick-lined tomb – probably initially intended to protect the body from the grave filling – which stopped the direct contact between the corpse and the sand, trapping moisture in close proximity to the body and encouraging putrefaction. Unfortunately, both coffins and tombs soon became essential components of a fashionable burial; the tomb served as protection against robbers, as a storehouse for grave-goods and, most importantly, as the permanent home of the soul, while the coffin carried the vital spells necessary to bring the deceased back to life. The resulting decomposition of the deceased was obvious, and led to ingenious attempts to preserve the body in a recognizable form.

Mummification techniques improved throughout the Dynastic period so that, although at the start of the Old Kingdom the majority of the embalmed bodies continued to decay, by the middle of the New Kingdom most professional undertakers could produce a remarkably lifelike embalmed corpse. The earliest attempts at preserving the body failed because no attempt was made to remove the soft tissue; the semi-dried corpses were simply wrapped in linen bandages complete with their already decomposing internal organs. As the bodies treated in this way simply disintegrated, resin or plaster was used to harden the bandages – although the body within the wrappings quickly rotted the hard outer shell retained a fairly natural appearance. It was only during the 4th Dynasty that the undertakers started to experiment with the removal of the viscera and the drying and stuffing of the now empty body cavity. This experimentation continued until, by the 21st Dynasty, the art of mummification had reached its peak.

Herodotus tells us that the good New Kingdom undertakers offered a range of services to their clients. The most successful method, which was naturally the most expensive, required that the body have its brain and entrails physically removed before undergoing a lengthy period of desiccation in dry natron powder. The hollow body cavities were then filled with rags and resin packing and the entire corpse was carefully bandaged. The whole process took seventy days to complete. The less costly embalming methods were generally less effective. The 'second' class of treatment involved the injection of fluids to dissolve the soft parts of the body without cutting open the stomach, while:

. . . the third method of embalming, which is practised in the case of the poorer classes, is to clear out the intestines with a clyster and then let the body lie in natron for seventy days, after which it is at once given to those who come to take it away.

Herodotus

Once it had returned from its lengthy stay at the embalming house the neatly wrapped and sweet-smelling body was placed in a coffin to await a burial befitting the rank of the deceased. As in modern times, the funeral served as an immediately recognizable indication of social status; a 'good' funeral conferred great prestige on the family as well as serving as a respectful tribute to the departed. Therefore, although the majority of Egyptians had a relatively simple ceremony followed by interment in the local cemetery, wealthy families paid for the most elaborate and ostentatious funerary ritual that they could afford. Just as the Afterlife was originally open to the king alone, so the traditional Egyptian funeral developed for the exclusive use of the monarch before being gradually usurped by the nobility. This royal origin was never completely forgotten, and tomb illustrations which depict funerals often include pictures of offering bearers carrying royal regalia such as crowns and sceptres which were not literally appropriate to the status of the deceased.

Specific funerary practices varied at different times and in different parts of the country according to local traditions, although the underlying ideas remained constant. The deceased was escorted to his or her new home, magic was used to ensure that he or she could be re-born, and the tomb was then sealed against intruders. The full Theban funeral developed into a particularly lengthy ritual with four basic stages: the mourning on the east bank of the Nile, the journey across the river, the procession to the necropolis and the arrival at the tomb. Each stage had its own particular religious actions and spells and each was presided over by one of several male priests who played different roles in the identification of the departed with the dead Osiris. Nine male officials escorted the funeral cortège, and ceremonial male dancers greeted the procession at the door of the tomb. Here the vitally important 'Opening of the Mouth' ceremony was conducted, as the mouth of the mummy or its anthropoid coffin was touched by magical implements to restore the faculties of the deceased, allowing him or her to breathe and eat in the next life. The major female participants in this ritual were the *djeryt*, two women who travelled with the body representing Isis and Nephthys, the loyal sisters of Osiris who had assumed the form of kites to search for their brother's dismembered remains. The role of the *djeryt* appears to have been entirely passive and their place was occasionally taken by large wooden models of women with wide protective bird's wings in place of arms. The grieving family followed the funeral procession to the tomb, their numbers increased by groups of paid female mourners and the family servants who carried the furniture needed for use in the Afterlife.

The contemporary funeral rituals performed at the northern city of Memphis have left far less archaeological evidence for us to unravel. However, we do know that temporary booths or shelters were erected near to the tomb, and that these were used for the funeral feast which was attended by the mourners and priests. This was followed by a ritual known as the 'smashing of the red pots' when, as its name suggests, the vessels used at the feast were destroyed.

The first-born son of the departed had an important role to play at his parent's funeral. Legend decreed that Horus, the loyal son and heir of Osiris, avenged his father's murder and performed his funerary rites before acceding to the throne. Taking this precedent to its logical conclusion, the Egyptians came to believe that the person carrying out the burial rites would become the acknowledged heir of the deceased, to the extent that a man with a legally dubious claim to inherit could reinforce his position by performing the necessary ceremony; 'let the possessions be given to him who buries' was apparently valid Egyptian law. Egyptian kings were careful, therefore, to accord a fitting burial to their predecessor, not because of a sense of natural decency but out of a more practical desire to strengthen their claim to the throne. Although it was desirable that the funeral rites should be performed by a son, the duty could be delegated to a paid priest without the son losing his right to inherit, just as a deputy could subsequently be employed to care for the tomb and perform the necessary daily offerings to the deceased. It was also possible, though perhaps less desirable, for a daughter or wife to organize the funeral. This was clearly an expensive business; the funeral of Huy, a native of Deir el-Medina, was financed by his wife Iy who had to sell a house in order to raise the necessary capital. Fortunately Iy then recovered her investment by inheriting all her late husband's property. By the Roman period the traditional funeral, including mummification, had become so costly that there could be considerable haggling within the family as to who exactly was expected to foot the bill. Some wills even included clauses explicitly stating that children had to pay for the funeral before they could receive any inheritance, while legal agreements between brothers and sisters, detailing exactly who would contribute what to the funeral expenses of a dead parent, were not uncommon.

His beloved wife who shares his estate, the Sole Royal Ornament, Priestess of Hathor, Demyosnai, good of speech. She who makes the offering of white bread, who pleases in every respect and who serves the heart in all that one could wish. The sister-of-the-estate, praised of Hathor, Lady of Dendera, Demyosnai.

>From the Middle Kingdom funeral stela of the butler Merer

Only the more privileged members of society could afford to build elaborate stone-cut tombs, and it is not surprising that very few women occupied prestigious tombs in their own right. Tomb ownership accurately reflected the social climate, and most women would have found it impossible to accumulate the wealth needed to pay for such a monument. Royal wives, mothers and daughters were often accorded a separate tomb close to that of the king but these burials, invariably far less imposing than the major tomb, should properly be seen as an extension of the king's funeral-complex. Even where the two tombs are completely separate, and again separate from the royal mortuary temple, as in the New Kingdom Valleys of the Kings and Queens, it is difficult to decide whether the burial of the queen should be interpreted as an extension of the king's burial–complex, as a separate monument reflecting the importance of the queen, or even as a separate monument reflecting the decreasing importance of the queen who was no longer worthy of burial with her husband.

Most women were included in stone–cut tombs in their role as wives and daughters, and in these cases the relevant male burial naturally took precedence, with the female taking a subsidiary role just as she would have done in her husband's or father's home. It is particularly noticeable that the decoration of these shared tombs relates almost exclusively to the male deceased and his survival in the Afterlife, while the text on the wall details the life and achievements of the man with only a passing reference to the activities of his wife. It would appear that the woman was expected to enter the Afterlife not so much as a person in her own right but as a part of her husband's entourage. As has already been noted, women are allocated a passive role in almost all tomb scenes so that often the only time a wife can be seen acting independently of her husband is when she is depicted mourning at his funeral. There is no standard scene showing a widower grieving for his lost wife.

Do not delay building your tomb in the mountains; you do not know how long you will live.

Late Period scribal advice

The majority of women were buried in individual graves dug into the desert sand of the village cemetery. These local cemeteries remained in use for remarkably long periods, slowly spreading and shifting as the number of interments increased so that the Late Period graves might be sited some distance away from the original Old Kingdom burial ground. Within the cemetery the graves of the less important people were either arranged around the more impressive tombs of the major local dignitaries or simply dug into the next available and unoccupied patch of desert. The location of each middle-class grave was then marked either by a simple wooden or stone stela or by a more impressive tomb superstructure; the graves of the illiterate peasants appear to have been left unmarked.

Local burial customs gradually evolved as the Dynastic period progressed, but the majority of interments always included a wooden coffin and an assortment of grave goods. Some of these goods were sex-specific so that while pottery and stone vessels or wooden headrests could be included in both male or female inhumations, some objects such as mirrors and certain items of jewellery were only found in women's graves. Ayrton and Loat, who directed the excavation of part of the Old Kingdom Abydos necropolis, have left us a detailed description of the recovery of a virtually intact female burial. It is worth quoting their description at some length, as it provides us with a vivid insight into the practicalities of an ordinary Egyptian woman's funeral:

The skeleton (a woman) lay on the left side, with the head to the north-west, arms to the sides and knees slightly drawn up. Under the left temple were the remains of a wooden pillow. Before the face stood a large alabaster vase, behind the head was a flat red pottery vase with handles, and at the back of the neck a small red polished pottery vase.

Before the breast lay a large copper mirror with a lotiform wooden handle, behind the knees was a large polished red pottery vase and a copper needle. Round the neck were two strings of glazed steatite beads, one with a large carnelian bead in the centre, and the other supporting a steatite button seal with the figure of a hornet cut on the face.

On the lid of the coffin, over the knees, was placed a small red pottery vase, and against the outside of the coffin at the feet leant a large globular vase of rough pottery, over the mouth of which was placed an inverted red polished pottery bowl with a spout.[6]

The strongly held Egyptian belief in ghosts and spirits meant that death did not necessarily bring an end to communications between husband and wife, and it was relatively common for the surviving partner to write to his or her dead spouse, asking for intercession in some personal or domestic problem. The 19th Dynasty letter written by a husband who believed that his dead wife was haunting him has already been quoted in Chapter 2. A similar letter, written during the Middle Kingdom on the surface of a red bowl, asks that the priest Intef, the husband of the widow Dedi, should use his influence to frighten off the evil spirits who are making his wife's serving-girl ill: 'If you don't help in this matter, your house will be destroyed . . . fight for her and watch over her, save her from all those who are causing her harm.' The bowl would have been used as an offering vessel in Intef's tomb. Less abrupt is the Middle Kingdom stela set up by Merirtifi to his dead wife Nebitef, asking that she should help him while he is ill. He promises that, if she appears to him in a dream, he will increase her mortuary cult:

. . . Look, I am your beloved on earth, so fight for me and intercede for my name . . . Drive off the illness of my limbs. May you appear as a blessed one before me, so that I may see you fighting for me, in my dream.

The dead in turn communicated with the living via their funerary stelae: commemorative stones or plaques which were set up either in the necropolis or the temple, and which usually included some autobiographical information together with a request that passers-by should repeat a prayer for the continued well-being of the deceased. Naturally, it was the prerogative of the husband to erect a stela for his dead wife, and it was he who chose the text. The stela of the Lady Taimhotep, who lived and died during the Graeco-Roman period, is unusual in providing us with some details of her life and early death. It tells how she married at fourteen years of age and bore three daughters and a long-awaited son before dying aged thirty. It then goes on to lament the cruel fate which has snatched her from her beloved husband and children, reflecting the stylized pessimism of the Late and Graeco-Roman Period approach to death:

Oh my brother, my husband. My friend and high priest. Do not weary of drink and of food, of drinking deep and loving . . . The west is a land of sleep where darkness weighs on the dwelling place. Those who live there sleep as mummies. They do not wake to see their brothers, and cannot see their fathers or mothers. Their hearts forget their wives and children . . . Turn my face to the north wind at the edge of the water. Perhaps then my heart will be cooled in its grief.

Historical Events

Years Before Christ	EGYPTIAN LOCAL CHRONOLOGY	EGYPT
3000	**Archaic Period** (Dynasties 1–2)	Unification of Egypt Queen Neith-Hotep
2500	**Old Kingdom** (Dynasties 3–6)	Djoser step-pyramid at Sakkara Great Pyramid of Khufu at Giza
2000	**First Intermediate Period** (Dynasties 7–11)	
	Middle Kingdom (Dynasties 11–13)	Theban Kings re-unify Egypt Queen Sobek-Nofru
1500	**Second Intermediate Period** (Dynasties 14–17)	Hyksos kings in Northern Egypt
	New Kingdom (Dynasties 18–20)	Queen Hatchepsut Queen Nefertiti Tutankhamen Ramesses II
1000	**Third Intermediate Period** (Dynasties 21–25)	BEGINNING OF Kings at Tanis Nubian kings
500	**Late Period** (Dynasties 26–31)	
	Ptolemaic Period	ALEXANDER
A.D.0		Egypt part of Roman Empire

NEAR EAST	EUROPE
	Standing stone alignments at Carnac, France
Sargon establishes the Akkadian Empire	
Ascendancy of Ur	Major building phase at Stonehenge, England
Hammurabi King in Babylon	Palace period in Minoan Crete
	Destruction of Minoan Crete
	Ascendancy of Mycenaean civilization in Aegean
THE IRON AGE IN THE EASTERN MEDITERRANEAN	
Solomon builds temple in Jerusalem Assyrian Empire	Traditional date for foundation of Rome
Nebuchadnezzer and the Babylonian Empire	Battle of Marathon Parthenon built in Athens
THE GREAT	
Parthian Empire in Persia	

Notes

Full details of books referred to in shortened form will be found in the Selected Bibliography.

Introduction

1   Although Herodotus wrote his book when Egypt was living under Persian rule, he is able to provide us with a wealth of data relevant to the preceding dynastic age. His observations, together with those of other visitors to Egypt – principally the historian Diodorus Siculus and the geographer Strabo – have proved a useful source of facts which would otherwise have been lost. However, it is wise to treat all such sources with a degree of caution. Herodotus was not a particularly discriminating observer, and at all times he placed a great deal of trust in the reported tales of others. Indeed, there is actually no direct proof that Herodotus ever visited Egypt, and some of the more obvious omissions from his text, such as his relatively short account of Thebes, have led several authorities to suggest that his guide may have been based on the reported observations of others. As Strabo himself stated: 'Both Herodotus and others talk much nonsense [about Egypt], adding to their account marvellous tales, to give as it were, a kind of rhythm to relish.'

2   This quotation now has a slightly ironic quality as the once substantial temple has almost completely disappeared.

3   The problem has been compounded by the reluctance of many egyptologists to examine and record domestic sites while impressive temples and tombs remain to be uncovered. All too often important finds have been equated with spectacular or valuable finds, and the

best-known egyptologists are generally those who have had the luck to uncover burials rich in gold.

4 Kahun was built as a temporary town lying at the mouth of the Faiyum and was occupied for about one hundred years during the construction of the pyramid of the Middle Kingdom Pharaoh Senwosret II. It was subsequently abandoned. The village at Amarna (ancient Akhetaten) was occupied for approximately twenty years by the workmen employed to build the capital city of the New Kingdom Pharaoh Akhenaten. In contrast, the village of Deir el-Medina, nestling in a valley of the Theban hills opposite modern Luxor, had a continuous occupation of over 400 years. This site has provided us with a veritable treasury of information on the daily lives of the ordinary people associated with the excavation and decoration of the royal tombs in the nearby Valleys of the Kings and Queens. For a detailed review of life in these and other model communities, consult Kemp (1989).

Chapter 1 Images of Women

1 Until relatively recently this potentially fertile field of research has been relegated to the background of archaeological and historical studies which have tended to concentrate on the élite and spectacular at the expense of the more mundane. Unhappily, the spectacular is usually associated with male achievements; it is almost invariably the more down-to-earth which is most relevant to women's studies. It is, of course, not only women who have suffered in this way. Our knowledge of all societies is based far more on the atypical actions of the most prominent citizens than on the daily labours of the masses, and the lives of large groups of men have also been ignored in our reconstruction of the past. While spectacular burials and impressive monuments still attract universal interest, there is now a growing demand for information about the more basic details of ordinary life. It is also recognized that the painstaking excavation of a domestic site, or even a rubbish dump, can provide a wealth of information which may not be as intrinsically valuable as a spectacular treasure-trove of

gold artefacts but which may be equally important for our understanding of the past.

2 These tombs do not necessarily demonstrate that the queens of Egypt were economically powerful in their own right. On the contrary, it is obvious that the Old and Middle Kingdom queens' pyramid and mastaba tombs were built as subsidiaries to the far larger pyramid complex of the king. Although the New Kingdom queens were important enough to be accorded an individual and expensive funeral, their high status was clearly a direct result of their marriage.

3 Most societies which normally expect their females to adopt a non-aggressive role do generally approve of their women fighting at times of national or local emergency. Petrie, W.F.M. (1897), *Deshasheh*, Egypt Exploration Society, London.

4 Following this reasoning, potentially threatening subsidiary figures included in tomb scenes, together with animal- and human-like hieroglyphs included in the commentary, were often depicted either without their legs or cut in half at the waist. This deliberate disablement was seen as a wise precaution, preventing the otherwise dangerous images from coming alive and menacing the principal occupant of the tomb.

5 Harris, J.E. & Wente, E.F. (1980), *An X-Ray Analysis of the Royal Mummies*, University of Chicago Press, Chicago.

6 Heqanakht was the priest of the funerary cult of the Vizier Ipi, based at Thebes. He lived during the early part of the Middle Kingdom, when Egypt was still suffering from the disruption of the anarchic First Intermediate Period, and was often forced to make business trips to the north of the country. While away from home he wrote a series of letters in which he attempted to impose long-distance control over both his local business interests and the behaviour of his quarrelsome and discontented family. These letters were preserved by their recipients, and eventually found their way into the shaft of a secondary grave dug into the courtyard of Ipi's tomb. The letters of Heqanakht have been published in translation by James (1962).

7 Christie, A. (1945), *Death Comes as the End*, Collins, Glasgow.

8 It is this type of bias in the written record which has led some

feminist historians to suggest that a clear distinction should be drawn between 'History', the recorded past written with an upper-case letter H, and 'history', the actual and complete past, recorded or not, written with a lower-case letter h. All men and women have played an equal role in the development of 'history', while 'History' was often made by an exceptional, educated and privileged male élite. Those interested in the use of this convention should consult Lerner, G. (1986), *The Creation of Patriarchy*, Oxford University Press: 4.

9   Abana, or Ibana, is the mother of Ahmose.

10 The Late Period 'autobiography' of the Lady Taimhotep, written by her husband after her death, is an exception to this general rule. An excerpt from this autobiography is quoted at the very end of Chapter 8 in this book.

11 English translations of the medical papyri are included in the selected bibliography at the back of this book.

12 Greek and Roman fiction always held a more ambivalent attitude towards women, and the scheming female was a standard character in classical literature.

13 Egypt received a variety of cultural influences from her neighbours, and it would be both interesting and informative to give some consideration to the prevailing social customs of all these states. Unfortunately, although women's studies are rapidly becoming an acceptable aspect of Near Eastern archaeology, there are still relatively few publications dealing with the women of the Near East; this lack of accessible information is particularly striking when compared to the attention which has been focused on the women of the classical world. Lesko (1987, ed.) has attempted to redress this problem and provides a useful bibliography for those interested in Near Eastern women's studies.

14 It would be a mistake to interpret the laws of Hammurabi too literally, as they appear to have been written as a guide to good behaviour rather than as a strict rule. We know that some women did conduct legal transactions on their own behalf, and wealthy widows were able to exercise a considerable degree of control over their private lives. Nevertheless, the rules do give a good

indication of the values of society, and of the legal position of women within the community.

15 For a concise discussion of the role of women in the classical world, consult Clark (1989).

16 Frazer, J.G. (1914), *The Golden Bough*, Part 4, Vol 2, London.

17 A matriarchy involves the dominance of the female line, with all property rights being controlled by women and transmitted from mother to daughter. It is now recognized that there has never been a true matriarchy anywhere in the world. The possibility that a matrilineal system may have existed in Egypt has more validity, but such a system would not necessarily explain the equal legal rights of women. Under a matrilineal system inheritance rights and kinship allegiance pass via the mother from mother's brother to mother's son, with the sister–brother relationship proving stronger than the wife–husband bond. Males, however, still exert the ultimate control over their society and females are no more equal than their sisters living under a patriarchal regime. The often-cited tomb of Paheri, which includes texts tracing the descent of the deceased along the female line, does not support the theory of a matrilineal society; Paheri was simply obeying human nature by listing out the more important branch of his family in preference to his less-exalted paternal line.

18 The case of Mose is discussed in detail in James (1984).

19 For further references on this subject consult Pestman, P.W. (1961), *Marriage and Matrimonial Property in Ancient Egypt*, E.J. Brill, Leiden.

20 Gardiner, A. (1945), Adoption Extraordinary, *Journal of Egyptian Archaeology* 26: 23–9.

Chapter 2 Married Bliss

1 Quoted in Lindsay, J. (1963), *Daily Life in Roman Egypt*, Frederick Muller Ltd, London: 17.

2 Women often have a depressed level of fertility for the first year or two following the onset of menstruation, but early teenage pregnancies must still have been a common occurrence.

3   This suggestion is based on the translation of a text concerning the division of the property of the workman Nekhmin. One very important but broken sentence reads 'While she was eating her . . . with Nekhmin.' For philological reasons, the missing word has been tentatively identified as salt. The woman referred to is Merut, Nekhmin's second wife, and it has been suggested that this line indicates that the couple were not merely living together but were formally married. This theory is discussed further in Janssen, J.J. (1974), An allusion to an Egyptian wedding ceremony?, *Goettinger Miszellen*, 10: 25–8.

4   For further references on this subject consult Pestman, P.W. (1961), *Marriage and Matrimonial Property in Ancient Egypt*, E.J. Brill, Leiden.

5   This theory is discussed in far more detail in Ward, W.A. (1986), *Essays on Feminine Titles of the Middle Kingdom and Related Subjects*, Beirut. See also Ward, W.A. (1983), Reflections on some Egyptian terms presumed to mean 'harem, harem-woman, concubine', *Berytus Archaeological Studies*, 31: 67–74.

6   See Janssen, J.J. (1988), Marriage problems and public relations (P.B.M. 10416), in *Pyramid Studies and other essays presented to I.E.S. Edwards*, Baines J. *et al* (eds.), Egypt Exploration Society, London: 134–7. Suggestions that this attempted assault may have actually represented an ancient Egyptian Skimmington, as described in Hardy's classic novel *The Mayor of Casterbridge*, are disproved in this article.

7   Translated by Burford (1976); quoted by Miles (Miles, R. (1988), *The Women's History of the World*, Paladin, London: 247), who discusses other instances where dung has been used as a contraceptive. Watterson (1991, p. 88) suggests that crocodile excrement soaked in sour milk, a contraceptive pessary recommended by the *Kahun Medical Papyrus*, may have had a weak acidic effect similar to that produced by the sponge soaked in vinegar which was a standard means of birth control in western Europe at the turn of this century, and which is still used by Egyptian peasants today.

8   This excerpt from the New Kingdom instructions of Scribe Any has often been compared with the comments of a modern Egyptian villager, recorded by Winifred Blackman in 1927:

My wife is good, and I am pleased with her, but she must remain there [pointing downward]. My mother is up there [pointing upward]. Did she not carry me for nine months [pressing his hands on his stomach]? Did she not endure pain to give me birth, and did she not feed me from her breast? How could I not love her? My wife may change and lose her love for me. My mother is always the same; her love for me cannot change.

9 *Mammisi* were small temples attached to a major temple, built to commemorate the birth of the god of the main temple. They are invariably decorated with scenes showing the birth of the god.

10 Baines, J. (1985), Egyptian Twins, *Orientalia*, 54: 461–82.

11 For further details concerning childhood in pharaonic Egypt, consult Janssen R.M. & Janssen J.J. (1990), *Growing up in Ancient Egypt*, The Rubicon Press, London.

Chapter 3 Mistress of the House

1 Hori's expanding and contracting household is illustrated diagrammatically in Kemp (1989), 157–8.

2 For a review of all aspects of Egyptian laundry practices consult Hall, R.M. (1986), *Egyptian Textiles*, Shire Egyptology, Shire Publications, Aylesbury.

3 For further references to the foods enjoyed by the ancient Egyptians see Darby, W.J., Ghaliongui, P. & Grivetti, L. (1977), *Food: the gift of Osiris*, Academic Press, London; Wilson, H. (1988), *Egyptian Food and Drink*, Shire Egyptology, Shire Publications, Aylesbury.

4 Emery, W.B. (1962), *A Funerary Repast in an Egyptian Tomb of the Archaic Period*, Nederlands Instituut voor het Nabije Osten, Leiden.

5 The downside of pig consumption is of course the danger of human parasitical infestation resulting from eating undercooked pork. For a fascinating discussion of the domestic pig as a free-range scavenger in urban Egypt consult Miller, R.L. (1990), Hogs

and Hygiene, *Journal of Egyptian Archaeology* 76: 125–40. This article provides a wealth of unexpected data, ranging from the percentage of serious injuries caused by free-range pigs in New Guinea, to the rituals of modern rubbish collection by the *zabbalin* of present-day Cairo.

6   It is of course equally valid to observe that it is far easier to depict someone pouring out a drink than it is to show a noble eating a goose in a dignified manner.

7   For additional references to wine and beer consumption consult Lesko, L.H. (1977), *King Tut's Wine Cellar*, B.C. Scribe Publications, California.

Chapter 4   Work and Play

1   Those scenes which depict women in association with writing equipment should, however, be approached with a degree of caution as their interpretation may be open to a certain amount of doubt. One famous Old Kingdom tomb scene, for example, shows the Princess Idut sailing on the Nile with a writing kit by her side, suggesting that this lady took a great deal of pride in her scholastic ability. We now know that the principal figure in this scene was originally intended to be a man – a 5th Dynasty (male) vizier called Ihui – and that the presence of the writing equipment may well be a form of ancient typographic error, unconnected with the princess herself.

2   Janssen, J.J. (1986), A Notable Lady, *Wepwawet* 12: 30–31.

3   For a detailed discussion of female titles in the Old and Middle Kingdoms, consult Fischer, H.G. (1976), *Varia*, Metropolitan Museum of Art, New York.

4   At least one woman, the Old Kingdom Lady Peshet, is known to have held the title of 'Chief of the Lady Physicians', suggesting that at this time there may have been a guild of professional female doctors, or perhaps a guild of female doctors who specialized in attending to women. However, Peshet was a member of a priestly family and her son Akhethope, who bore the title of 'Overseer of the Ka priests of the Mother of the King', ultimately

inherited his mother's title of physician, indicating that this is more likely to have been a purely honorary accolade. We have no other information concerning the work of Egyptian female doctors.

5 Although the gods and goddesses were usually served by priests of the same sex the chief local priest of each cult was usually a man and, of course, the male king was the supreme priest of all cults male and female.

6 There is no doubt that the title of vizier is accorded to Nebet and not her husband Huy. However, Huy is given the title of 'Overseer of the Pyramid City', which is normally a part of the vizier's title during the Old Kingdom, and it seems likely that it was actually Huy who acted as vizier on his wife's behalf. In his review of the evidence concerning this unusual lady, Fischer, H.G. (1976), *Varia*, Metropolitan Museum of Art, New York, has concluded that Nebet's title was almost certainly an honorary one, designed to enhance the status of a relatively low-born woman who married well and eventually became the grandmother of a king of Egypt.

7 Ward, W.A. (1984), The case of Mrs Tchat and her sons at Beni Hassan, *Goettinger Miszellen* 71: 51–9.

8 For a guide to Egyptian music and musicians, consult Manniche, L. (1991), *Music and Musicians in Ancient Egypt*, British Museum Publications, London.

9 Penelope, the faithful wife of the absent Odysseus who spent her days working at the loom while awaiting her husband's return, was performing a socially approved female task intended to emphasize her virtuous wifely behaviour.

10 James (1984): 175–7 gives full details of the case of the missing servant girl.

11 Experts are still divided over the extent that slavery was practised in ancient Egypt, as it is now very difficult for us to distinguish between those whom we would class as slaves and those who are merely servants. Certainly, the pyramidal structure of Egyptian society combined with the well-developed system of *corvée* labour to make slaves peripheral to the Egyptian economy. The most complete discussion of this question is given in Bakir, A.M.

(1952), *Slavery in Pharaonic Egypt*, Institut Français d'Archéologie Orientale, Cairo.

12 For further details of dynastic pricing, consult Janssen, J.J. (1975), *Commodity Prices from the Ramessid Period*, Brill, Leiden.

13 Janssen, R.M. & Janssen, J.J. (1989), *Egyptian Household Animals*, Shire Publications, Aylesbury.

Chapter 5 Good Grooming

1   For a review of the evidence for male circumcision in Ancient Egypt consult Janssen, R.M. & Janssen, J.J. (1990), *Growing Up in Ancient Egypt*, The Rubicon Press, London.

2   Where it has become accepted practice, female circumcision is usually explained as a necessity both to prevent the girl's sexual organs from growing like those of a man and to decrease her sexual appetites by reducing her chance of achieving orgasm; all available evidence indicates that ancient Egyptian women were expected to get as much enjoyment out of their love lives as their male partners, suggesting that there may have been no perceived need for female circumcision.

3   For further details of wig manufacture consult Cox, J.S. (1977), The Construction of an Ancient Egyptian Wig, *Journal of Egyptian Archaeology* 63: 67–70. It would appear that not even the best of the Egyptian wigs were as natural-looking as the somewhat ideal-ized tomb paintings would suggest.

4   Riefsthal, E. (1952), An Ancient Egyptian Hairdresser, *Bulletin of the Brooklyn Museum* 13.4: 7–16; (1956), Two Hairdressers of the 11th Dynasty, *Journal of Near Eastern Studies* 15: 10–17.

5   Keimer, L. (1948), *Remarques sur le Tatouage dans L'Égypte Ancienne*, Institut Français d'Archéologie Orientale, Cairo.

6   For a review of all aspects of Egyptian textile manufacture see Hall, R.M. (1986), *Egyptian Textiles*, Shire Egyptology, Shire Publications, Aylesbury. The changing styles in women's garments are detailed in Riefsthal, E. & Chapman, S. (1970), A Note on Ancient Fashions, *Bulletin of the Museum of Fine Arts, Boston* 68: 244–59.

7   At least some of the dresses which have been recovered from tombs

seem to have been designed exclusively as grave-goods, as they were both too long and too narrow to actually fit the occupant of the tomb. This tradition of providing the deceased with garments may be compared with the provision of specific tomb-jewellery which is mentioned later in this chapter; magical intervention would ensure that both dresses and jewellery would become fully functional in the Afterlife. For details of actual recovered garments and interesting comments on the role of the sleeve in Egyptian clothing consult Hall, R.M. (1981), Two linen dresses from the 5th Dynasty site of Deshasheh, *Journal of Egyptian Archaeology* 67: 168–71; Hall, R.M. and Pedrini, L. (1984), A pleated linen dress from a Sixth Dynasty tomb at Gebelein, *Journal of Egyptian Archaeology* 70: 136–9.

8   For further information concerning the oracle of Amenhotep I at work see McDowell, A.G. (1990), *Jurisdiction in the Workmen's Community of Deir el-Medina*, Nederlands Instituut Voor Het Nabije Oosten, Leiden.

9   Where the gold contains a high proportion of silver it forms the valuable alloy electrum, a metal which can often be mistaken for silver and one which was very much prized by the Egyptian jewellers.

Chapter 6 The Royal Harem

1   The correct interpretation of terms commonly translated as 'harem' or 'royal harem' has been discussed in detail in Ward, W.A. (1983), Reflections on some Egyptian terms presumed to mean 'harem, harem-woman, concubine', *Berytus Archaeological Studies*, 31: 67–74.

2   In sharp contrast, the contemporary tombs of the nobles buried at Sakkara were also surrounded by neat rows of subsidiary inhumations but these graves were reserved for craftsmen and minor administrators who were far less intimately connected with the occupants of the main tomb.

3   Emery, W.B. (1954), *Great Tombs of the First Dynasty*, Vol 2, Egypt Exploration Society, London: 142.

4   For a detailed and poignant description of the excavation of the

Royal Cemetery, consult Woolley, L. (1934), *Ur Excavations*, Vol 2, The Royal Cemetery, The Trustees of the British Museum, London.

5 Consult Ward, W.A. (1983), Reflections on some Egyptian terms presumed to mean 'harem, harem-woman, concubine', *Berytus Archaeological Studies*, 31.

6 There is no record of an actual title of secondary wife being used, but it is clear that these foreign princesses – who, with one exception, were not accorded the superior rank of 'King's Great Wife' – were not classed as simple concubines of the king.

7 Commemorative scarabs recording lengthy hieroglyphic texts were a standard means of publicizing important events during the reign of Amenhotep III such as royal marriages, major hunting expeditions and even the building of a large pleasure lake for Queen Tiy.

8 We know that the Hittite queen of Ramesses II and her retinue lived for at least some of the time at *Mer-Wer*, as her personal laundry list was found by Professor Petrie during the excavation of the site.

9 The body of Ramesses III does not show any signs of a violent assault but poison, supposedly a woman's weapon, would of course have left no mark.

10 The cartouche is a hieroglyphic symbol used to indicate a royal name from the early Old Kingdom onwards. It consists of an oval-shaped loop representing a double thickness of rope drawn around the name, with the ends of the 'rope' tied to form a straight line at the base of the oval. Two of the names of the king, the throne-name and the birth-name, were invariably written within a cartouche.

11 The question of the changing role of the Egyptian queen-consort, including a scholarly register of titles and epithets of royal women, has been discussed in Troy, L. (1986), *Patterns of Queenship in Ancient Egyptian Myth and History*, Acta Universitatis Upsaliensis, Uppsala.

12 There is evidence to suggest that as many as six remarkable women (Meryt-Neith, Nitocris, Sobeknofru, Hatchepsut, Nefertiti and Twosret) were able to take the throne of Egypt and rule in

their own right as queen regnant or queen-consort. The detailed evidence relating to these atypical reigns is considered in Chapter 7.

13 Scenes showing these ladies visiting a farm and drinking fresh milk while the cow and her calf stand watching are perhaps more likely to represent imagined events in the bucolic Afterlife than royal day-to-day happenings.

14 For a learned discussion of the arguments for and against the 'heiress-princess' theory of inherited Egyptian kingship, including an extensive bibliography of relevant references, consult Robin, G. (1983), A Critical Examination of the Theory that the Right to the Throne of Ancient Egypt Passed Through the Female Line in the 18th Dynasty, *Goettinger Miszellen*, Heft 62: 67–77.

Chapter 7 Female Kings

1 *Maat* was personified in the form of a goddess of the same name. This goddess, the daughter of Re, wore a distinctive headdress consisting of a single tall ostrich feather held in place by a golden fillet. She was closely associated with truth and the administration of justice.

2 This discrimination against female succession is at least partially explained in European royalty by the desire to maintain a pure patrilineal descent. However, this solution is not particularly applicable to Egypt where at various times the pharaoh actually nominated a totally unrelated successor, apparently preferring to pick the best man for the job rather than relying on family ties.

3 The notorious Queen Cleopatra VII, the last Egyptian monarch, reigned during the Graeco-Roman period which followed the Dynastic era, and therefore falls outside the scope of this book.

4 An alternative interpretation of these early royal graves suggests that each king built himself one tomb at Abydos, the royal cemetery of their southern homeland. In this case the larger Sakkara tombs must have belonged to the highest-ranking courtiers and priests. Unfortunately, this does not explain the presence of the solar boats at Sakkara; with the exception of Meryt-Neith, these boats were provided for the use of kings only.

5   The text of this announcement, preserved in Hatchepsut's
    magnificent mortuary temple at Deir el-Bahri, is almost identical
    to the Middle Kingdom co-regency decree of Amenemhat III and
    Senwosret III, and is presumably a straight copy. By replicating an
    existing text Hatchepsut would have been seen to be reinforcing
    the strength of her message, confirming a direct link not only with
    her royal father but also with the earlier kings of the 12th
    Dynasty. This continuous aspect of kingship was very important
    to the Egyptians as it indicated the presence of *maat* in the land.

6   For further references to Senenmut, consult Dorman, P.F. (1988),
    The Monuments of Senenmut, Kegan Paul, London.

Chapter 8   Religious Life and Death

1   Juvenal, Satire 15, quoted in translation in Lindsay, J. (1963), *Daily
    Life in Roman Egypt*, Frederick Muller Ltd, London: 113.

2   The New Kingdom Tale of the Destruction of Mankind tells how
    Re decided to eliminate all human life as the people were plotting
    against him. He created the 'Eye of Re', Sekhmet, who started the
    slaughter, but later repented of his hasty actions. In order to
    prevent Sekhmet from carrying out a wholesale massacre he
    mixed red ochre into beer; the goddess, thinking that the red
    liquid was blood, drank it and became too inebriated to continue
    her mission of death.

3   For further references to domestic religion consult: Pinch, G. (1983),
    Childbirth and Female Figurines at Deir el-Medina and el-Amarna,
    Orientalia 52: 405–14; Kemp, B.J. (1979), Wall Paintings from the
    Workmen's Village at el-Amarna, *Journal of Egyptian Archaeology*
    65: 52–3.

4   Meskhenet's unusual headdress, which is bound to her head by a
    circlet, has also been interpreted as two long palm shoots with
    curved tips.

5   Budge, W. (1910), *Book of the Dead, Text II*, Kegan Paul, London.

6   Ayrton, E.R. (1909), Untitled report in F.Ll. Griffith (ed.), *Egypt
    Exploration Fund Archaeological Report 1908–1909*, Egypt Explora-
    tion Fund, London: 3.

Selected Bibliography

Many books and articles include information relevant to our understanding of the life of the Egyptian woman. However, this information tends to form only a minor part of a more general study, and there are very few works devoted exclusively to female-oriented topics. The references listed below include some of the more important and accessible publications with preference given to those written in English; all these works include bibliographies which will be of interest to those readers seeking more detailed references on specific subjects. More specialized references to points raised in the text have been included in the notes.

Female-oriented Archaeology

Cameron, A. & Kuhrt, A., eds. (1983), *Images of Women in Antiquity*, Croom Helm, London.

Clark, G. (1989), *Women in the Ancient World*, New Surveys in the Classics 21, Oxford University Press, Oxford.

Desroches-Noblecourt, C. (1986), *La Femme au Temps des Pharaons*, Stock/Laurence Pernoud, Paris.

Lesko, B.S., ed. (1987), *Women's Earliest Records From Ancient Egypt and Western Asia: Proceedings of the Conference on Women in the Ancient Near East, Brown University*, Brown Judaic Studies 166, Scholars Press, Atalanta.

Moore, H.L. (1988), *Feminism and Anthropology*, Polity Press, Oxford.

Pomeroy, S.B. (1984), *Women in Hellenistic Egypt*, Schocken Books, New York.

Watterson, B. (1991), *Women in Ancient Egypt*, Alan Sutton, Stroud.

Wenig, S. (1969), *The Woman in Egyptian Art*, translated by B. Fisher, Edition Leipzig, Leipzig.

Contemporary and Modern Observers

Atiya, N. (1984), *Khul-Khaal: five Egyptian women tell their stories*, American University in Cairo Press, Cairo.

Blackman, W.S. (1927), *The Fellahin of Upper Egypt*, Harrap, London.

Breasted, J.H. (1930), *The Edwin Smith Medical Papyrus*, University of Chicago Press, Chicago.

Diodorus Siculus, *Bibliotheca Historica*, translated by Oldfather, C.H. & Sherman C.L. (1933–67), Loeb Classical Library, New York.

Ebbell, B. (1937), *The Papyrus Ebers*, Levin & Munksgaard, Copenhagen.

Griffith, F.Ll. (1898), *Hieratic Papyri from Kahun and Gurob*, Bernard Quaritch, London.

Herodotus, *The Histories*, translated by A. de Selincourt, revised with Introduction and Notes by A.R. Burn (1983), Penguin Books, London.

James, T.G.H. (1962), *The Hekanakhte Papers and other early middle documents*, Metropolitan Museum of Art, New York.

Lichtheim, M. (1973) *Ancient Egyptian Literature I: The Old and Middle Kingdoms*, University of California Press, Los Angeles.

Lichtheim, M. (1976) *Ancient Egyptian Literature II: The New Kingdom*, University of California Press, Los Angeles.

Lichtheim, M. (1980) *Ancient Egyptian Literature III: The Late Period*, University of California Press, Los Angeles.

Parkinson, R.B. (1991), *Voices from Ancient Egypt: an anthology of Middle Kingdom writings*, British Museum Press, London.

Rugh, A.B. (1986), *Reveal and Conceal: dress in contemporary Egypt*, American University in Cairo Press, Cairo.

Simpson, W.K., ed. (1972), *The Literature of Ancient Egypt: an anthology of stories, instructions and poetry*, Yale University Press, New Haven.

Strabo, *The Geography of Strabo VII*, translated by H.L. Jones (1932), Loeb Classical Library, New York.

Watson, H. (1992), *Women in the City of the Dead*, Hurst & company, London

History and Geography

Aldred, C. (1973), *Akhenaten and Nefertiti*, Brooklyn Museum, New York.

Baines, J. & Malek, J. (1980), *Atlas of Ancient Egypt*, Facts on File, New York.

Brovarski, E., Doll, S.K. & Freed, R.E., eds. (1982), *Egypt's Golden Age: the art of living in the New Kingdom*, Museum of Fine Arts, Boston.

Emery, W.B. (1961), *Archaic Egypt*, Penguin, London.

Gardiner, A. (1961), *Egypt of the Pharaohs*, Oxford University Press, Oxford.

Hayes, W.C. (1953), *The Scepter of Egypt Vol I: from earliest times to the end of the Middle Kingdom*, Metropolitan Museum of Art, New York.

Hayes, W.C. (1959), *The Scepter of Egypt Vol II: the Hyksos Period and the New Kingdom*, Metropolitan Museum of Art, New York.

Kemp, B.J. (1989), *Ancient Egypt: anatomy of a civilization*, Routledge, London.

Daily life

Bourriau, J. (1988), *Pharaohs and Mortals: Egyptian art in the Middle Kingdom*, Cambridge University Press, Cambridge.

James, T.G.H. (1984), *Pharaoh's People: scenes from life in Imperial Egypt*, Oxford University Press, Oxford.

Janssen, R.M. & Janssen, J. (1990), *Growing Up in Ancient Egypt*, The Rubicon Press, London.

Manniche, L. (1987), *Sexual Life in Ancient Egypt*, Kegan Paul International, London.

Morenz, S., *Egyptian Religion*, translated by A. Keep (1973), Methuen, London.

Spencer, A.J. (1982), *Death in Ancient Egypt*, Penguin Books, London.

Stead, M. (1986), *Egyptian Life*, British Museum Publications, London.

Wilkinson, A. (1971), *Ancient Egyptian Jewellery*, Methuen, London.

Index

Figures in bold refer to a picture caption on that page.